Marketing
in the
Soviet Union

Thomas V. Greer

The Praeger Special Studies program—utilizing the most modern and efficient book production techniques and a selective worldwide distribution network—makes available to the academic, government, and business communities significant, timely research in U.S. and international economic, social, and political development.

Marketing in the Soviet Union

PRAEGER SPECIAL STUDIES IN INTERNATIONAL ECONOMICS AND DEVELOPMENT

Praeger Publishers   New York   Washington   London

Library of Congress Cataloging in Publication Data

Greer, Thomas V
  Marketing in the Soviet Union.

  (Praeger special studies in international
economics and development)
  1. Marketing—Russia.   I. Title.
HF5415.12.RaG73   1973   380.'0947   72-90666

PRAEGER PUBLISHERS
111 Fourth Avenue, New York, N.Y. 10003, U.S.A.
5, Cromwell Place, London SW7 2JL, England

Published in the United States of America in 1973
by Praeger Publishers, Inc.

Printed in the United States of America

To my family

An ongoing concern of academicians in the marketing field is the documentation and analysis of the varying ways in which marketing meets human needs in the diverse cultures of the world. The aim of this book is to contribute to such a knowledge of the Soviet culture. A more current interpretation of the Soviet marketing system and the changes associated with it is necessary to the continuing development of a comprehensive body of knowledge on comparative marketing systems. Although several fine books already exist on Soviet marketing (notably Goldman's Soviet Marketing: Distribution in a Controlled Economy, 1963; and Felker's Soviet Economic Controversies: The Emerging Marketing Concept and Changes in Planning 1960-65, 1966), the present work is broader in scope and is focused on development since the publication of the Goldman and Felker books.

Throughout, a deliberate effort has been made to avoid cultural bias and to refrain from criticisms of the Soviet system based solely on any presupposition of the innate superiority of capitalism. It is hoped that the book will accomplish for Soviet marketing the important goal expounded by Robert Bartels of making "marketing practices socially explainable from their [other nations'] viewpoint, although perhaps not economically justifiable from ours."*

It is also hoped that the book will be of considerable assistance to marketing executives who may wish to market goods or services in the U.S.S.R. or obtain them there, and to officials in the public sector who need information for interpretation, comparison, planning, and policy-making. Contextual material such as that presented here is essential to an understanding of the marketing process in the Soviet Union. Such understanding must always precede effective marketing transactions with another culture.

---

*Robert Bartels, Comparative Marketing: Wholesaling in Fifteen Countries (Homewood, Ill.: Richard D. Irwin, 1963), p. viii.

CONTENTS

ABBREVIATIONS USED IN NOTES

JPRS   Joint Publications Research Service.
TOUTAS   Translations on U.S.S.R. Trade and Services.
TUEA   Translations on U.S.S.R. Economic Affairs.
       The numbers given with the above abbreviations in the notes
refer to documents in the microfilm series from CCM Information
Corporation, New York, New York.
CDSP   Current Digest of the Soviet Press. A printed series
       from Association for the Advancement of Slavic Studies, The
       Ohio State University, Columbus, Ohio.
       References to other translation services are not abbreviated.

Marketing
in the
Soviet Union

Several aspects of products, the physical results of the workings of an economic system, are explored in this chapter. Unfortunately, in the West there is little organized information on Soviet products and several stereotypes are held. Goods are thought to be extremely scarce in the U.S.S.R., and it is also believed that only one item is offered for each generic type of product. Still another stereotype is that all goods produced are of abominably low quality. The specific subject areas to be examined regarding products are shortages, extra-legal markets, quality, technology and new products, assortments, product differentiation, and fashion.

SHORTAGES

During the 1960s and early 1970s the supply of consumer goods and services rose substantially, and the trend is continuing. A very few products are in general oversupply: stockings, radios, metal beds, and some types of washing machines. Sometimes a particular item is in oversupply in a particular area; an American scholar reported that one area received enough women's socks for ten years—but all in one size.[1] Pravda has scolded editorially: "Still far from rare are cases in which one locale suffers from a shortage of certain goods while another locale has a surplus of the same goods laid up in a warehouse."[2] The reasons for this type of shortage include errors in basic planning, errors in timing or physical distribution or both, and "localism." This last factor refers to a fairly widespread practice of favoring customers in one's region or even stockpiling in anticipation of local needs while delaying action on requests from organizations far away.

The 1971-75 Ninth Five-Year Plan gives considerable attention to consumer goods and raising the standard of living. More than two years late in appearing in draft form, it aroused substantial enthusiasm when it did appear February 14, 1971. The feature mainly responsible for Western reaction was that output of consumer goods is to rise faster than output of producer goods. The output of Industries A (producer goods) is supposed to increase by 41 to 45 percent, while the output of Industries B (consumer goods) is supposed to increase by 44 to 48 percent. If the lower projection of the range for producer goods and the upper projection of the range for consumer goods were realized, a quite significant change in priorities would have taken place. Even if only the midpoints of the ranges were realized, a noteworthy change in priorities would have occurred. However, one should note that if the high end of the range for producer goods and the low end of the range for consumer goods were realized, producer goods would again have triumphed and maintained the tradition established in 1928. Even if output of consumer goods were at the maximum projected rate, the structural change in output could not be massive, since consumer goods accounted for only about one-fourth of production in 1970.

That the Five-Year Plan gives great attention to producer goods can be seen readily in this statement of Alexei Kosygin:

> The plan envisages the further powerful development of heavy industry—the basis for the steady expansion of social production and for ensuring the country's defense capability. This will make it possible to carry out the substantial technical re-equipment of the national economy, to bring about a significant rise in the productivity of social labor and to expand greatly supplies to branches producing goods for the population and to all spheres of everyday services.[3]

In order to reach the consumer goods goals of the Five-Year Plan, machine building[4] and output of some synthetics must be stepped up drastically. Capital investments in machine building will almost double compared with the Eighth Plan. In order to meet consumer needs and to take pressure off agriculture and forestry, the manufacture of synthetic materials will grow rapidly too. Output of plastics and synthetic fibers, for instance, will more than double.[5]

The 1971-75 Five-Year Plan specifies increases in countless categories of products. It requires 90 percent increases over the level of 1970 in the supply of furniture, wallpaper, chinaware, earthenware, glass and enamelware dishes, silverware, clocks and watches, sporting goods, stationery, furs, photographic goods, electrical goods, lace curtains, pillows, headgear, blankets, towels, women's toilet articles, and motorcycles with sidecars.[6]

Several misunderstood points about Soviet shortages should be briefly noted. One is that the industrial executive is probably not as unconcerned about consumer welfare as popular thought may assume. Probably this is true of the central planner also. However, one finds it somewhat easier to be sympathetic with the enterprise official than with the central planner. One must remember the constraints on the executive's behavior, constraints mostly in the form of quantitative norms imposed on him. Only a modest amount of flexibility was introduced through the reforms of the 1960s. The planner, too, has numbers thrust on him and suffers from severe research deficiencies, especially in determination of demand, throughout the economic-political apparatus. Many fundamental decisions on allocation of resources are made by politico-economic leaders, and the central planners must work with these guidelines and restrictions. It must be remembered that most central planners are technicians. Nevertheless, their great power is clear.

Second, consumer goods manufacturing plants in the U.S.S.R. traditionally have been rather small, and even so do not usually specialize in only one or two products. Many products are made in twenty or even thirty different plants. Growth of Soviet consumption levels may have been significantly constrained by the failure to reach the same potential economies of scale in production of consumer goods that they have reached in capital goods. The firmy (combines) of the early 1960s and the production associations of today (see the section "Technology and New Products" below) seemingly have economies of scale as one of their simple purposes.

Third, new Soviet plants seem to require an extremely long time to get into full production after they are constructed. Moreover, most well-established enterprises operate distressingly far below capacity, as Central Statistical Administration research has indicated.[7]

Consumption levels for consumer goods have developed unevenly in the Soviet Union. In fact, they have shown wide fluctuations since 1917.[8] Philip Hanson concludes that "the structure of private consumption in the U.S.S.R. is still in some respects that of a backward country."[9] Chapman shows, for example, that the per capita meat, milk, and egg supply and housing and clothing conditions of the Soviet Union were seven decades behind that of the United States.[10] On the other hand, some services, such as medicine and public transportation, are well-developed by U.S. standards, and household durables are somewhere between those extremes. Detailed measurement of levels of consumption, product by product, relative to each of the leading Western nations, has barely begun. The complexity of the task is compounded by the problem of determining valid purchasing power equivalents for conversion among currencies. Quality, assortment, convenience, credit, and availability of consumer goods further complicates the potential measurement problem. Obviously, too, the relative access to public-sector services makes for measurement difficulty. One Soviet study puts U.S.S.R. consumption well below that of Czechoslovakia, Hungary, and Poland, and, by implication, well below East Germany.[11] Schroeder notes the additional difficulty of declining but still great disparity between urban and rural consumption levels in the U.S.S.R.[12]

There are various degrees of severity in the shortages of consumer goods. Some shortages do not receive great publicity because they pale in comparison with other shortages or because significant progress has been made toward alleviation. The well-known Soviet thinker and reform economist Evsei Liberman has found it necessary to state that "Socialism does not espouse asceticism. Material needs must be satisfied."[13]

For many goods there are "rational norms" of consumption set by the central planners with the assistance of the scientific-academic community. They represent "need" as experts see it. And yet, output of some of these goods is so low that the consumption norms cannot be met. Examples of products whose rational norms will still not be reached at the end of the Five-Year Plan in 1975, despite scheduled large increases in production, are knitwear, meat, and milk. Output of leather footwear by 1975 should allow the consumer to slightly exceed the rational norm for the first time. Obviously there are some methodological difficulties in comparing production with these prescriptive norms for consumption: quality, feasible substitutes (if any), prices asked, nonuniformity in access to goods, and differential rates of consumption.

Many goods are in very short supply. For example, despite high prices, stepped-up production, and realistic plans for even more production, automobiles remain scarce. The buyer must pay well in advance of delivery, from as little as three months in some jurisdictions to as much as one year in others. Thus buyers finance the automobile dealership and the factory.[14] However, of infinitely more importance is the fact that industry experiences shortages of parts and supplies. Izvestia has reported that "a lack of spare parts is causing much downtime of equipment and is forcing enterprises to organize their own makeshift production of spare parts locally."[15] It is well worth remembering that the 1966-70 Five-Year Plan had severe shortfalls in steel, electricity, gas, and coal, as well as in many consumer goods.

In a 1970 editorial Izvestia specifically pointed to shortages of blankets, bath towels, hardware, table flatware, pencils, drawing pads, quilted jackets, thermos bottles, and other consumer goods.[16] The newspaper went on to state that the shortage of some products could make quite a story. For example, despite countless official and unofficial complaints and comments about oilcloth table covers during the 1966-70 period, they were still in short supply. The editorial noted that five years was surely long enough to build new oilcloth factories, especially since the product was simple and well-established. Moreover, the editorial noted that, although sales of dishes were up 21 percent over the previous year, the industry was still filling only two-thirds of the orders of trade enterprises. Perhaps most important of all, Izvestia editorialized as follows:

> It is time to have a fresh look at the very appraisal of the activities of the ministries in charge of the industrial branches manufacturing consumer goods. Managers account for themselves before the people not only through statistical reports, but also the goods on shelves; and, moreover, this kind of accounting should be the main one. Fully meet the demands for products of the industrial branches! This should become the first precept for the ministries and their chief administrations. How can one talk about the satisfactory work of the branches if the statistical report attests to the fulfillment of the plan by one or another branch, while the consumer finds the products of these branches in short supply? Besides, the question then arises as to whether the plan drawn up for that branch of industry was sufficiently substantiated. Can one regard as satisfactory a plan that envisages a shortage year after year?

The story of one consumer's experience in trying to obtain a scarce product through the bureaucracy is enlightening. A resident of Voronezh had suffered from severe hand wounds received in military service in World War II. From July to October he combed his home city in an attempt to find a pair of gloves, but without success. He was told by the sales attendants that, if there were any gloves, they would buy them themselves. Finally he wrote the Russian Republic Ministry of Trade. A high official wrote in his behalf to the director of the Trade Administration of the Voronezh Province Soviet Executive Committee. That body in turn wrote the director of the Voronezh City Manufactured Goods Trade Association, asking him to give the man preference. None of the organizations got directly in touch with the consumer. Finally, by January, after additional inquiries about his first inquiry, he found that his original letter had been referred down to the Thousand Trifles Store in his home town. He rushed there, only to find that the store did not consider gloves part of its trade. Then he went to the Trade Administration, "where he was told in person that everyone was tired of him and that if he needed gloves so badly, he ought to get them wherever he could."[17]

The Deputy Minister of Trade for the Russian Republic recently protested that the planning agencies do not think in terms of combinations of goods. There are enough cameras but not enough photographic paper, enough television sets and high frequency cables but not enough voltage regulators. There are some tape recorders but few tapes.[18] Furthermore, he noted that some production plans are still stated in terms of tonnage. This is the policy responsible for the shortage of enameled kitchen ware. The factories producing such goods, primarily those of the Ministry of Ferrous Metallurgy, avoid producing small items and still reach their tonnage goals with large, heavy items. He argued that the goals should be rewritten to specify quantities of various items.

EXTRALEGAL MARKETS

The black market is vigorous and involves traffic in foreign goods, scarce Soviet goods, currency, precious metals, and jewels. It is subject to continuous police investigation and prosecution, although the complex legal provisions covering black market operations suffer from poor draftsmanship and inconsistent, dubious judicial interpretation. Soviet law has overlaps, gaps, and other problems in treating and distinguishing between the categories of illegal private trading and the embezzlement of property.[19]

The following selected quotations from a case history of a black market operator are illuminating:

> I am 23 years old. My parents were divorced when I was one. I was raised by my grandfather, a well-known professor of biology. I left school when I was 15 and took a job as an apprentice machinist. My "apprenticeship" consisted basically of carrying heavy loads and going on errands to the nearest store for vodka.
>
> Later I got a job as a laboratory assistant at a research institute at 70 rubles a month. It was then that my petty speculation began. At a secondhand commission store that I visited while searching for recording tape, I learned of the possibility of recording music from the records that were being sold there. The average record cost 25 or 30 rubles, and the especially "popular" ones cost as much as 100. I couldn't resist the temptation of making enough money by speculation to get a beautiful tape recorder, tapes, and other illicitly obtained items.

For a long time, acquiring and having these things was virtually my sole purpose in life. My idea of happiness was a Grundig tape recorder, a stack of Presley and Holiday records, a package of chewing gum, and jeans of various colors. I sat amid this splendor smoking Marlboros, drinking gin and tonic, and looking through the latest issue of Playboy.

I quickly acquired a circle of acquaintances with similar inclinations. We bought and sold everything that came along—records, tape, chewing gum, shoes, jeans, etc. I spent my money as fast as I made it, for I was only 17 or 18 at the time.

[   ]

I had finished school, but decided to remain a speculator rather than go to an institute. I bought currency and goods from foreigners. The articles I sold through the commission stores and the currency I "pushed through" the Birch Tree Store, when they would take it, or sold to "fences" and speculators whom I knew.

Despite my increasing disgust with this way of life, I was powerless to abandon it. In early 1969 I quit my job and didn't take another until the end of the year, and that only for the sake of being employed somewhere. After a month I arranged for others to work in my place and gave them my wages.[20]

Foreign-made merchandise, especially that from the Western countries, carries a certain mystique for Soviet citizens and constitutes a standard for comparison. Visitors from abroad are still often stopped on the street and asked to sell their belongings. Much of the Soviet press criticizes purchases from foreigners and disapprovingly refers to such purchases as overly stilyaga (style-conscious). However, such transactions are motivated not only by fashion and attractive design but also by durability, reliability, workmanship, and novelty. In addition, the goods may be resold profitably. The black market for foreign merchandise is so active that the Presidium in 1970 decreed more severe penalties for buying goods from foreign visitors, including up to one year of hard labor.[21]

The black market is broad-based. There is illicit traffic in foreign and Russian religious objects, especially icons and crosses.[22] There is illicit traffic in jewelry, gold coins, clothing, and furs. In one well-publicized case, a foreign student in Moscow and several Russians cooperated in a ring that speculated heavily in jewelry and coats. They bought hundreds of fur coats and raincoats from dollar stores and resold them. It is interesting that the same group's transactions in currency assumed a value for the ruble of about U.S. $.25 at times and U.S. $.50 at other times instead of the then official rate of U.S. $1.10.[23]

There is an active black market for fur pelts that substantially supplements the income of many rural dwellers. Government procurement prices are much too low to reflect the relative scarcities. For example, Sovetskaya Rossia reports:

> . . . almost none of the muskrat fur obtained by the hunters of eastern Siberia goes to the state procurement agents.
>
> There are only two ways to combat the black market in furs, which is growing rather rapidly: to suppress it by administrative methods or to restructure procurement and wholesale prices. The first is not very effective. . . .
>
> There are many absurdities and complicated categories in the price system for sable. But at the market in Irkutsk "hunters" get 70 to 100 rubles for a sable pelt, and people don't care whether it's black or red, as long as it's in decent condition.
>
> What would change if the state procurement office paid that kind of money to the hunters? First of all, the state would get the pelt, which is worth at least 200 rubles in Moscow. Secondly, the hunters themselves would get the money that now goes to speculators. The speculator would disappear and there would be no need for administrative methods.
>
> But instead the procurement agents prefer to make the maximum profit on each pelt, thus inevitably losing a large quantity of fur. According to experts, the hunters in one small area of eastern Siberia trapped more than 800 sables, but only 87 were turned over to the state procurement agent.[24]

A leading Soviet newspaper recently reported a revealing story of a Soviet citizen who rented a Moskvitch automobile for a Sunday drive.[25] The car proved defective in several ways. Nevertheless, the customer was financially responsible for repair of the defects, replacement of a fender damaged because of the way in which the tow truck was operated, and the minimum daily mileage of 310 miles; he was also informed that he would have to pay the daily rental charge until the car was completely repaired and in service again—some months in the future. First, the customer had to bribe the tow truck operator, and then he was referred by the mechanic to a black market dealer in automotive parts. In order to avoid the rental charges that would come with waiting for an officially priced fender, he had to pay more than twice that figure to the illicit dealer. An American news magazine commented that publication of the story in the U.S.S.R. was, in part, an officially sanctioned attempt to persuade Soviet citizens that they are better off without this rental service.[26]

Organized Black Market Crime

Better-known in the West is the black market for capital goods which business managers and engineers desperately need. The lack of a machine or a replacement part can mean the failure to reach planned production goals and interfere seriously with the careers of the concerned persons.

In one celebrated case in the 1960s a ring of several managers and engineers in several plants sold more than 900 lathes through the black market. Spreading across the Caucasus, Soviet Central Asia, and several other locations, the dispersion of the ring was impressive. One of the plants illegally sold lathes in 35 cities. The ring included two women engineers in a central government agency that oversees the machine building industry who issued false sales documentation. The ringleader was executed and the other members imprisoned.[27] In a scandal in the northern Caucasus involving the black market for spare machine parts, one official said that he recognized that it was a crime but that it was their daily life in industry. The investigation revealed that black markets in that region had become almost legalized and open operations.[28] Sometimes the economic crime is not illicit sale of the goods but systematic understatement of the materials inventory and equipment, as in a 1972 Armenian case.[29] Such deviation gives the enterprise an operating cushion, violates the planning norms, and can create the circumstances leading to illicit sale.

There have been many instances of black market operations that do not fit the classic model of capital goods shortages. A notorious case in the 1960s was a 54-member ring in Kirghizia, among whose leaders were the head of the State Planning Committee of the Kirghiz Republic, the Deputy Minister of Trade of the Kirghiz Republic, two textile factory managers, and several retailing executives. They were convicted of conducting a black market operation that did U.S. $3.5 million dollars in sales volume. They operated complete factories turning out carpets and curtains. Four leaders were executed and the others imprisoned.[30]

Another operation yielded the convicted black marketers over U.S. $3 million in profits and involved a total of 52 firms and institutions. An elaborate plant making knitwear was set up in a mental hospital. Subcontracts were let to other factories for dye work. Channels of distribution were set up involving many retailers. The leaders were executed and several others given prison terms.[31]

In a case that ended in early 1972, it was determined that an exceptionally well organized ring operated in the Tashkent Cooperative Wholesale and Mail Order House. Officials of that enterprise demanded bribes from managers of retail stores that they supplied and, in turn, some of the retail managers sold some of the merchandise to speculators. Such prosaic items as rugs, woolen kerchiefs, embroidery thread, silks, and beads were involved. The director of the Tashkent wholesale base was even daring enough to offer for sale the best positions in his enterprise. For example, the job of warehouse chief was sold by the director for 5,000 rubles. In light of proven theft of at least 366,000 rubles, the director was sentenced to death and several others to long terms in "strict-regime colonies."[32]

Automobile theft and resale are rising rapidly. Although some appears to be on an individual basis, much of it appears to be organized crime. Cars are still scarce and will be for several years, even if plans for increased production are accomplished. Moreover, there is incentive for car theft just to supply the demand for parts. Prices on the black market for both cars and parts are well above official prices. Adding to the incentive is the relatively low penalty, a maximum of one year for the first offense. Even if total automobile production came in line with total demand, there might still be incentive for theft because of assortment factors or geographic dispersion of inventory.

Expediters

Several Soviet and Western journalists have noted that industry uses traveling expediters, sometimes called tolkachi, to solve shortages of equipment, parts, and materials that are urgently needed. One Soviet writer has observed that this practice is more evident in the last few months of each calendar year, as each enterprise tries to meet or surpass its goals for that year.[33] Attempts to stop the practice have not succeeded.

A Russian engineer has related how a plant director openly exhorted an expediter as he left on a trip:

> Keep your eyes open, don't be caught napping, act according to the situation. If you have to offer someone a bottle, don't be shy. We'll cover all expenses. But I warn you: Don't come back empty-handed.

A purchasing agent strongly supported expediters:

> No enterprise can get along without these "ex-
> pediters" . . . the assignments they get are difficult,
> they need special talents.
> They really are selfless people . . . their efforts
> are not for themselves, but for the good of the cause.

The Russian engineer asserted: "At many enterprises the 'expediter'
has already become a necessary production unit, a kind of official
who might as well be entered in the table of organization."[34]

The director of the Fighters of the Revolution manufacturing
plant in Omsk, M. Ryzhov, has written that expediters are an acute
problem. They "introduce disorder in the supply system and violate
economic plans. . . . Their activity has somewhat enlivened recently." He admitted that his own firm used an expediter for 150
days in 1971 to assure that it received the necessary goods from just
one supplier. Of the expediter, the plant director said: "Production
was delivered for us, though with difficulties, when he was present,
but as soon as he left, deliveries stopped." Ryzhov tried to get at
the underlying cause: "It seems to me that a pusher exists as a result
of shortcomings and errors in planning." The plant director added
that the number of expediters is not declining, although "their only
economic levers are the capacity to push a deal through and put a
bottle of perfume in the pocket." He also noted two techniques. Some
expediters send birthday cards to appropriate people and their families. One sometimes wears his old military uniform in order to impress people more.[35]

One Soviet journalist has related how the assistant director of
the Berdyansk Machinery Plant bribed several persons at the
Chelyabinsk Tractor Plant to get priority deliveries, but the recipients
merely kept the money and did not help. Then he found the right
person, a middle-aged woman manager who enjoyed an impeccable
professional reputation. Berdyansk paid her by putting her on its
payroll as an engineer, although the two plants were more than a
thousand miles apart. For 18 months Berdyansk received everything
it ordered—just as it ordered it and without delay. Upon discovery,
the recipient but not the giver of the bribes was imprisoned.[36] The
bribe-giver lost his job and several other executives of the Berdyansk
facility were reprimanded, which Pravda considered a fair outcome.[37]

In addition, Soviet industry practices barter, in which expediters
are sometimes involved. A chief engineer who needs metal sheeting
to keep production going but has an excess of copper pipe may find
it advisable to trade with a friendly chief engineer in a nearby enterprise. Although technically illegal, industrial barter apparently

arouses little reaction in the government. It can do much to offset mistaken calculations of need or timing errors.

QUALITY

Although quality is not a concept lending itself to purely objective measurement, it is without doubt a major component of consumer satisfaction. The range of quality in goods and services is still not adequate in the Soviet Union, in that consumer desire for higher quality is not fully appreciated by the central planning agencies and specific manufacturing enterprises. To be sure, as in all nations, some consumers accept lower quality, some medium quality, and some higher quality in their effective demand. However, most Soviet-made goods are of lower quality.

Probably the most vivid example of the quality problem one could encounter came in a major editorial in Izvestia. After scolding industry for many instances of slipshod work, it noted that some glassware factories were quite busy turning out drinking glasses that could not even be washed in hot water.[38]

One investigation of quality is revealing. An inquiry was conducted concerning the output of the Yerevan Tire Plant, the stimulus for which was the protest of a resident of Ordzhonikidze who bought a new Moskvich 412 car. After less than 1,600 miles of cautious driving, the tires blew out. He filed a complaint and the State Automobile Inspection Service agreed with him that the tires failed to meet minimum state standards. The plant was ordered to replace the tires. After more than three months the replacements arrived, but the buyer found them unsatisfactory. Since the State Automobile Inspection Service also found cracks three to six centimeters long and up to three millimeters deep, it ordered the plant to send another round of replacements.[39] Many other persons who had had comparable experience with Yerevan tires then complained, whereupon the plant issued a statement in which it reported that it had reprimanded the director of the technical control department for negligence in handling complaints, transferred a technician, and taken measures to improve quality. Pravda noted that the statement was evasive and suggested that the plant was taking remedial action only on the review of complaints and not on the quality of the output.[40]

Some quality investigations result in legal action by the state against executives. The chief engineer and long-time acting director of Moscow Furniture Factory Number 1 and the head of his quality control department were both imprisoned and heavily fined for supplying six stores with beds, mattresses, and sofas that fell short of state standards. The rationale for the decision was lack of proper supervision over assigned activities under article 152 of the Russian Republic Criminal Code.[41] Under the same legal provision the managing director and chief engineer of the Kursk Diary Combine were imprisoned for substandard output. The firm had had previous warnings and fines. It was shown that, when the quality control department rejected goods, the defendants arranged for at least half the production to bypass the department and go directly to grocery stores. The defendants argued that in all their actions they had only the interests of the state at heart. As a matter of fact, for the periods in which the misdeeds occurred, the plant won several awards for overfulfilling production goals.[42]

For many years the authorities, retailers, and consumers have had trouble with the Bolshevskiy Metal Dish Plant, but the situation is still unresolved. Recently it was found that the plant was turning out defective galvanized pails with, interestingly enough, an unclear rendering of the trademark on the defective goods. Central planning authorities have been remarkably patient with this factory.[43]

For a very long time there have been quality standards for Soviet output, but no coherent overall system for grading. For several years the consumer, the industrial buyer, and the buyer for trade organizations have been helped by the existence of the seal of quality. This seal is awarded to especially meritorious products, those that are "on a level with the best achievements of domestic and foreign technology."[44] In 1969, for example, over 200 brands of food products received the seal.[45] In his annual report to the nation, N. K. Baibakov, Vice-Chairman of the U.S.S.R. Council of Ministers and Chairman of the State Planning Committee, stated that the number of items receiving the seal of quality was growing every year and contended that the percentage of Soviet-made goods whose quality equaled the best in the world was increasing.[46] In 1972 over 1,500 products in the industrial sector encompassing fabrics, apparel, footwear, and chinaware carried the seal of quality; but a Soviet writer stated that this was insignificant as a share of total output in those industries.[47] Although such output is scheduled to grow, the plans in this sector of the economy specify that only 1.9 percent of 1975 output will be good enough to earn the seal.[48]

In a related development, Pravda announced in an editorial that starting in 1972, some industrial ministries were to certify all their "basic" products by quality category: highest, first, or second quality. This editorial went on with a stirring call to instill in people "a sense of proprietary responsibility for the honor of the factory trademark."[49] This was clarified later to indicate that "highest" would mean the category receiving the seal of quality.[50] It is intended that most products will fall into the category of "first" quality and that goods categorized as "second" will be redesigned or removed from production.

However, another aspect of the total quality problem is getting extremely little planner attention: The various standards utilized sequentially in turning out a final product do not mesh well and often are in disagreement. The standards in use at stage one may preclude ever reaching the standards set up for stage two or three.

However, the well-known and much decorated chief engineer of an industrial machinery company has raised several questions about the seal of quality. He recommended that it be given to machine tools in whole units rather than to individual machines and assemblies, and that the mark be given for longer time periods. He called attention to the great amount of paper work necessary to confer the mark and added:

> Experience suggests that enterprises should be rewarded more tangibly for putting out products with the seal of quality. Our plant, for example, produced 5,700,000 rubles' worth of certified output last year, but the increment over the usual price came to only 111,000 rubles in all. Yet it requires extra expenditures—of labor, of resources, of time—to manufacture articles with the seal of quality. In fact, the bonuses are meager, too: In all, 43,000 rubles were paid out to our personnel for manufacturing certified products. These sums thus have no appreciable influence on either the plant's economic indicators or the earnings of its production workers.[51]

Moreover, this man reported that his plant had given its 169 best production workers the right to affix their own personal mark to their work. While recognizing that some levels of quality would exceed the customers' needs, the general manager of another industrial plant complained that there was no economic incentive to produce a level of quality above the state standards.[52]

Increasingly there is organized resistance to poor quality. In part this development results from consumer protest and in part from the outraged feelings of professional buyers, store managers, and government officials. The authoritative magazine Sovetskaya Torgovlya reported, for example, that in the second quarter of 1971 alone trade enterprises ceased taking deliveries from 100 light industry enterprises, 16 metal, glass, and chinaware factories, and 47 furniture factories. Quality control inspection in that three-month period either completely rejected or reduced in grade between 15 and 30 percent of all goods produced. About 48 percent of all toys were completely rejected. Such inspection showed that one-third of television sets had defective workmanship.[53] The worst offender is the footwear industry. Izvestia reports that 20 million rubles' worth of shoes were rejected in 1970 alone, up 17 percent from 1969. Various footwear plants paid over 2 million rubles in fines in 1970 for such output. It was noted that some plants turned out certain lots containing not a single unit that could be accepted. Four shoe plants were specified as particularly derelict: The Paris Commune Factory, Fashionable Footwear Factory Number 1, the Ray Association of Minsk, and the Moscow Leather Combine.[54] The State Standards Committee of the U.S.S.R. in 1971 suspended shipments of shoes from the Ussuri Combine, clothing from the Baku Volodarsky Clothing Factory, and SK-4 combines from the Rostov Farm Machinery Association.[55] One trade planner with over 40 years' experience has stated that the samples of merchandise shown the wholesalers and retailers look as if they would please the consumer. However, when the goods arrive, "It's the same old story every time—outright defective output, low quality. The articles don't sell in the stores. The shelves become empty, but the warehouses are full."[56]

In a sympathetic yet critical report, Pravda has noted that the Omsk Footwear Factory delivered many thousands of pairs of shoes in 1971 that did not match the samples shown. However, the newspaper explained, not once during the year did this plant receive first-grade raw materials from its suppliers. Most were grades five, six, and seven.[57] However, the Chairman of the U.S.S.R. Council of Ministers' State Standards Committee, Professor V. Boitsov, categorically rejected the low-quality-materials defense for low-quality output. He maintained that if "closer business contact" is practiced, standard materials can be obtained. He gave three examples of enterprises where this problem had been solved: the Kiev Red Excavator Plant, Volgograd Red October Metallurgical Plant, and the Moscow Likhachev Vehicle Plant.[58]

A potentially very important step was taken in 1970 on the subject of quality, but its practical significance remains to be seen. The U.S.S.R. Council of Ministers and the Central Committee of the Communist Party passed a resolution entitled "On Enhancing the Role of Standards in Improving the Quality of Goods Produced" on November 10, 1970, stipulating that in cases of the sale of goods manufactured with deviations from legal standards and technical specifications, the proftis so obtained will be diverted to the state treasury and the production and sales will not count toward enterprise goals.[59] After the first year of operation of this policy, the Chairman of the State Standards Committee announced that 51 million rubles' worth of output was excluded from plan fulfillment and funds amounting to 11.5 million rubles confiscated.[60] This latter figure may have represented profits, but it may have also included some penalties. The Georgian Republic unit of the Standards Committee reported that it disqualified 2.5

million rubles' worth of output from plan fulfillment and confiscated net earnings of 223,000 rubles on such sales in 1971.[61] It was a modest but not unimpressive beginning for this national policy. Much of the value lies in the example set for others.

The quality of Soviet goods is dependent in part on the characteristics of quality control departments in the nation's manufacturing plants. There is widespread dissatisfaction with such organizational units, as exemplified in studies conducted by the Standardization Research Institute.[62] Such research is highly critical of the lack of autonomy of quality control departments in industry and points to the frequent, documented cases of plant officials overriding the quality controllers. This research is critical of the practice whereby the bonus-incentive program for quality control workers is dependent on the fulfillment of the plant's assigned quotas rather than maintenance of standards. In addition, the average quality control employee makes only about two-thirds of what an average production employee makes and the labor turnover is relatively high. Measurement equipment is not uniformly available. Moreover, the poor quality control in factories forces duplicate quality inspection further down the channels of distribution. The Standardization Research Institute concludes that this duplication of inspection has reached "intolerable proportions." Its director has advised that a large-scale experiment be conducted in which quality control departments would be put under the jurisdiction of ministries and/or the State Standards Committee rather than the plant executives. This proposed arrangement has been used by East Germany for many years with some success. A republic-level official of the State Standards Committee urged only that the plant directors' choices of quality control managers be subject to confirmation by higher authorities.[63] From 1969 on, these issues have given rise to considerable professional dialogue and many letters to the editors of leading publications in the U.S.S.R.

Meanwhile, harassment of quality control workers to the point of physical abuse occurs on occasion. In one well-documented case the aggrieved women quality controllers complained that it required two years to get the local law enforcement officers to start action. Finally a brigade leader and a foreman were found guilty of continuously beating them in an attempt to force acceptance of output.[64]

Even if the problems of organization structure, conflict of interest, pay, equipment, and duplication in quality control can be solved, there remains the obsolescence of standards that hold quality unnecessarily low. The State Standards Committee castigates industry for failure to formulate appropriate plans for updating and raising standards and failure to follow through after the plans are formulated. Once the standards are changed, industry does not implement them with revised blueprints and bills of specifications. Some industries that have been singled out for especially strong criticism are chemicals, petrochemicals, lumber, and pulp and paper. All have a particularly wide effect on other industries and services.[65]

The Association: Concept and Institution

At the 24th Soviet Communist Party Congress in 1971, Party Chairman Leonid Brezhnev and Premier Alexei Kosygin made important policy statements about products. They stressed a reorganization plan that would make for more product redesign and new products. They stated that the 1971-75 Five-Year Plan will establish "large production amalgamations" which will bring research, development, and production under a common management. This reorganization is mainly for the purpose of overcoming the traditional reluctance of Soviet manufacturing executives to halt production long enough to improve techniques or to change product characteristics. Moreover, Brezhnev announced that Soviet planners will reduce their traditional emphasis on gross quantities of product and move instead toward plans that will reward factories that seek innovation and factories that turn out quality goods. However, the real potential for change is in the day-to-day behavior of the large industrial ministries and professional planners rather than the general wishes of the top leadership.

In order to help carry out the general mission sketched by Brezhnev and Kosygin, the concept of the obyedineniye (association) is being developed further and promoted vigorously. This idea, not new, is essentially the bringing together of several naturally related enterprises for purposes of pooling some functions, particularly research on products and production processes and utilization of computer equipment, and sharing ideas and information on a wide range of items from labor productivity to supplier dependability. The highest incidence of this managerial concept is in consumer goods manufacturing, where about one-third of the enterprises belong to such a group. Growth of output in such affiliated enterprises is much higher than in other enterprises. The concept has had especially wide application and development in the Leningrad area, where by May 1971, there were "more than 50" large associations covering 233 manufacturing companies and 42 research, design, and construction firms.[66] By March, 1972, this had grown to 72 such associations covering "more than 300" manufacturing companies and "upwards of 50 research organizations and design organizations."[67] Pravda claimed

17

enthusiastically in an editorial that the association form of management modernizes the product line and improves the quality of goods more rapidly than traditional forms. The newspaper went on to say:

> In addition to their plants and research institutes, the large industrial associations often have major project designing, technological and industrial design organizations. This allows a closer connection between the processes of designing and introducing new items. It steers the interests of the scientists closer to the needs of the plants and makes for better coordination of the plans for scientific research with the plans for the development of production. As a result, scientific and technical progress is accelerated. The Positron Association, for instance, has reduced the period for mastering the output of new items from between two and five years to one year.[68]

Economist L. Blyakhman has argued vigorously for the association concept in order to reduce the research-to-production cycle. He has castigated the chemical engineering industry in particular for a 9-to-12-year cycle when, he contends, the new equipment and processes are obsolete in 6 to 7 years. He stresses the informational ties within an association that are missing when the researchers and developers are organizationally isolated.

> For example, reductions in the time spent in expert examinations, coordination sessions, the argument-and-reconciliation process, etc., alone have made it possible to shorten by one-third the schedules for the development and assimilation of comparable innovations at the Plastic Polymers, Positron, Svetlana and Paper Machinery Associations in Leningrad. . . .[69]

He goes on to extol the Food Industry Automatic Machinery Association in Odessa and its work. It consists of a scientific unit, two design units, a technological unit, an office for the acquisition of equipment, a start-up and adjustment unit, an experimental unit, a factory producing the new equipment, and a unit that trains people from food processing companies how to use the equipment. Blyakhman states that well-thought-out associations provide for the coordination of "technical and economic planning, financing, capital construction, supply and marketing on the scale of the whole complex."

There are obstacles in the way of forming associations, however, One province-level party secretary, N. Morosov, explained it this way:

Why is such a major matter advancing so slowly?
The executives of small enterprises oppose joining an
association for reasons of prestige. Cooperation within
an association would cause the previously independent
enterprises to lose their individuality on the micro-
territorial, province, and district levels. Departmental
barriers also retard this process.

Here is an example. The Proletarian Freedom
Woodworking Machine Tool Plant and a design bureau
are located on the same industrial site in Yaroslavl.
The design bureau designs machinery, and the plant's
shops turn and mill parts and put together subassem-
blies for these machines. The entrance gate is not all
that unites the two enterprises. In essence these two
organizations have been working for a long time to solve
common problems. It would seem that very little stands
in the way, but the association has not come into existence. The designers fear that they will be swamped with
unaccustomed work; and the plant's executives, concerned
about fulfilling current production plans, view union with
the designers as a burden. It seems too that the ministry's chief administration does not want to part with its
role of coordinator.[70]

Morosov gave other examples and indicated that additional attempts
were being made to combat localism by associating some enterprises
that were in differing geographic administrative areas.

Soviet economist I. Shifrin strongly endorses the need for associations. However, he has been critical of some that have formed,
claiming that they are associations in name only. At the same time
he is anxious to establish the policy that association executives receive higher pay than enterprise executives, which does not always
occur now. He is interested in formulating a clear legal and economically rational basis for the association type of organization:

It would be advisable [to clarify] the legal status
of a firm's branches. It is also necessary to provide
a clear formulation of possible means for the organizational consolidation of enterprises, an annexation of
one or several enterprises by a larger one, the opening
by existing enterprises of branches in other cities or in
rural areas, and so forth. In order to avoid the mechanical, irrational consolidation of enterprises, it is
necessary to formulate basic principles for the achievement of industrial and technical unity in new structural

19

formations. Included in these basic principles would be
similarity in the type of output, close cooperative ties
based on industrial affinity, etc.[71]

It is by no means settled that the association form will become
universal in Soviet industry, although the prospects are bright for it
to reach a majority position in a few years. The key is whether
ministries and central planners in Moscow can forgo a level of detail
to which they have long been committed personally, if not by instruc-
tion from above.

Management strategies and organization structure are intimately
related. In a nonsocialist economy the master strategy of the firm
is highly influential in determining the structure. But after it is in
place, the structure is critically important in determining how the
firm defines its risks, identifies its opportunities, and measures
accomplishment against criteria. In the U.S.S.R. the emerging master
theme for organization structure is, as stated, the association. The
early instances of the form indicate a patchwork quilt of improvisa-
tions. Whether this almost ad hoc coalescing will be permitted to
continue or only two or three combinations will gain Moscow's stamp
of approval remains to be seen.

Innovations and Inventions

Managerial resistance to product and process change has been
considerable, according to countless Soviet sources. Sometimes
where there was no demonstrable resistance, the slowness with which
the innovation was adopted was impressive. Former premier Nikita
Khrushchev phrased it in his own colorful manner:

In our country some bureaucrats are so used to the
old nag that they do not want to change over to a good
race horse, for he might tear away on the turn and even
spill them out of the sleigh! Therefore, such people will
hold on to the old nag's tail with both hands and teeth.[72]

The main reason for this state of affairs is that the reward system
has stressed fulfillment of assigned figures, not the taking of risks,
no matter how carefully calculated and researched. Also important
are the facts that inadequate resources and combinations of resources
are assigned for or available to improvements, and innovations
seemingly have grossly inadequate dissemination through channels
and across jurisdictional boundaries. Another reason is the inadequate price, and resultant inadequate margin, on most new items.
(See Chapter 5.)

The time horizon, too, should be noted. Ironically, it is short-run by American standards. Even a five-year plan is not long compared with the planning of large U.S. corporations. In practice, however, the Soviet enterprise executive has even a shorter framework, usually one year or less. This factor is given virtually no attention in Soviet literature. However, Derbisher and Glichev, who were interested more in incentives than in planning per se, have stated that the determination of the results of an enterprise's work on a yearly basis rather than a longer time discourages innovation.[73]

Two scientists, one heading up a mining mechanics research institute and the other an electrochemistry research institute, wrote that research organizations and industrial establishments sometimes are unable to find any common professional language and that industrial executives sometimes have no time for research matters. They gave an example of one plant where they had been delayed for three years from finishing a simple improvement to the production line. They acknowledged that in some circumstances there would have to be significant interference with output while they conducted pilot studies and perfected the experimental setups. They noted that, despite the instructions from appropriate directive authorities, ministries and departments often plan output from pilot installations. Sometimes the new industrial designs originated by the scientists and their research engineers are obsolete before production men let them be installed. One of their most interesting conclusions was that some ministries that successfully fill the production goals year after year never implement more than 70 to 80 percent of the goal for introduction of new production equipment.[74]

Inventions and what later happens to them have been causing much controversy. Patent protection is really not the problem, although some of what the Soviet government says apparently attempts to put patents in this perspective. The problem is to get inventors to register the designs in a timely manner; process them swiftly; screen them for type, uniqueness, and potential; disseminate the information throughout appropriate sectors of the economy; and accomplish implementation. Registration seems to come more rapidly when the invention takes place in a research institute than in an industrial enterprise. Several engineering schools offer, and some require, a course in patent studies. At the Sverdlovsk Polytechnical Institute the students "must make a study of the level of technology, using patent searches in the given spheres of production."[75] The Vice-Chairman of the U.S.S.R. Council of Ministers' State Committee on Invention and Discovery has emphasized the acute need for objective screening by scientific experts.[76] Occasionally something important that might command even a foreign market is isolated in the screening. An example is a pneumatic punch developed by the Siberian

Mining Institute of the U.S.S.R. Academy of Sciences and now exported to 30 countries.[77]

There is little incentive for an enterprise to register its invention, since the plant cannot, of course, really own the patent and license its use. There is some prestige for the enterprise, however; and this kind of reward, coupled with an appeal to patriotism, must not be discounted. Also not to be discounted is professional prestige for the inventors-innovators. However, the monetary compensation for such persons is usually slight and always unpredictable in amount. A Soviet legal scholar has stated:

> There is no clarity in the rules on remuneration for inventions, especially if their utilization will not yield savings but, for instance, will improve output quality or working conditions. In such cases, the appropriate instructions indicate that the remuneration is to be determined according to the "real value" of the innovation. Because there is still no uniform set of rules for determining the amount of the remuneration due to the innovators, the executives of enterprises and organizations decide this question by "rule of thumb." This practice often violates the innovators' rights.
>
> Here is an example confirming this point. A group of innovators created an original device for transmitting information on the operation of an automated complex of equpiment. Specialists in the Ministry of Instrument Making, Means of Automation and Control Systems set 311 rubles as the total remuneration for the innovators, on the basis of the innovation's "real value." Feeling that this sum was too little, the innovators appealed to the Committee on Inventions and Discoveries. As a result, the remuneration due them was increased to 9,000 rubles, taking into account the scale of introduction, the complexity of the problem they had solved and other factors.[78]

The inventions that are acted on most rapidly are those that fit neatly into existing niches in the structure of organizations and into budget categories, and that derive from inventors employed by the industrial organization. Those that cross lines suffer. One scientist recently gave several case examples of products and processes and the amount of delay they suffered.[79] Then he recommended that a special administrative category of inventions be created by the U.S.S.R. Council of Ministers' Committee on Inventions and Discoveries. This would be restricted to a small number of inventions perceived as of great economic value. The necessary work to refine the invention and apply it in industry would be compulsory and cut through all existing plans and commitments of research and development organizations and manufacturing firms. Although idealistic and replete with assumptions, the recommendation does have merit. One must note, of course, that some delay occurs in all types of economic systems and all countries.

The U.S.S.R. Council of Ministers' Committee on Inventions and Discoveries has reported that the flow of patent applications is at an unprecedented level and that 170,000 were expected in 1972 alone. The backlog of unexamined applications amounted to 104,000 at the beginning of that year. Additional personnel had been hired and a review board set up for disputed patent applications.[80]

Another scientist has documented several cases of inventions and discoveries, for some of which he could quantify the savings, all of which have received absolutely no use. He noted bitterly that many research and development planners and industrial executives do not even acknowledge notification of proven major inventions.[81] However, two other scientists who conducted a study of research institutes in Siberia were more conciliatory. They concluded that 9 percent of the discoveries and inventions were turned down on their merits when they were presented to industry or to intermediate organizations for further development. The rest of the rejections were attributed to extreme shortages of testing equipment, materials, and funds.[82] The U.S.S.R. Minister of Light Industry has stated that new technology and use of that technology on the production line is the key to a radical improvement in the quality of goods during the 1971-75 Plan.[83]

Considerable controversy has erupted concerning whether a patent should be credited to the principal investigator or to the collective in which he works. The great bulk of the credits and rewards go to groups. The factors of individual creativity versus group interaction and support, and the advantages of group laboratory facilities, both enter into the controversy. The dispute extends also to the proper authorship of journal articles treating the invention or discovery.[84]

Soviet banking officials have become more generous in lending policy for industry to renovate its machinery and equipment and to modernize its production lines and techniques. The duration of capital loans for production improvement has been changed from three to six years. The amount that can be approved at the local Gosbank level has been raised to 100,000 rubles and, at the Republic level, to 500,000 rubles. During the four years 1966-69 the Ukraine Gosbank extended 33,311 such loans, amounting to 736.3 million rubles, which was two and a half times the amount loaned in the five years 1961-65. Although his calculations are at best unclear, the head of the Ukrainian

Gosbank contends that the bank's production loans in 1969 alone enabled the production of an additional 55 million rubles in goods and the saving of 63 million rubles in Ukrainian industrial operations. This banker praised the chemical industry for particularly effective use of such credit and stated that for each ruble loaned to that industry, 3 rubles, 80 kopecks in sales resulted.[85]

New product development receives an as yet unmeasured amount of stimulation from the funds-handling techniques created by the economic reforms of the middle and late 1960s. In 1969 about 13 percent of all the profit in the national economy went into the enterprise material-incentive accounts, versus about 8 percent in 1968. Part of the material-incentive fund goes into bonuses, part into fringe benefits, and part into the production-development fund. Besides drawing on enterprise profits, the production-development fund has access to 15 to 45 percent of the depreciation allowances on fixed assets and proceeds from sale of unwanted fixed assets. Soviet analyst V. Pereslegin states:

> The quotas for the deductions from profits to the production-development fund are established as a proportion of the average yearly value of the fixed productive assets. The deductions are calculated: for each percent by which the sales volume (or balance sheet profit) exceeds that of the past year, as envisaged in the yearly plan; for each percent of the accounting profitability provided for in the annual plan. The quotas for the deductions from profits to the production-development fund are fixed for groups of enterprises and take account of the composition and the service life of the assets, notably of their wear.[86]

Wills and Hayhurst have said of the production development fund:

> It provides not, of course, the new capital for major extensions of enterprise which are derived from the central planning authority, but the resources for product improvement and improvement in productive efficiency. This fund seldom falls below 2-3% of the fixed capital employed with direct profits supplemented by an allowance for depreciation. It can rise to 15% in certain industrial sectors.[87]

ASSORTMENTS

The assortment situation has improved considerably since the early 1960s.[88] Manufacturing plants in the U.S.S.R. are today offering a wider variety of goods and some assortment within many varieties of goods, instead of only one model of each generic type of merchandise. The variety and assortment, of course, leave much to be desired by Western standards. Nevertheless, most Russian citizens are quite pleased at the trend. While noting that assortments are still too limited on many household appliances, Izvestia recently complained that there are already so many models that getting replacement parts is complicated and repair service fragmented. The newspaper recommended some standardization of assemblies and parts.[89]

A generic type of product may be in undeniable oversupply and yet the consumer not be satisfied. An example is socks and stockings. According to one outspoken Soviet economist, this is because the assortment is inappropriate in size and color.[90] This economist goes on to say:

> . . . it is necessary now to improve the planning of consumer goods production in such a way as to bring about timely revision of the assortment, enlarge the range of goods and improve the quality and appearance of the goods. . . .
>
> . . . the retail stores and wholesale bases can, in theory, present the mills with a "note" protesting "distortions" in goods shipments. But in practice this occurs only after the mills have turned in their reports of "good work" and their staffs have received bonuses; "memoranda" from trade officials are, moreover, quite rare and unpopular, and they are pitched in pleading, not a demanding tone.
>
> [   ]
>
> . . . trade orders, which reflect Soviet public demand, should be fulfilled not only "in general and on the whole" in terms of ruble volume, behind which one cannot perceive either the goods or the buyers, but also and invariably in terms of the full range of assortment specifications corresponding to public demand. This was the intention in the transfer of industrial enterprises to operating on orders from retail outlets, trade trusts and wholesale bases. . . .
>
> In clothing, these specifications would be, say, the cloth, color, cut, model, size, and build; in short, the specifications for which the buyer "votes."
>
> We consider it advisable that profit obtained from the output of goods that were not ordered be turned over to the [national government] budget, rather than left with the producer, as now happens.[91]

25

A. I. Struyev, veteran trade official, issued the following appeal to store managers in the U.S.S.R.:

> One cannot remain silent today about the fact that in a number of stores . . . the assortment of goods is narrow.
>   . . . in connection with the increase in the population's income, the demand for clothing, footwear, and household articles has risen sharply. The trade organizations are called upon to work in a more concerted and more efficient manner, to intensify their influence on production and to press for the fulfillment and overfulfillment of plans and for the improvement in the assortment and quality of goods.[92]

Economist I. M. Khrekin, Director of the All-Union Research Institute for the Study of the Population's Demand for Consumer Goods and the Conditions of Trade, criticized one industry in the following manner:

> The institute has established that the assortment of washing machines is clearly out of step with demand. Analysts have submitted specific recommendations. But industry has turned a deaf ear to them and keeps on increasing the production of precisely those machines that are not always marketable. This has affected trade; the growth of home washing machine sales has slackened and inventories of these machines have increased sharply over the past five years.[93]

Production of washing machines for household use began in 1950. By 1970 over 40 million had been built and about half the households had one. In that year over 5 million were produced. Also in that year, the number of days' stock on hand doubled. Over the years more and more plants have begun production of this appliance. By the end of 1971, 33 plants, each with one or more brands and some with several models per brand, produced washing machines.[94] By mid-1972 the number had declined to 31.[95]

A modicum of assortment has been created throughout the washing machine industry, but some brands are quite similar. Only one brand carries the seal of quality. One brand, Batumi, was recently discontinued because of its quite poor reputation. There were three conspicuous problems with the assortment in this industry as of 1972. First, "semiautomatic" machines made up only a "small part" of production volume, and most of these had only one washing cycle. About 85 percent of production was of the tub and manual wringer type. Second, there was no completely automatic machine made. Third, there was no mini-machine for sale, although one organization of professionals had long recommended it. One manufacturing firm claimed to have such a design ready for production; but the Ministry of Machine Building for Light Industry and the Food Industry and Household Appliances vetoed production, on the grounds that another plant was "mastering the production of the same item." However, that plant has been in that awkward stage for six years—without success.[96]

The experience of one brand of washing machine is informative. The SMR 1.5 from the Searchlight Plant was put into production many years ago by the simple expedient of copying a model that was discontinued simultaneously by the Vladimir Ilyich Plant. Production peaked out in 1970. By 1971 the plant's production assignments were cut in half. At that time it began to design a new generation of laundry appliance. One Soviet trade writer commented: "It made a serious mistake from the beginning: In order to keep in step with demand, one must already be working on the next model while offering the market a new item. . . ."[97] Under pressure from many sides, the firm did an about-face and by early 1972 had designed a semi-automatic washer with the sales theme of suitability for synthetic fabrics. It was named the Eureka. To what extent it incorporated design ideas from other plants in unknown. Moreover, the firm's designers were working on a project to convert the Eureka to a fully automatic device. The first orders for the semiautomatic Eureka had just been received at the time. Thus it appears that some organizations can change their outlook, at least in the short run.

Another enterprise that found it necessary to change its washing machine line was Cheboksary Rubber Goods, after it found sales off drastically, inventories mounting, and rejections common. It has attempted to increase the assortment in the line, has redesigned the old products, and has cut production on the unpopular model. This plant has had quality problems as well.[98] Obviously the problems of assortment in this industry, such as sketched above, overlap the problems of technology and new product development.

Trud has called attention to a problem of size assortment that is developing in refrigerators. Only 4 percent of units being manufactured are "large capacity." It also notes the extreme bias in screen sizes of television sets and the great difficulty in finding a large size. Moreover, it points to the washing machine debacle and the almost classic problems of footwear assortment.[99]

PRODUCT DIFFERENTIATION

Very closely related to, and somewhat overlapping, the subject of assortment is the subject of product differentiation. By utilizing policies of product differentiation, according to Harry L. Hansen, "the seller has the opportunity to distinguish his product from that of competitors in the minds of consumers; hopefully to establish an image as a progressive company among them; and to steal a march on competitors. . . ."[100] Wendell R. Smith describes product differentiation as being "concerned with bending demand to the will of supply." Such a set of policies is often contrasted with policies of "segmentation of the market," which Smith defines as "rational and more precise adjustment of product and marketing effort to consumer or user requirements."[101] Smith further states that market segmentation "consists of viewing a heterogeneous market (one characterized by divergent demand) as a number of smaller homogeneous markets in response to different product preferences among important market segments."[102] On analysis it is possible, of course, that the two sets of policies are not always opposites and that product differentiation may be superimposed on market segmentation, while market segmentation may be a necessary prerequisite for product differentiation. At any rate, the practice of product differentiation is usually associated with relatively small functional distinctiveness, if any, and at least some, but often much, product identity and psychological distinctiveness.

In the Soviet economy there is a long-run trend toward substantial use of product differentiation. Marks indicating the manufacturing plant which produced a particular produce were utilized by the Communists as early as the 1920s, and these production marks gradually led to a resumption of the use of "trademarks." Employing standard party terminology, Pravda recently stated: "Since it is disadvantageous to retain articles in stock, the struggle in behalf of the plants' trademarks has been intensified."[103] What this amounts to, in Soviet phraseology, is a hearty endorsement of the usefulness of trademarks.

There are at least five reasons explaining the adoption of product differentiation in the U.S.S.R. First, pinpointing of responsibility for the product is easily accomplished because the manufacturing firm is readily identified. Second, there has been a recognition, at times grudging and at other times bewildered, that not all consumers want perfectly standardized, spartanly designed merchandise. Third, participation in a choice-making process is an important behavioral need. This need gains importance as various physical signs of affluence appear around the ordinary man. One way of indulging this need without spreading much effective power among the masses is to offer variety and assortment of goods. Fourth, there is a need to impress foreign visitors to the Soviet Union, both from highly developed and less developed countries. Fifth, the financial incentives program for manufacturing executives and workers, the mainstream of which is normally attributed to economist Evsei Liberman of Kharkov University, has made some of those persons much more concerned with sales and enterprise earnings and consonance with integrated goals' than ever before. Despite severe difficulties, reservations, and shortcomings in implementing the plans, some manufacturing organizations want to differentiate their products in order to develop repeat customers, create stable channels, and build identities and even "images" for specific products.

Liberman's program has encouraged new developments in the product line of an enterprise, especially if they involve any technological improvement or greater reliability or durability. He has taken this position:

> At present, profitability is reduced if the enterprises are mastering many new products and a great deal of new technology. For this reason, we have worked out a scale of supplements to and reductions in incentive payments in accordance with the proportion of new products in the plan. The incentive payments will be somewhat reduced for the output of items established in production and raised substantially for the introduction of new products.[104]

One must be very careful to note that the ideas and procedures in the above quotation can apply even if the managers of the industrial establishment have little authority, i. e., even if the basic product line decisions are made at the level of the ministries or central planners in Moscow.

The Deputy Minister of Trade for the Russian Republic, S. Sarukhanov, proposed that all consumer goods manufacturers be given an exemption from the turnover tax on the first year's mass-production volume of any new consumer product. This proposal used the term "new" in the normal Western manner to include substantial change, not just a totally new product.[105]

Some examples of product differentiation might be helpful. Although there are many manufacturers of refrigerators, the brand produced by the Likhachev Works in Moscow has been successfully differentiated from the rest. It is widely regarded as the best by far and carries a price 15 to 25 percent above functionally comparable models of other industrial firms. The core of the explanation for the perceived difference is that Likhachev is primarily a producer of industrial equipment and automotive goods, and the refrigerator is one of the few consumer goods it produces in significant quantity. A highly placed trade official told the author that consumers ascribe a technological sophistication and high quality to Likhachev's refrigerator. How much of this differentiation is due to the factory's marketing initiative and how much to the consumers' curiosity and drive is unknown, but the factory is certainly not passive in this regard. The complex of differentiation is doubly interesting in that one refrigerator maker, Erevan, presents itself as the master of refrigerator manufacturing and specializes its efforts in that device. There is, of course, no way to quantify the possibility that consumers will create a greater measure of product differentiation than producers intend.

Another example is in the motorcycle and motorbike industry. Although there are several producers, both Lvov Motorcycle Works and Izhevsk, with its Izh-350, have differentiated their products from all the rest. Lvov is particularly interesting in that it has developed a continuous flow of questionnaire data from wholesale buyers and samples of consumers on the characteristics of the product and potential demand. The Izh-350 has been associated thematically with speed. A third example is in the bicycle industry. There are several manufacturers, but Riga brand and Kharkov brand have differentiated themselves from the industry at large. Through adroit word-of-mouth promotion, the Riga Works has subtly and carefully exploited the fact that it was already an outstanding producer of bicycles long before the Communist take-over and the implication that its standards and professional integrity have never suffered.

FASHION

Fashion is one of the most interesting manifestations of economic and social change in the U.S.S.R. Although Karl Marx disapproved of what he termed the "murderous, meaningless caprices of fashion,"[106] the concept and practice did not end immediately following the Revolution. It declined and existed in attenuated but fairly vigorous form in the 1920s.[107] Fashion almost disappeared between 1928 and the mid-1950s but then began a slow comeback. Today the Soviet government no longer disapproves of or disparages fashion in apparel. Furthermore, it does not utilize fashion merely to get rid of surpluses of certain materials, as it once did. After long years of dialogue on the subject, designers and policy makers have agreed on the psychic utility of fashion, provided the fashion cycle is slow enough for the physical utility of the garments to be consumed. This is made easier by the general avoidance of fads and the emphasis on "restraint, simplicity, practicality."[108]

Consumer interest in fashion is still growing, and more segmentation of that interest is being recognized. As one Soviet fashion executive explains, fashion concepts vary "according to age-group categories and the tastes of individual groups in society."[109] One segment is the high fashion of the designer, "a fashion for displays, exhibitions and wishes,"[110] not intended for production. Izvestia has criticized this state of affairs as failing to meet the needs of the "ultrafashionable" segment of the population.[111] A currently emerging segment of the fashion market is men's apparel, indicated by the long lines of male and female shoppers waiting patiently for an opportunity to purchase the small supplies of fashionable ties, shirts, and trousers. However, Levashova states that the "decisive" and most important segment is that of young people.[112] Interest in fashion has now risen to the point that retailers are quite anxious to gain authority to reduce prices on goods going out of style, for they realize such merchandise is far less apt to be sold than in years gone by.[113]

Each republic has its own fashion designers, and there is an overlay of ethnic type in their offerings. Many of their products utilize the applied and decorative arts of their republic and cater to the local taste. For example, apparel designed for the three Baltic republics must be quite subdued, while that for the Ukraine, Belorussia, and Moldavia includes bold patterns and bright, contrasting colors.[114]

There are virtually no specialty shops for ready-made, high-fashion items and extremely few for mass fashions. Better-quality clothing is usually tailor-made, and there is surprisingly large use of such shops. Some department stores regard their tailoring departments as the highest-quality unit of the organization, and some seek to differentiate themselves from other stores by this means. Often the only way to obtain the clothes exhibited in the stores' fashion shows is through the tailoring department by individual order.

NOTES

1. Marshall I. Goldman, Soviet Marketing: Distribution in a Controlled Economy (New York: Free Press of Glencoe, 1963), p. 69.

2. "Editorial: Reserves of Trade," Pravda, August 4, 1970, p. 1. CDSP, 22 (September 1, 1970), 14-15.

3. Alexei Kosygin, "On the State Five-Year Plan for the Development of the U.S.S.R. National Economy," Izvestia, November 25, 1971, pp. 2-4. CDSP, 23 (December 21, 1971), 12-24, at 13.

4. See A. Butov and I. Pogosov, Vestnik Statistiki, no. 6. (1971), 2-13. JPRS, 53786; TUEA, 276.

5. Kosygin, "On the State Five-Year Plan," pp. 12-24, at p. 15.

6. "In the C.P.S.U. Central Committee and the U.S.S.R. Council of Ministers: On Measures for Ensuring the Further Development of Production of Goods in Mass Demand," Pravda, October 29, 1971, pp. 1-2. CDSP, 23 (November 23, 1971), 2.

7. See L. Tairov, "Before Cutting the Ribbon: Why the Facilities of New Enterprises Are Being Slowly Assimilated," Pravda, April 1, 1972, p. 2. CDSP, 24 (April 26, 1972), 30, 35.

8. For example, see Janet G. Chapman, Real Wages in Soviet Russia Since 1928 (Cambridge, Mass.: Harvard University Press, 1963); and Philip Hanson, The Consumer in the Soviet Economy (Evanston: Northwestern University Press, 1968).

9. Hanson, The Consumer in the Soviet Economy, p. 41.

10. Chapman, Real Wages in Soviet Russia Since 1928.

11. Ya. Ya. Kotkovsky, O. K. Rybakov, and A. P. Strukov, cited in Gertrude E. Schroeder, "Consumption in the U.S.S.R.: A Survey," Studies on the Soviet Union, 10, no. 4 (1970), 1-40, at p. 22.

12. Schroeder, "Consumption in the U.S.S.R.: A Survey," pp. 17-18.

13. E. G. Liberman, Economic Methods and the Effectiveness of Production (White Plains, N.Y.: International Arts and Sciences Press, 1971), p. 71. Originally published by Ekonomika Publishing House, Moscow, 1970.

14. Ya. Orlov and L. Margolin, "Around the Steering Wheel," Izvestia, March 10, 1970, p. 4. CDSP, 23 (April 6, 1971), 34-35.

15. "Ensure a Regular Supply of Spare Parts," Izvestia, October 7, 1971, p. 4. CDSP, 23 (November 2, 1971), 32.

16. "Editorial: More Goods for the People," Izvestia, August 12, 1970, p. 1. CDSP, 22 (September 8, 1970), 18.

17. I. Shatunovsky, "Footdragging," Pravda, January 16, 1972, p. 6. CDSP, 24 (February 9, 1972), 5.

18. S. Sarukhanov, "Returning to What Was Printed: But Why Are They Not on Sale?," Pravda, August 7, 1970, p. 2. CDSP, 22 (September 8, 1970), 18.

19. V. Tatsiy, "Delimiting Illegal Private Trading from the Embezzlement of Socialist Property," Sovetskaya Yustitsiya, no. 18 (September 1970), 17-18. JPRS, 51783, TUEA, 181.

20. "Path to a Blind Alley," Komsomolskaya Pravda, February 12, 1971, p. 2. CDSP, 23 (April 6, 1971), 26-27.

21. "Decree of the Praesidium of the U.S.S.R. Supreme Soviet," Vedomosti Verkhovnovo Soveta SSSR, no. 13 1515 (April 1, 1970), items 108, 134. CDSP, 22 (May 19, 1970), 31-32.

22. A. Basov, "Dried Fish with Diamonds," Selskaya Zhizn, February 13, 1971, p. 4. CDSP, 23 (April 6, 1971), 27.

23. A. Shliyenkov, "Case Number 425," Komsomolskaya Pravda, January 31, 1971, p. 4. CDSP, 23 (April 6, 1971), 26.

24. A. Linnik and A. Rakov, "Where the 'Soft Gold' Comes from," Sovetskaya Rossia, January 31, 1971, p. 2. CDSP, 23 (April 6, 1971), 27.

25. E. Parkhomovsky, "Look out for the Car!," Izvestia, January 22, 1971, p. 3. CDSP, 23 (February 23, 1971), 13-15.

26. "They Don't Try Harder," Time, March 1, 1971, p. 24.

27. Albert Parry, The New Class Divided (New York: Macmillan, 1966), p. 181.

28. Ibid., p. 191.

29. "Strict Accountability for Materials," Izvestia, April 13, 1972, p. 4. CDSP, 24 (May 10, 1972), 21.

30. Parry, The New Class Divided, pp. 181-82.

31. Ibid., pp. 183-84.

32. P. Barashev, "A Case Is Heard: Not Subject to Appeal," Pravda, February 18, 1972, p. 6. CDSP, 29 (March 15, 1972), 16-17.

33. Yu. Shpakov, "Agent's Demise," Pravda, November 16, 1971, p. 3. CDSP, 23 (December 14, 1971), 27.

34. V. Biletsky, "Sending Out 'Expediters,'" Pravda, February 25, 1972, p. 3. CDSP, 24 (March 22, 1972), 19, 21.

35. M. Ryzhov, Pravda, February 25, 1972; and Murray Seeger, "Russia's 'Pushers' Deal in Efficiency, Not Drugs," Washington Post, May 4, 1972, p. G-2.

36. Shpakov, "Agent's Demise."

37. "Accomplices Get Their Just Deserts," Pravda, February 11, 1972, p. 2. CDSP, 24 (March 8, 1972), 20.

38. "Editorial: More Goods for the People," Izvestia, August 12, 1970, p. 1. CDSP, 22 (September 8, 1970), 18-19.

39. M. Kryukov, "Neither Car nor Tires," Pravda, October 29, 1971, p. 3. CDSP, 23 (November 23, 1971), 27, 31.

40. "What Was Done After the Pravda Report: Formal Response," Pravda, December 9, 1971, p. 3. CDSP, 23 (January 4, 1972), 49.

41. Ed. Polyanovsky, "Called to Account for Defects," Izvestia, June 5, 1971, p. 6. CDSP, 23 (July 20, 1971), 23; and Polyanovsky, "The Price of Substandard Goods," Izvestia, June 20, 1971, p. 4. CDSP, 23 (July 20, 1971), 23.

42. Yu. Feofanov, "The Skeleton Key and Kefir," Izvestia, December 9, 1971, p. 6. CDSP, 23 (January 4, 1972), 40.

43. Al. Yemel'yanov, "Defective Goods Producers with Seniority," Sovetskaya Torgovlya, December 13, 1969, p. 3. JPRS, 50264; TOUTAS, 104.

44. "Editorial: Seal of Quality," Pravda, June 21, 1972, p. 1. CDSP, 24 (July 17, 1972), 25.

45. "Figures and Facts," Sovetskaya Torgovlya, no. 4 (April 1970), 58-63. JPRS, 50700; TOUTAS, 130.

46. N. K. Baibakov, "On the State Plan for the Development of the U.S.S.R. National Economy in 1971," Pravda, December 9, 1970, pp. 1-3. CDSP, 22 (January 5, 1971), 8-16, at 10-11.

47. K. Michurin, "We Complete Review of Quality of Consumer Goods," Pravda, June 23, 1972, p. 2. CDSP, 24 (July 17, 1972), 24-25.

48. Ibid.

49. "Editorial: Planning Quality," Pravda, December 21, 1971, p. 1. CDSP, 23 (January 18, 1972), 16.

50. "Editorial: Seal of Quality."

51. A. Vernik, "Problems and Judgments: Certified for Quality," Pravda, October 3, 1971, p. 2. CDSP, 23 (November 2, 1971), 31-32.

52. A. Shmakov, "Verified by the Ruble," Izvestia, May 16, 1972, p. 2. CDSP, 24 (June 14, 1972), 26.

53. I. Tsitovsky, "The Basic Criterion Is Consumer Demand," Sovetskaya Torgovlya, September 18, 1971, p. 2. CDSP, 23 (December 14, 1971), 9.

54. M. Karzanova, "Industry, Trade and the Contract," Izvestia, December 17, 1971, p. 3. CDSP, 23 (January 11, 1972), 13.

55. "Editorial: Planning Quality."

56. P. Zakabluchny, "Letter to the Editor: What Does Conscience Dictate?—Invitation to a Discussion," Pravda, January 13, 1972, p. 3. CDSP, 24 (February 9, 1972), 5.

57. G. Ivanov, "If the Chain Is Broken: Why the Footwear Factory Did not Fulfill Its Annual Assignment," Pravda, January 11, 1972, p. 2. CDSP, 24 (February 9, 1972), 4-5.

58. V. Boitsov, "Planning Quality," Pravda, March 3, 1972, p. 2. CDSP, 24 (March 29, 1972), 24.

59. N. K. Baibakov, "On the State Plan for 1971," p. 11.

60. Boitsov, "Planning Quality."

61. G. Zedginidze, "Goods for the People: Incentive to Renewal," Pravda, March 28, 1972, p. 2. CDSP, 24 (April 26, 1972), 30.

62. For example, see A. Derbisher and A. Glichev, "Routes of Technical Progress: How to Control Quality," Pravda, September 21, 1969, p. 2. CDSP, 21 (October 15, 1969), 9-10. See also A. Derbisher, "Problems and Judgments: Are Quality-Control Services Perfect?," Pravda, October 9, 1971, p. 3. CDSP, 23 (November 9, 1971), 30-31.

63. Zedginidze, "Goods for the People."

64. F. Mustafayev, "Follow-up: Good Lesson," Komsomolskaya Pravda, February 12, 1971, p. 2. CDSP, 23 (April 20, 1971), 29, 48.

65. Boitsov, "Planning Quality."

66. "Editorial: The Policy Is to Create Associations," Pravda, May 24, 1971, p. 1. CDSP, 23 (June 22, 1971), 23-24.

67. G. Romanov, "According to a Single Plan," Pravda, March 16, 1972, p. 2. CDSP, 24 (April 12, 1972), 28.

68. "Editorial: The Policy Is to Create Associations."

69. L. Blyakhman, "The Factory Sector of Science: Experience and Prospects of the Association," Pravda, December 1, 1971, p. 3. CDSP, 23 (December 28, 1971), 1-3.

70. N. Morosov, "Science of Management: On the Road to Becoming an Association," Pravda, March 27, 1972, p. 2. CDSP, 24 (April 26, 1972), 29-30.

71. I. Shifrin, "The Right to Be Called an Association," Izvestia, June 2, 1971, p. 3. JPRS, 53535, TOUTAS, 255.

72. Quoted in Barry M. Richman, Soviet Management (Englewood Cliffs, N.J.: Prentice-Hall, 1965), p. 189. Also see Richman, "Managerial Opposition to Product Innovation in Soviet Union Industry," California Management Review, 6 (Winter 1963), 11-26.

73. Derbisher and Glichev, "Routes of Technical Progress."

74. A. Dzidziguri and N. Landia, "The Tempos of Scientific Quest: The Experiment at the Plant," Pravda, August 26, 1970, p. 3. CDSP, 22 (September 22, 1970), 19.

75. V. Eventov, "Patent on One's Work," Pravda, March 23, 1972, p. 3. CDSP, 24 (April 19, 1972), 27.

76. V. Tsaregorodtsev, "The Law Protects Inventions," Pravda, December 28, 1971, p. 3. CDSP, 23 (January 25, 1972), 20.

77. Ye. Yefimov, "The Innovator and the Law," Pravda, February 4, 1972, p. 2. CDSP, 24 (March 1, 1972), 14-15.

78. Ibid.

79. V. Rassokhin, "The Fate of the Major Invention," Izvestia, May 25, 1971, p. 3. CDSP, 23 (June 22, 1971), 26-27.

80. "After Criticism," Pravda, January 10, 1972, p. 2. CDSP, 24, (February 9, 1972), 24.

81. M. Rostarchuk, "Stopped-up Horn of Plenty," Izvestia, November 21, 1971, p. 1. CDSP, 23 (December 21, 1971), 5.

82. Yu. Kanygin and A. Mironenko, "Apply Innovations in Production: Creative Shops," Pravda, November 21, 1971, p. 2. CDSP, 23 (December 21, 1971), 5-6.

83. N. Tarasov, "How Is the Introduction of New Trade Methods Proceeding?," Izvestia, December 29, 1971, p. 2. CDSP, 23 (January 25, 1972), 25-26.

84. See, for example, the following articles in Literaturnaya Gazeta: Zory Shokhin, "The Scientist's Ethic: Discovery Made—But Who Made It?," January 26, 1972, p. 11; 'We Discuss the Article 'Discovery Made—But Who Made It?," March 1, 1972, p. 12; V. Perevedentsev, "Collectivism True and False," April 19, 1972, p. 11; Ye. Kopylova, "At No Loss to Society," April 19, 1972, p. 11; L. Makash, "Everyone Loses," April 19, 1972, p. 11; "The Majority Opinion: 'This Is Intolerable!," April 19, 1972, p. 11.

85. G. Pavlenko, "Credit Strengthens Relations," Pravda Ukrainy, August 8, 1970, p. 2. JPRS, 51754; TUEA, 179.

86. V. Pereslegin, Finance and Credit in the U.S.S.R. (Moscow: Progress Publishers, 1971), pp. 109-10.

87. Gordon Wills and R. Hayhurst, "Marketing in Socialist Societies," European Journal of Marketing, 5, no. 1 (Spring 1971), 13-28, at 18.

88. Compare Philip Hanson, "The Assortment Problem in Soviet Retail Trade," Soviet Studies, 14 (April 1963), 347-64.

89. "Specialization of the Production of Consumer Goods," Izvestia, November 30, 1968, p. 2. CDSP, 20 (December 18, 1968), 26-27.

90. Ya. Orlov, "Consumer Demand Is the Guideline—How to Develop Trade," Pravda, April 15, 1971, p. 3. CDSP, 23 (May 11, 1971), 43-44.

91. Ibid.

92. "Today Is Trade Worker's Day: In the Customer's Interests," Pravda, July 23, 1967, p. 1. CDSP, 19 (August 19, 1967), 28-29.

93. A. Krivel and I. M. Khrekin, "How Trade Should Be Developed: The Buyer Calls the Tune," Pravda, May 6, 1971, p. 3. CDSP, 23 (June 1, 1971), 36.

94. L. Margolin, "Demand, Production and Trade: The Instructive Story of the Washing Machine," Sovetskaya Torgovlya, January 8, 1972, p. 3. CDSP, 24 (February 9, 1972), 1-4.

95. "When Will Automatic Washers Appear?," Izvestia, June 20, 1972, p. 3. CDSP, 24 (July 17, 1972), 26-27.

96. L. Margolin, "Demand, Production and Trade."

97. Ibid.

98. "Poor Workmanship Costs You More," Pravda, April 17, 1972, p. 2. CDSP, 24 (May 17, 1972), 26-27.

99. D. Ukrainsky and Ye. Galkin, "Goods That Everyone Needs: The Plan and Shortages—Two Aspects of a Single Problem," Trud, August 5, 1971, p. 2. CDSP, 23 (December 14, 1971), 8-9.

100. Harry L. Hansen, Marketing: Text, Techniques, and Cases (3rd ed., Homewood, Ill.: Richard D. Irwin, 1967), p. 455.

101. Wendell R. Smith, "Product Differentiation and Market Segmentation as Alternative Marketing Strategies," Journal of Marketing, 21 (July 1956), 5.

102. Ibid., p. 6.

103. "Summer Goods," Pravda, May 12, 1970, p. 1. CDSP, 22 (June 9, 1970), 19-20.

104. E. G. Liberman, "Enterprise Profits as Basis for Incentive Payments Improve Economic Management and Planning: The Plan, Profits and Bonuses," Pravda, September 9, 1962, p. 3. CDSP, 14

(October 3, 1962), 13-15. Also see Voprosy Ekonomiki, no. 6, 1955; Kommunist, no. 10, 1956; and Kommunist, no. 1, 1959.

105. S. Sarukhanov, "Returning to What Was Printed."

106. Quoted in Dwight E. Robinson, "The Economics of Fashion Demand," Quarterly Journal of Economics, 75 (August 1961), 376-98.

107. See L. E. Hubbard, Soviet Trade and Distribution (London: Macmillan, 1938), p. 274.

108. Irina Andreyeva, "We Reply: Fashions Die Young," Sovetskaya Kultura, December 3, 1966, p. 4. CDSP, 19 (March 15, 1967), 11-12.

109. A. Levashova, "This Season's Fashions," Izvestia, March 18, 1972, p. 5. CDSP, 24 (April 12, 1972), 12.

110. Ibid.

111. A. Yezhelov and I. Karpenko, "The Ins and Outs of Clothing," Izvestia, April 11, 1972, p. 4. CDSP, 24 (May 10, 1972), 6-7.

112. Levashova, "This Season's Fashions."

113. See M. Iosilevich, "Problems and Polemics: Goods with Buyer Appeal," Izvestia, February 26, 1972, p. 2. CDSP, 24 (March 22, 1972), 29.

114. Nikolai Tarasov, Light Industry (Moscow: Novosti Publishing House, 1972), pp. 39-40.

2

RETAIL TRADE

HISTORY AND STRUCTURE

Retail trade in the U.S.S.R. consists of two large sectors, the state stores and the cooperative stores, and a small sector, the kolkhoz marketplaces. (The marketplaces are considered in the agricultural marketing section of Chapter 5.) This chapter considers the two main sectors.

Retail and wholesale trade was nationalized November 21, 1918, 13 months after the beginning of the Bolshevik Revolution on October 26, 1917. The Bolsheviks recognized some need for the cooperative sector, and thus the constitution recognizes both state and cooperative activity. However, philosophically there is a Soviet preference for state activity. The state sector is by far the larger and has been since the middle 1930s. It currently conducts about 70 percent of retail sales. The state sector's increase in share of the market has come about in part because of the philosophical preference for that sector by people in power but, more important, because of a long-run shift of population from the countryside to the city. The state store network is mostly urban and the cooperative store network mostly rural.

Also involved in the state store sector are the Ministry of Culture, which operates some of the book shops; the Ministry of Health, which operates the pharmacies; and the Ministry of Communication, which operates some of the newsstands. Jurisdictional boundaries tend to be rigidly enforced. For example, a municipal official recently protested that newsstand clerks ran out of stock in two or three hours but could then be productive for the rest of their shift by selling inexpensive convenience goods if the various government departments would only allow it.[1] There are also "workers' supply departments," which are stores selling meals and a very limited variety of merchandise to employees of particular factories, and military post exchanges. Their sales are included in those of the state store network.

Beginning in 1953, the cooperative network was permitted to operate some commission shops and stalls to which kolkhoz farms, and kolkhoz farmers acting as individuals, might send their goods for sale. The cooperative society earns a commission on such transactions, often as large as 10 percent. The prices charged in such stalls can legally exceed the state prices.

The cooperative societies do not exactly fit the pattern to which Westerners are accustomed, especially in utilization of the Rochdale principles. Soviet retail cooperatives are different in that the basic units possess little autonomy. For example, decisions on staffing managerial positions and setting budgets are made in the cooperative system hierarchy, well above the basic unit. Payment of dividends to members is not common practice and, when payment is made, it may have no relationship to individual patronage. Pricing is almost never the prerogative of the cooperative. The system is headed by a central union of cooperatives known as Centrosoyuz but is under the authority of the Council of Ministers for highest-level decisions and fundamental policy. However, in practice the top officials of the government store network are extremely influential in the policies of the system of cooperatives and in naming store managers.

In the years following the 1917 Revolution many private enterprise retailers remained in business, but their situation was uncertain and their relationships with the government erratic and usually strained. For a short time it appeared that private retailing would be wiped out. Traditional channels of distribution were giving way to new forms. All institutions and their legal, physical, and communications ties were in a state of change. Economic historian Lancelot Lawton records that many products passed through channels containing 15 middlemen during the harried, confused years of the 1920s.[2] The 1920s were dominated by the NEP (New Economic Policy), which ran from 1921 to 1928.[3] It served to legitimize the legality of private trade and small industry. Hubbard records that in 1926, private enterprise retailers conducted 43.8 percent of the trade. These private organizations were very small and comprised 83.6 percent of all retail organizations in the economy. However, taxation of private shopkeepers increased, their opportunities to obtain merchandise decreased, and the economy began to utilize central planning to a greater extent and give detailed attention to trade. Thus in 1927-28, private retailers' share of sales fell to 23.4 percent.[4] The First Five-Year Plan was being created during these years and was inaugurated in October 1928. By the early 1930s the private enterprise shops all but disappeared, and private trading was categorized as against the public interest.

As of 1968 there were 671,300 stores, a large increase over the 407,200 of 1940.[5] The state and cooperative sectors had a sales volume of 164 billion rubles in 1971, a claimed real increase of 7.0 percent over 1970.[6] This, however fell short of the 7.4 percent goal for that year.[7] State and cooperative retail trade in 1972 was 174.9 billion rubles, a claimed real increase of 6.9 percent over the previous year.[8]

Retail sales of the government and cooperative store networks for each of the years in the eleven-year period 1962 through 1972 are given in the table on state and cooperative retail trade. The claimed real growth, i.e., after adjustment for price changes, is also given there. These data show a peak growth rate in 1965. From that year on, they show a fairly high growth rate tempered by a strong trend of declining rates of increase. Because the population growth rate declined throughout the 1960s, retail sales on a per capita basis increased fairly rapidly.

State and Cooperative Retail Trade,
U.S.S.R., 1962-72

Year	Sales Volume (billions of rubles)	Claimed Real Growth Over Previous Year (percentage)
1972	174.9	6.9
1971	164.0	7.0
1970	153.6	7.4
1969	142.8	7.4
1968	132.8	8.7
1967	122.2	9.4
1966	111.7	8.7
1965	103.5	10.0
1964	95.2	5.3
1963	91.6	5.0
1962	86.3	6.0

Source: Compiled from annual reports on the results of the previous year's plans published at various dates during January, February, and March every year in Pravda and Izvestia.

The Ninth Five-Year Plan contains the following sales volume goals, expressed as percentages of the 1970 performance: 1971, 106.4 percent; 1972, 114.6 percent; 1973, 123.3; 1974, 132.3; 1975, 141.8.[9] However, these goals were announced on November 25, 1971, and represent a sizable retrenchment of the 1971 retail sales volume goal announced on December 9, 1970.

As in Western economies, there is some inconsistency in measuring aggregate retail sales in the U.S.S.R. However, it appears that the extent of the measurement problem is greater in the U.S.S.R. The most bothersome aspect of the problem is that retail trade includes "goods sold on a small-scale wholesale basis to establishments, organizations, enterprises, and kolkhozes for current administrative needs and for collective use."[10] Goods sold on a large-scale and/or on a quasi-constant basis are excluded from the count. Fortunately, a small amount of separating out can be done. Nonfood sales of retailers to enterprises and organizations included in the reported aggregate retail sales came to 2.349 billion rubles in 1967 and 1.353 billion rubles in 1962. The Russian writer V. Nikitin states that this is an "ever larger distortion" year by year.[11] If adjusted for this alleged distortion, the ruble growth of retail sales between those two years would be about 3 percent less than reported by the Ministry of Trade. The distortion is not uniformly handled. Occasional sales by retailers to sovkhoz farms (state farms) are not counted as retail, but such sales to kolkhoz farms (collective farms) are so counted. Retailers' food sales to nurseries, kindergartens, boarding schools, rest homes, and sanitariums are treated as retail; but sales of nonfood items to those types of institutions are not treated as retail. Moreover, the sales of cooperative stores on a commission basis for kolkhoz farms and individual kolkhoz farmers are not counted as retail. Some small details, such as deposits on containers, are handled differently from one geographic jurisdiction or type of store to another. Nikitin offers this concise and reserved criticism:

> . . . the volume of retail trade turnover can to a certain degree fluctuate substantially not under the influence of changing economic conditions, but exclusively because of changes in the concept of goods turnover itself. . . . The basic economic criterion of retail goods turnover should be the sale of goods for the purpose of final consumption.[12]

Retail sales from 1928 fo 1940 were grossly exaggerated and distorted, according to Naum Jasny. Corrections were issued in 1956 but still appeared overstated.[13]

A Russian financial analyst and banker, K. Zigangirov, also has considered this problem. Zigangirov's seemingly careful analysis indicates that retail sales in Tselinogradskaya Oblast were overstated by 4.6 percent in 1967, 4.4 percent in 1968, and 3.6 percent in 1969. He concludes that in 1969 the Central Department Store of Tselinograd conducted 3.9 percent, or 687,000 rubles, of its sales at wholesale.[14]

It is tempting to assume that Soviet trade is labor-intensive, mainly because huge amounts of capital have been invested in heavy industry for several decades and because Soviet trade facilities, for the most part, are not physically impressive. However, research by Skurski indicates that, using current prices, the factor proportion of labor in retailing and wholesaling fell from 69.3 percent in 1940 to 50.9 percent in 1966, while the factor proportion of capital was rising from 30.7 to 49.1. Using constant 1955 prices, the factor proportion of labor fell from 74.5 percent to 42.0 percent, while capital was rising from 25.5 percent to 58.0 percent. The reversal in factor proportions can be attributed to several causes. There has been a rapidly increasing inventory level, about nine times as large in 1966 as in 1950 and almost 16 times as large as in 1940, in constant terms. Moreover, there have been advances in trade technology, equipment, displays, and prepackaging. There also has been an insufficient number of new employees in trade in recent years, thus bringing about more reliance on capital. Furthermore, the cost of labor has risen much more rapidly than capital. In addition, consumer desire for more capital in trade may have had some influence. Using comparable statistical techniques for industry, it has been demonstrated that by 1960, trade had become more capital-intensive than most heavy industries of the U.S.S.R.[15]

SOME PHYSICAL FACTORS

One aspect of Soviet administration over retail trade has been indecision and changeability on the issue of small-scale versus large-scale merchandising and small specialty shops versus larger, departmentalized establishments. Stores such as Moscow's Detski Mir, which has over 2,000 employees, loom very large in the array of retail establishments but are not typical or dominant. A Soviet economist has argued persuasively in behalf of an emphasis on large establishments:

Inasmuch as several small stores are always more costly to build and operate than one large store with an equal amount of floor space, the planning agencies of local Soviet executive committees should have no fear of large-scale enterprises. The important thing is that the territorial radius served be convenient for the customers.[16]

The smallest stores have tended to become relatively less important in the overall picture. In 1963 the state stores which employed over 10 persons represented only 3.3 percent of all state stores, but by 1968 the proportion had risen to 6.2 percent. Because of the growing use of self-service in stores, the rising proportion probably under-states somewhat the real change in the situation. These larger stores employed over one-third of the personnel and accounted for almost 40 percent of the sales volume of state stores in 1968.[17] The Russian Republic Minister of Trade has a strong preference for larger stores. The average size of the store facilities in his jurisdiction rose by about 160 square feet between 1965 and 1970.[18]

The production association concept (see Chapter 1 for discussion), which attempts to take advantage of economies of scale and rational integration of functions, equipment, and staff services, may find a rough parallel in retail trade. Two highly placed planners in the retailing industry have called for the attachment of small stores to large stores:

> The problem of the complete economic accountability of the trade network is also most closely linked with enlarging trade enterprises and broadening the range of goods that each sells. That is why it is very important not only to build and put into operation new trade centers and large department stores, but also to set up associations on an economic-accountability basis by transferring relatively small adjacent trade enterprises to the balance sheets of larger stores, or by placing them under such stores' day-to-day management. This should be done regardless of the departmental jurisdiction of these smaller enterprises.[19]

There is some potential for joint development of the above ideas and the idea of the self-service chain, an institution discussed later in this chapter. However, there is considerable feeling that a store should have as much independence as possible. The system of co-operative stores has an experiment underway in one province to gauge the results of the association concept.[20]

Large Soviet cities devote a relatively low fraction of downtown space to retailing, a fact resulting in part from the policy of using retailing facilities intensively and in part from the planned dispersion of these facilities throughout the metropolitan area. Retailing facilities traditionally were in the center of the city; but because of increasing populations in the large cities, logistical difficulties in movement of shoppers and goods, and some physical deterioration downtown, considerable geographical decentralization has occurred. Shops of many types are now found on arterial streets throughout the metropolitan area and on the street floors of countless apartment house developments. An emerging practice is to construct complexes of shops, offices, and apartments.

The massive reconstruction of the Novoslobodskaya Street district in Moscow, begun in early 1972, is perhaps indicative of the future. The first street in that district to receive attention, Seleznevskaya Street, is getting retail facilities and 15-story apartment houses to replace deteriorated two- and three-story apartment houses. The new buildings occupy only one-fifth as much ground space as the old, thus freeing large tracts for recreation and parks. The first two floors contain only retail facilities and various service trades. Included is a department store with about 31,000 square feet of floor space. These two commercial floors run for several hundred feet, linking the various apartment house towers. On some adjacent streets within the district, 24-story office buildings are scheduled. The service establishments, such as dry cleaning, shoe repair, and tailoring, are particularly welcome in such developments, for there is a nationwide shortage of such facilities.[21]

The retailing-transportation interface is noteworthy. Subway and bus system generally mesh well with major retail clusters in outlying areas as well as with the central business district. Streets have been so remarkably uncongested that even the multiplied automobile ownership and permanently increased automobile production scheduled in the 1971-75 Ninth Five-Year Plan will not saturate them by Western standards. However, the Russians are concerned about adequate preparation for the automobile age. Planning and construction are well advanced to divert the increases in vehicular traffic away from downtown areas. Some high-speed beltways are finished, and elaborate expressway systems are on the drawing boards. Planners are studying the feasibility of prohibiting vehicular traffic from certain downtown commercial streets in sizable cities, a policy which Baku has already adopted and implemented. In the central business district of Kiev there is a children's pedestrian street one block long. This attractively designed mall contains 11 children's specialty shops, a children's pharmacy, and a library. Facilities for selling and servicing the stream of new automobiles are grossly inadequate, but considerable investment is so earmarked and major construction has begun.

Long-range planning for large cities may bring further changes in locational patterns of retail trade. The planners' goal is to make each extremely large city into several smaller cities, each with an employment-creating base, recreational and cultural facilities, services, and both centralized and decentralized retailing. Moscow would have eight such communities. This planning work is proceeding also for Leningrad, Baku, Kiev, and Kharkov.[22] The General Plan for the Development of Moscow, constantly under review and revision, is a joint product of three research organizations: the Institute of the General Plan, the Scientific Research Institute of the Economics of Construction, and the Central Scientific Research Institute of Urban Development. The personnel of these agencies are using as a theme for their work this passage from the directives of the 24th Party Congress: "Implement a broad system of measures directed toward saving the time of the population. . . . Improve all forms of commodity servicing."[23]

An explicit characteristic recurring through the plans is much more investment in below-ground installations. The dominant reasons appear to be the potential saving of time for shoppers and the avoidance of developing agricultural land. Making more land in the metropolitan area available for parks and reducing the number of pedestrians on the street are secondary reasons for the subsurface emphasis, while the harsh winter climate ostensibly is of little, if any, importance.

The Moscow General Plan calls for construction of several arterial streets underground and elaborate shopping areas underground surrounding subway stations. Subsurface shopping has been used in some large foreign cities, such as Stockholm and Montreal, but never on the scale the U.S.S.R. plans. Although all kinds of goods and services will be affected, initial priorities go to department stores and service institutions, including savings banks, restaurants, cafes, hairdressers, and laundries. In addition, virtually all automobile parking would be below ground. The grocery store network would be only slightly modified. However, this somewhat inconsistent arrangement could conceivably be changed. Two factors appear to account for the separate treatment of grocery stores: the significant investment in new supermarket-type food stores and additional investment already scheduled; and the allowance of growth of advance ordering, primarily in non-supermarket-type food stores (See "Other Factors in Retailing Operations," below). Where there is a practice of advance ordering, it "can be organized according to a system of morning formulation and evening pickup of completed orders along the path of movement."[24] Chertanovo Center, a planned complex of stores and about 5,000 apartment units begun in 1972 on Moscow's south side, will have no vehicular surface traffic. Tunnels will link all buildings, and every building will have a parking garage below ground. One planning specification is quite interesting, in that it unveils some of the thinking on the extent to which automobile ownership will expand: there will be one parking space underground for every two households in the area.[25]

Large downtown stores in Moscow include Gosudarstveny Universalny Magazin (State Department Store), better known as GUM; Tsentralny Universalny Magazin (Central Department Store), better known as TsUM; Mostorg (Moscow Trade Organization Department Store); Vesna (Spring); and Detski Mir (Children's World). The structure that houses GUM, the showcase store for the economy, was completed in 1894 but has been maintained reasonably well. Designed by Pomerantzev for a large shopping bazaar, it has a skylighted central hall three stories high. Although many separate small shops originally occupied the building, it is similar in design to many Western European department store buildings of the late 1800s and constituted one of Europe's largest merchandising facilities in that period. GUM averages over 200,000 customers a day, and it claims to carry about 330,000 different items in inventory. Most of the other retail establishments in Moscow's central business district are rather specialized and small, typically under 2,000 square feet of selling area. Many are inadequately housed. The facilities for one small department store are novel indeed. The river workers of the Moscow Steamship Company have a floating store contained in a ship designed and built in East Germany in 1970 especially for this purpose.

Portable stalls and kiosks are common. In the central areas of most cities, scattered along the streets near the large stores and major transit stops, are vendors in portable stalls and kiosks offering foods, beverages, novelties, and printed materials. In several cities some of these operations are directed by one or two large department stores. When the weather permits, a sizable number of stores operate portable branches in selected noncommercial neighborhoods and handles a variety of merchandise. An example of a large operation is Luzhniki Fair Center is Moscow, which has about 250 such shops. A more typical example is the seven stalls in Leningrad's Haymarket Square.

Soviet cities devote more space downtown to grocery stores than do American cities. All Soviet cities have several small grocery establishments and one or more gastronoms (departmentalized grocery stores) downtown. On central Moscow's Gorky Street stands an intriguing reminder of the past, the prestigious Gastronom Number 1, the gilded and chandeliered food store known as the Eliseev Grocery Store before the 1917 Revolution. Another elegant Eliseev Grocery Store operates on central Leningrad's Nevsky Prospect. As in Western Europe, some large department stores have sizable grocery divisions. For example, GUM allocates about one-eighth of its selling area to foods.

The physical facilities for retail trade tend to be much poorer in the countryside than in urban areas. General stores, the most common type of establishment, are maintained in thousands of farming villages. The average rural store has a sales volume much below the average urban store, a major reason for which is self-supply by rural families, especially in foods and home-sewn apparel. The availability of mail order goods is also important. Further monetization of the rural areas will probably raise the average sales volume of establishments in those areas. Philip Hanson states:

> That the rural network consists of rather small shops
> selling at higher costs a more limited and lower-quality
> range of goods, follows from the relative poverty and
> greater self-supply of the Soviet countryside. It is not a
> reflection on the efficiency of the cooperative network.[26]

Programs are in progress to provide rural areas with better facilities. Apparently much of this will consist of small centers containing a small department store, a restaurant, and a cafe.[27] An architect and an engineer researching rural needs and options have noted that many areas exhibit a "belt type of settlement, whereby various settlements actually merge into unbroken bands of built-up areas along river valleys or gorges, forming rural agglomerates." One example that they analyzed was the farm villages in Skvirskiy Raion, Kiyevskaya Oblast. They stretch unbroken for 10 miles along the Rostavitsa River. Trade officials treated each village separately, providing stores and other services but "failing to provide an optimal solution to the whole problem." The newer research specifies placement of specialty stores in one cluster in the agglomerate and general stores in each village. The research team asserts that every village is part of a complex spatial system, defined in part by transportation facilities and availability of transportation.[28]

A complete inventory of all fixed assets held by the government store network was scheduled for late 1971, the first such control project since 1961. In the Russian Republic alone this was to involve over 2 million separate fixed-asset accounts. The ambitious project was to include an appraisal of wear and tear and an estimate of current replacement cost. Despite the still-prevailing shortages of fixed assets in retailing, it appears that they more than doubled in book value in those 10 years. Results of the project may not be released for several years.[29]

Progress on physical characteristics is erratic and spotty. The press of the U.S.S.R. often points out that "some organizations of the construction ministries are impermissibly slow in building stores . . . these organizations consider them 'second-rate' facilities."[30] Perhaps in some way related to the results of the 1971 evaluation of fixed assets in state trade, the national government announced on January 30, 1972, that it would permit jurisdictions, if they so desired, to shift 5 percent of capital funds previously allocated for construction of housing to the construction and equipping of trade facilities and public catering establishments.[31] This announcement is a good indication of the severity of shortages of retail facilities and equipment, for housing is also in short supply and carries emotional overtones.

Equipment for stores is a severe problem. Such equipment as loading and unloading apparatus, slicing machines, and automatic scales are being introduced quite slowly. Display windows facing the street are not yet common and lighting is exceedingly poor. Refrigeration rooms and refrigerator cases are extremely limited, although the Five-Year Plan specifies a 1975 production of open refrigerator cases seven times as great as that of 1970. Production of self-service counters is supposed to be 70 percent higher in 1975 than in 1970. Elevators and escalators are uncommon except in a fraction of the stores completed in the 1970s. Even there the elevators are usually restricted to freight and the escalators usually go up only. The abacus is in common use, for there has been a great shortage of cash registers. Use of computers by retailers is extremely rare. GUM put in its first installation, a Minsk-22, in 1969 and applies it mainly to the reordering of standard items and screening of merchandise for potential markdowns. A large department store in Leningrad, Gostiny Dvor (Merchants' Yard), installed a computer in 1971 for similar purposes.

There has been so little cash register equipment, and especially so little sophisticated cash register equipment, that self-service stores have felt it necessary to have not only cashiers but checkers for the cashiers. A one-to-one ratio has usually been maintained. In other words, the shopper goes through the same procedure twice. Another reason is that there is some anxiety about protecting the resources of the store. An Izvestia staff reporter recently noted with great admiration that the Zanevsky Supermarket in Leningrad had acquired the self-confidence, and the automatic cash registers, to get rid of the second-stage checkout.[32] According to the U.S.S.R. Minister of Trade, this "regular rechecking of the cashier's calculation of every buyer's purchases . . . evokes just criticism from customers." The practice was prohibited by the Ministry of Trade in 1970 but was still in use by some stores, he complained, as of the close of 1971. He threatened to try to withhold their portion of the profit-sharing plan unless they obeyed his orders. He has authorized the use of occasional spot checks on accuracy of cashiers.[33]

Self-service is certainly not assisted by the prevailing layout designs of Soviet stores. The model designs for specialty shops on the street floors of apartment houses were not meant for the self-service era. However, it is costly for each small shop that is scheduled to adopt self-service to redesign its own layout. At the end of 1971 there was no coordination of this acute need for redesign and reinstallation.[34] One of the senior city planners for Moscow recently noted the obsolescence of "standard plans" for stores.[35]

A few larger stores are converting the traditional "set of boxes" layout system to a grid system. One critic has said of the box system:

> This is not a convenient floor plan, inasmuch as the shoppers' path around the salesroom is lengthened by the necessity of crossing the "barren" spaces separating one "box" from another. In stores lacking a proper knowledge of trade organization, an employee is stationed at the entrance to the box in such a way as to limit the shoppers' access. A "linear" arrangement of facilities needs to be introduced. This will make it possible to cut down the excessive staff and to serve more customers.[36]

Several critics have pointed out that Soviet stores usually departmentalize their goods on the basis of only one factor, the traditional clusters of goods, such as clothing, notions, or recreational products. They call for more ingenuity in setting up department boundaries.[37]

Research in retailing management has been almost nonexistent in the past. There is some room for optimism, however, in the founding of a new agency, the Central Institute for the Scientific Organization of Labor and Administration and Rationalization of Trade. It will work on physical facility problems and operating policy matters. However, like many other agencies, especially new ones, the Central Institute may not fare well in budget allocations or manpower allotments. Moreover, its area of influence may well be restricted to cooperative stores, for the founding organization is the Central Union of Consumers' Cooperatives.

The Soviet planning process that generated such prototypic cities as Karaganda is Kazakhstan and Magnitogorsk in the Urals is now being forced to turn its attention to the even more difficult problems of urban renewal, especially in the central business districts of older cities. This has already affected retail trade and has implications for its future patterns. Urban renewal for the older cities is a distinctly controversial topic. Arguments revolve around preservation of historical sites, maintenance of subcultural and/or period atmosphere, provision of green areas, and concentration of retailing facilities.

Moscow is a particularly perplexing case because of its medieval physical heritage centering on the Kremlin compound, St. Basil's Cathedral, and the serpentine Moscow River, and because of the national-symbolic role of central Moscow. This symbolic role is two-sided: the mystical Holy Mother Russia, repository-of-truth role of the pre-1917 Empire, and the contemporary role of artistic heritage, economic direction, and seat of government. The inner city, characterized by crooked streets and irregular plazas, has been slashed through by several wide thoroughfares constructed in the Soviet era and is served well by the subway system. A few high-rise buildings have been allowed in the city, but this type of construction sparks controversy. For example, much objection has been raised to a proposed 60-floor building on a major square. And one of the most senior of Moscow's city planning officials has lamented the "chaotic building up of the center."[38] In the central part of Moscow delineated by the Sadovoye Ring, a middle-speed thoroughfare, population decreased 47 percent between 1960 and 1968.[39] This occurred because officials wanted certain land and structures for new uses, many residential buildings had deteriorated, and many residents preferred space in the new apartment buildings farther out, for which they had applied years earlier. The appropriate number of residents in central Moscow is still to be determined. It is worthwhile to note that a few cities have developed two central business districts. For example, Tbilisi has done so, and Riga is tentatively planning in this direction. Of current concern to Moscow's central city officials is the pollution of the Moscow River resulting from sewage and barge traffic. The pollution issue aside, commerce and public recreation are competing claimants of the river.

Attempts at replacement of the venerable but outmoded and overcrowded facilities for specialty shops and department stores in Moscow and elsewhere will also cause disagreement among liberals and conservatives in city planning and the trade officials involved. It will be recalled that even the hallowed GUM, largest store in Moscow and a showcase for the national economy, was closed down by Stalin but later reopened by Malenkov. And when the large Detski Mir department store was constructed in the late 1950s in central Moscow, the traditionalists won out and a medium-rise structure of innocuous design resulted.

One completed development, Kalinin Prospect, gives some limited evidence of what the future may hold. Located in the central business district, it is a planned complex of specialty shops, a department store, office buildings, and apartment houses using high-rise structures. Architect Yu. Yaralov notes that officials will use the experience of Kalinin Prospect in erecting the much larger Chertanovo Center in Moscow.[40]

SELF-SERVICE

In an attempt ostensibly to help shoppers examine merchandise, a considerable number of stores have adopted Western-style self-service or modified self-service to replace the rigid and time-consuming clerk service at the counter. The official goal for the end of the 1971-75 Five-Year Plan is that self-service techniques will account for 40 percent of all retail trade,[41] a figure that appears somewhat on the optimistic side but not impossible. It is not publicized, but it is highly probable that the stress on self-service is also for the purpose of conserving labor in retail establishments.

The typical Soviet practice, called <u>kassa</u> (literally "cashier"), has been to wait in line to be admitted to the shop or particular department in a large store, then wait in line to see the goods, then wait in line to pay the cashier and obtain a claim slip, then wait in line again to obtain the package. The modified self-service usually consists of the elimination of the line to enter the shop or department and the line to examine the goods, but retains the line to pay for the goods and obtain the claim slip and the line to pick up the package. Under this technique the salesperson does not handle the money. At extremely crowded hours the entry line may be reinstated. The pure kassa system probably still exists in at least 80 percent of Soviet stores and probably prevails in 75 percent of the business transacted. However, self-service and modified self-service are growing and show promise of much more growth.

Despite major editorial support from the media, including <u>Pravda</u>,[42] the self-service movement has been growing unevenly, in terms of both geography and type of store. It is much further along in large cities than it is in towns and villages. For example, in Bashkiria, only about 5 percent of city shops and less than 1 percent of village shops have adopted this practice.[43] By early 1973 about 25 percent of sales in state stores in the Russian Federation utilized self-service techniques.[44] The movement is further along in the Ukraine and some other European portions of the nation than in Central Asia but poorly developed in the republics lying between the Caspian Sea and the Black Sea.

As of July 1, 1969, 16.1 percent of the country's state stores, excluding pharmacies, had adopted self-service, a gain over the 14.8 percent on that date one year earlier.[45] Only about 50 department stores in the nation have any self-service departments. A major innovator is the Central Department Store in Vinnitsa, a city in the Ukraine. Business economist V. Kuzin argues that it comes "close to the best foreign stores."[46] However, self-service is making headway in the food trade. In 1969, 920 such food stores opened and in 1970 another 2,777.[47] By mid-1970, 10 percent of food stores were on the self-service plan.[48] In Uzhgorod, the Carpathian Grocery Store saw its sales volume almost triple when it converted to self-service.[49] A few small chains of self-service grocery stores have formed, one of which is known as Universam. Already operating in the Lyublino and Kuibyshev boroughs of the capital, this chain of quasi supermarkets is adding at least three more stores in other parts of the city. Each store is designed to handle about 10,000 customers per day. Universam will probably merge with Novelty, a Leningrad-based chain. However, the only supermarket-type food store in central Moscow is exclusively for foreigners with hard currency.

A. I. Struyev, Minister of Trade for the Soviet Union, said:

> The growing requirements of today's customers can be satisfied only by a trade system that allows them to acquire needed goods not only with a minimum expenditure of time but also with the maximum convenience. Therefore, the developing in every way of progressive methods for the sale of goods is the first and foremost task of trade workers.[50]

The excessive time that it takes Soviet citizens to complete their shopping was traditionally omitted from national planning for the retailing industry:

> These losses were for a long time left out of account by economics and especially by trade practice. That was the personal, the private matter of the customer, so to speak. Actually this is an important social problem. People make their purchases in their free time and they pay dearly for this, very dearly.[51]

However, the Trade Ministry is now showing some concern. It reports research studies which concluded that self-service enables each Soviet family affected to save at least 10 hours per week, on the average.[52]

Always concerned about theft, Soviet store managers have become more so since the rise of self-service. A Kaliningrad engineer complains of it in this way: "I don't like to go to the self-service store. When I go there . . . I am a suspicious person in the eyes of the service personnel—in short, a potential thief."[53] The Ministry of Trade, attempting to meet consumer criticism, issued an order in 1971 prohibiting stores from "requiring customers upon entering to show the goods they have purchased elsewhere or to leave their personal belongings at the door."[54] A few overhead cameras have begun to appear in self-service stores.

The extent to which the self-service movement can be developed will be greatly influenced by the amount of prepackaging available. This point is especially true for the food trade. At the close of 1971 less than 40 percent of foodstuffs were prepackaged.[55] Two republic-level deputies stated in late 1971 that only between 15 and 20 percent of all goods sold at retail were in prepackaged form. These aggressive critics stated that there were four possible institutions where the packaging could be done: the manufacturing plant, the wholesale establishment, the headquarters for a large retailing organization, or the retail store itself. They expressed no preference but felt that explicit policy must be forthcoming on how much packaging work each level is to do, if any. They suspected that it must vary by type of product. They noted the heavy costs of packaging equipment and the relatively large space it requires. They further stated that they had the impression that there was no coordination among the ministries, naming specifically the Ministry of Trade and the Ministry of the Food Industry, and no coordination among the divisions of the Ministry of Trade.

The same two officials criticized the quantity and quality of packaging materials, especially polymer wrappings.[56] Moreover, the Minister of Trade has criticized the Ministry of the Chemical Industry and the Ministry of the Pulp and Paper Industry regarding packaging materials.[57] The Deputy Minister of the Chemical Industry replied to the criticisms, alleging that everything was all right. He stated that such packaging materials measured up to the technical standards agreed to by the Ministries of the Food Industry and of the Meat and Dairy Industry. He enumerated the types of polymer wrappings available at the end of 1971: two-layer polyethylene and cellophane, two-layer polyethylene and lavsan, two-layer polyethylene and paper, and polyethylene netting. The Ministry's plans for expansion of the product line call for introducing "Saran" thermosetting film and rigid polyvinyl chloride film in 1974.[58] To all of this, the First Deputy Minister of the Food Industry replied that the "need for polymer materials goes unsatisfied from year to year. As a result, the state plans for the packaging of foodstuffs are not fulfilled." He added that some automated packaging lines go unused for lack of materials.[59]

An executive of the Ukraine Wholesale Grocery Organization in Kiev noted in 1970 that over 3,000 food stores in the Ukraine Republic took advantage of the available prepackaged goods. He went on to stress that development of a network of self-service stores was being held back by shortages of prepackaged products and the complete absence of prepackaging for some kinds of products. For example, only 16 percent of macaroni and 6 percent of candy, and none of the granulated sugar or starch produced in the Ukraine, is in prepackaged form. This executive noted the extremely protracted disagreement over whether trade or production enterprises should take care of packaging, and concluded that it was more appropriate at the production level. However, he stated that for some goods the wholesaler perhaps should take the packaging responsibility if the producer was a very long distance from the retailers. He also bemoaned the fact that the latest packaging equipment is not automatic but requires large expenditures of manual labor.[60]

Another aspect of prepackaging and self-service is the shipping of several units of prepackaged merchandise in a container suitable for setting out on a store shelf. In this way the producer can make possible a saving of labor at the retail level. However, this is only in the research and study stage in the U.S.S.R.

CUSTOMER RELATIONS AND PERSONNEL ASPECTS OF RETAILING

Countless Soviet writers have lamented the unconcern and general lethargy of the shops and employees of the retailing industry. An _Izvestia_ staff journalist commented that solution of most people's grievances does not require expenditure of great effort or capital but instead involves around perceived organizational passiveness and the lack of administrative ability on the part of many trade enterprise leaders.[61] Moreover, the employees receive extremely little training, are not knowledgeable about the merchandise, and are undermotivated to perform their work.

A Kharkov wholesaling executive has forcefully argued that, although shortages and low quality of products are important contributors to shoppers' dissatisfaction, the inability of sales attendants to deal with people is also very important.

> Psychology, together with the managers, whose duty it is to act as trainers, are called upon to help workers in the service sphere to grasp the importance of observing routine and rhythm in labor work, the importance of a lofty sense of personal responsibility and discipline when serving customers. It is necessary to help sales personnel increase labor productivity, acquire good manners and become courteous, tactful, and patient.[62]

This executive goes on to expose the general morale problem of employees in the retailing industry and to note the need for behavioral research on the retail transaction:

> Trade needs the serious attention of psychologists. The trade employee should be helped in acquiring a more profound awareness of the social importance of his labor, so that his labor will exalt him. . . . Scientists could provide answers to many of the questions arising in the interrelationships of salesclerk and customer.[63]

A staff article in <u>Pravda</u>, trying to raise the prestige of retail employees, stated that the labor of the salesclerk is "just as honorable as the labor of the miner, the metallurgist or the construction worker."[64] Moreover, in an editorial that newspaper directed attention to the need to inculcate new retail workers with "love for work and respect for their occupation."[65]

A Russian economist asserts that the retailing industry needs an organization that would intensively train store personnel in the latest methods before the establishment is even turned over to the management to operate.[66] The retailing industry maintains some training courses through the Correspondence Institute of Soviet Trade.[67]

There is a substantial shortage of employees in retailing. For example, in Leningrad and Moscow alone there is a permanent deficit of 8,000 to 10,000 sales personnel and cashiers in grocery stores. Trade officials have been scolded for not giving adequate attention to forecasts of needed additional personnel.[68] In an attempt to remedy the difficulty, the Young Communist League has pledged to recruit and send 1 million young people into trade during the 1971-75 Five-Year Plan.[69] Two examples of recruiting and training have encouraged retail managers. In the Kalinin Cooperative Technicum several textbooks on retail trade have been written, a program of occupational guidance set up that gives detailed attention to trade, and a program established that puts interested pupils to work in stores while they are still in school. The Kiev Central Department Store also has created a highly successful work-study program with two high schools.[70] Such programs are uncommon in the U.S.S.R. In another attempt to take care of the shortage of employees in retailing, retired people are being urged to work part-time. The government is allowing pensioners to work as salesclerks, cashiers, and as department and section heads who also sell, while retaining their pensions up to a combined income ceiling of 300 rubles a month.[71] By Soviet standards this ceiling is a liberal incentive. Although most observers and commentators feel that there is a shortage of sales people in the stores, a Russian business writer, V. Varavka, believes otherwise. He contends that most stores are already overstaffed.[72] He adds that the number of persons assigned to a given department relative to other departments seems to follow no pattern of logic.

Varavka also decries the still-legal personnel regulation, dating from January 4, 1967, that divides retail salespeople into the three grades of junior, ordinary, and senior. This regulation stipulates that a graduate of a secondary school must work six and a half years before advancing to senior grade. The stipulations are no longer enforced—a fortunate development, in his opinion. The stores have extremely large numbers of persons even in management who have not completed a secondary education. In Chelyabinskaya Oblast, for example, 890 of 1,469 management-level personnel have not finished that level of school.

In most stores there is a complaint book, where aggrieved shoppers may record their comments on merchandise, shortages, assortments, and the sales personnel. Not a new technique at all, it nevertheless had no significant effect until the mid-1960s. It acts as a mild deterrent generally; but on rare occasions it is the basis for reprimand, transfer, or minor penalties.

The potential of commission plans for paying retail sales personnel has been of interest to the Russians since at least the early 1960s and has been discussed in Russian journals and newspapers.[73] Although it has made no headway in state stores, it exists in a few cooperative stores. One Soviet economic writer praises the Chebarkulskiy Raion Department Store in Chelyabinskaya Oblast for its commission scheme.[74] He goes on to state that commission plans are seldom used, not for philosophical reasons but because managers are fearful that sales people's earnings would be artificially restricted by unpredictable shortages of goods completely beyond the control of the employees or the store, and because managers have so little managerial training that they do not know how to work out the mechanics of the policy in advance. He states that the commission plan would work on a large scale but would require the same timeliness and managerial flexibility that the store under discussion demonstrated.

In stores that have introduced the economic accountability reform and incentives plans, the sales personnel and cashiers can earn premium pay for fulfilling the sales volume goal and "observing the essential conditions of customer service."[75] No premium pay is available even for exemplary customer service if the sales goal is missed. The other employees and the store manager can earn premium pay too, but it is contingent on several indexes—mainly profit—rather than sales volume. Izvestia reported in late 1972 that retailing employees could earn a 10 percent bonus over base pay if store sales reached the quota and 1 percent of base pay for every 3 percent the store went over quota, up to a limit of 40 percent bonus over base pay. Thus the employee's material incentive ceased when the store went beyond sales quota plus 10 percent. In addition, a pay experiment began in mid-1970 in five Moscow stores and was still running in late 1972. It included bonuses for high service standards and for savings from more efficient operations. Initial results were mildly encouraging, but the Ministry of Trade has not reacted to expand the experiment.[76] Occasionally there are motivational fringe benefits. For example, one large department store awarded a group of outstanding sales personnel a trip to visit a large retail enterprise in East Germany.[77] Despite reforms and improvements in many stores, the following statement by an Izvestia staff journalist is instructive:

When I reached a store just 15 minutes before closing time one day, I was given a thorough explanation why I was not wanted there at that moment. The store had already fulfilled its plan; exceeding it too much might prove dangerous. The plan might be drawn up for the next quarter according to "what had been achieved during this quarter," and there would be no bonus then. I was told that the store had changed over to the new system of planning and economic incentive, but I found little consolation in this.[78]

A widely held view blaming manufacturing firms and, indirectly, wholesalers for many problems of retailers is exemplified in this statement:

> . . . the lack of rhythm in the supplying and shipment of goods to the stores disrupts the set routine of work, disorganizes the sales personnel, and has an irritating effect on their psyches. Industry regularly plays havoc with the rhythmic delivery of its output. As a result, the bulk of the commodities scheduled to be sold at an even pace in the course of the month is sold in five or six days. The work load on the salesclerk is more than tripled. This violation of routine and rhythm in work and the attendant inordinate overload are the prime reasons for nervous strain among trade personnel.[79]

Other executives who have analyzed the flow of retail work have concluded that it is quite uneven and that shopper traffic tends to concentrate in the final few days of the month.[80] Moreover, daily shopper traffic shows a sharp peak in the late afternoon and early evening. Most urban stores of most types end their business day between 7:30 p.m. and 8:30 p.m.

MAIL ORDER RETAILING

Mail order sales are small but growing. In the Russian Republic 0.21 percent of retail sales in 1968 were of this type.[81] The chief organizations in this business are the U.S.S.R. Central Union of Consumers' Cooperatives Mail Order Trust, which handles over 1.75 million packages a year, and the Mail Order Trade Trust, which handles over 5.5 million packages a year. The Mail Order Trade Trust employs 2,400 persons and has a sales volume of nearly 150 million rubles annually. Its sales volume almost doubled between

1955 and 1960 and more than doubled between 1960 and 1968. The average order size fell from 21.2 rubles in 1960 to 13.2 rubles in 1968, which possibly pushed its unit costs up. It publishes a catalog listing about 13,500 items. The usefulness and timeliness for the customer is reduced in that its catalogs are published only once every two or three years rather than seasonally or even annually. New price lists are issued once a year. Although there is a need for several times as many, only 100,000 to 125,000 copies of the catalog and 150,000 to 200,000 copies of the price list are printed.

The Mail Order Trade Trust operates 12 warehouses. Five of these are general merchandise houses and are in Novosibirsk, Sverdlovsk, Rostov, Irkutsk, and Moscow. Seven specialized houses, all concentrating on spare parts, assemblies, and accessories for consumer goods, are widely scattered but each is located immediately adjacent to a large industrial complex producing the line of goods. Each warehouse has a special branch of the postal system. Nevertheless, the extremely overburdened and underautomated condition of the postal system is a limiting factor for this kind of business.[82] The Mail Order Trade Trust is planning to construct Europe's largest mail order facility, with a capacity of 10 million parcels a year, at Odintsovo. It has already carried mechanization rather far and is getting into computer applications.

The work of this organization is made slower, more detailed, and more costly by its insistence that there be absolutely no averaging out or rounding of shipping costs. No credit is given. The customer must pay in advance if the parcel goes by rail carrier, while he has the choice of paying in advance or C.O.D. if the parcel goes through the postal system. The customer pays the insurance. In recent years this organization has been studying the operations of Swedish, East German, and North American mail order firms with regard to shipping, insurance, and payment, in an attempt to see what it might copy or modify.

Many Soviet citizens live in remote areas with severely limited retail facilities, poor selection of goods, and harsh climate. Thus the mail order houses perform a badly needed function. About 60 percent of the Mail Order Trade Trust's sales are to inhabitants of the Far North, the Soviet Far East, and Siberia. About one-sixth of its sales are to residents of the completely new towns on the frontier.

The Mail Order Trade Trust deals directly with manufacturers for almost all its merchandise and with wholesale organizations only when unavoidable. Apparently some price concessions are given by wholesalers when they deal with the Trust. An operating policy that poses some minor product choice problems for non-European residents of the ethnic republics is that the Trust, although selling to the entire nation, buys only from suppliers in the Russian Republic.[83]

This mail order organization does 55 percent of its sales volume in spare parts for consumer goods, assemblies, and accessories for consumer goods. Other large selling categories are radios, records, toys, musical instruments, and photographic goods. It carries no leather footwear or toiletries. The Moscow branch received 250,000 orders in 1968 for kinds of merchandise it did not stock. It does not have its own house brands but, according to its president, is quite interested in adopting that practice and is studying the already existing East German system for so doing.[84]

CREDIT

Installment credit for consumers was introduced on an experimental basis in the late 1950s, received official authorization in 1960, and was allowed to grow substantially through the rest of the decade. Although its use is common for durable goods, it is frequently allowed for major purchases of clothing. The exact features of installment plans, such as the percentage down payment, the repayment period, and the categories of merchandise for which this form of selling is available, vary considerably from one administrative jurisdiction to another. Higher trade officials in the republics and regions, rather than store managers, make these policy decisions. The manager of one of the largest specialty stores in Moscow has urged that the large stores be permitted some initiative in selecting the types of goods on which to extend credit, subject to veto by higher trade officials. He was chagrined that all men's coats, but no men's suits, in the Moscow area were covered by credit at the time. He believed that the credit policies interfered with reaching sales goals.[85]

One scholar reported in a 1966 research project that trade officials tried to restrict the ruble volume that a consumer could acquire at one time on the installment plan. In the Ukraine a limit equal to three months' wages was set, while in the Russian Republic it was four months' wages and in Azerbaijan there was no ceiling.[86] However, as of early 1972, there was still no organized credit information exchange among stores and the limits were not really enforceable. Repayment periods vary widely by type of product and region of the country but appear to be only slightly less generous than those in the United States. Three years for a major durable and up to one year for a large purchase of apparel are not uncommon. Some loans are repaid directly by the consumer; but some others, not necessarily delinquent, are repaid by deductions from wages. The employer then remits to the store. The direct payment plan emerged well after the indirect type.

The goods to which installment credit is applicable at any given time tend to coincide with abundant supply and oversupply, but there are occasional exceptions. A scarce product category may qualify, as did television sets in the 1960s. However, a British scholar cautions that some of the models of television receivers in the mid-1960s may have been rather old.[87] On the other hand, sometimes the erratic flow of marketing information and the vagaries of the trade hierarchy delay a suitable product category from qualifying for installment credit for an unreasonable time. One academician reports that, although 380,000 sewing machines were clogging warehouses, the Russian Republic Ministry of Trade waited almost two years before approving this product for installment credit.[88] The Vice-Chairman of the Board of Directors of the Union of Rural Consumers' Cooperatives, writing in 1971, described credit as "effective trade strategy" and concluded that it constituted "necessary commercial tactics in certain problem areas." He went on to decry as "artificial" the withholding of credit on several products.[89] He added:

> As adopted by the Rostov Province Executive Committee, the list of goods sold on credit in the province had 56 entries in 1968; today it has 32. Volgograd Province has 1,387 stores this year that trade in everyday goods but do not sell them on credit. As a result, trade on credit has decreased by 12% there.[90]

Almost all trade organizations borrow from the State Bank (Gosbank) from time to time. They commonly need loans at least for temporary purposes, such as high seasonal stocks or buying a long time in advance of the actual selling season. As of 1971, over 60 percent of all working capital in trade was supplied by the State Bank and about one-third of all short-term credit extended by the Bank was to retailers.[91] Writing in 1965, American lawyer Leonard Goldberg reported that most Soviet retailers were subject to a control policy whereby part of their working capital allowance had to be deposited in the State Bank and withdrawn in an elaborate procedure as if it was a loan.[92]

Soviet bankers have sought to influence the day-to-day operation of retail trade for many years. Apparently they try to influence the management process mainly in order to reduce the stores' need for credit.[93] They occasionally serve on voluntary advisory committees attached to business establishments. Moreover, they often serve in auxiliary control units attached to the lower levels of the government and the party to monitor business operations.[94]

Gosbank officials are interested in improving their operations that bear on retail trade. They want to sharpen the thought and

analysis behind lines of credit and relate credit more closely to
sales forecasts. In addition, they are concerned about interest rates.
The standard rate for amounts up to the approved line of credit is 2
percent per annum and, above the line, 4 percent. Russian financial
analysts P. Novoselov and S. Mezhiborskaya report a recent change.
Loans extended on a temporary basis to stores because of "failure
to fulfill the plan" carry an interest rate of 4 percent. They suggest
that Decree No. 280 of the U.S.S.R. Council of Ministers, which increased the penalty for late payment to 10.8 percent per annum, compounded daily, is effective.[95] All of this indicates that interest rates,
largely ignored as a strategic factor in business from the early 1930s
until the 1960s, are again showing up as a potentially important tool
in general finance and trade. The real core of the changes will probably be differentiation of rates by many factors revolving around
purpose of the loan and maturity of the loan and, perhaps later, the
financial condition of the borrower. The fact that there has been
little expert utilization of the interest rate is a result of ideological
hurdles, very little experience, and considerable rigidity.

OTHER FACTORS IN RETAILING OPERATIONS

There are several other noteworthy developments and trends
in retailing operations. One is both popular and official concern
about tie-in deals. It has been common to require a customer to buy
something he did not want in order for him to get what he wanted.
For example, in one food store the customer had to buy a fish if he
wanted half a kilogram of yeast. In another shop he had to buy two
iron kettles if he wanted a teapot and cups. In one sporting goods
store he had to buy two nine-year-old, bedraggled felt hats if he
wanted a motorcycle or tennis racket. Many retailers have defended
this practice and termed the combinations "gift sets." Obviously it
expedites sale of obsolete and overstocked products. The Ministry
of Trade issued Special Order No. 199 in late 1971 to require shops
to break up "gift sets" if customers so requested, but compliance
has been discouraging and the Ministry not very aggressive about it.[96]
Concern for public health and standards of sanitation is growing.
In particular, it affects stores, food service establishments, and
farmers' markets. However, the extent and effectiveness of the
movement varies greatly from one jurisdiction to another. The explanation for the variation appears to be differences among cultures
and differences in personal concern among local officials of trade,
regulatory, and law enforcement organizations. For example, in
Uzbekistan's Tashkent Province, August 1970 was proclaimed Hygiene
and Public Amenities Month. Public health doctors successfully

closed 200 stores and farmers' market stalls and numerous restaurants
for substandard conditions and then processed fines against them.
However, in the case of two food stores, the chairman of the affected
workers' cooperative immediately broke the seal on the door and
permitted business to continue. Protests from public health personnel
to local law enforcement officials were futile.[97]

In part, the increasing use of vending machines is a result of
the concern for public health, for such devices can reduce the problems
of sanitation involved in the common drinking glass of street vendors.
Nevertheless, most vending machines use the same cup over and
over again instead of disposable cups. In addition, vending machines
have the potential to conserve manpower. Some people laud their
potential for reduction of stores' evening hours. New and better
vending machines are being made, such as a specialized design introduced in 1971 that has a capacity of 800 newspapers. The Five-
Year Plan specifies that 1975 production of vending machines will be
90 percent higher than 1970. There are a few shops consisting only
of vending machines. For example, the Smetana Store in a Moscow
residential neighborhood handles liquid milk, powdered milk, cheese,
animal lard, tobacco products, and several other items in about 50
vending chutes. However, any cost saving is reduced by the presence
of a cashier to make change; and the convenience and usefulness are
reduced by the fact that it is open only from eight a.m. to nine p.m.

Several other types of stores are noteworthy. Consumer goods
manufacturers received permission in the 1950s for "new product
stores," the first of which opened in 1957. There are several hundred
of these factory-owned establishments where new goods are displayed
and offered for sale prior to their going into mass production. Obviously they should not be equated with the test market found in many
Western economies, but they are helpful. A Western scholar reported
the opening in 1961 of the first "factory retail outlet" stores, which
can stock any of the factory's product line, new or well entrenched.[98]
In this way the management of the plant can get almost instant feedback
on some aspects of the product, although the statistical representative-
ness of the information is challengeable. One suspects the inclusion
of some substandard output. Despite a rising standard of living,
secondhand shops abound and do a brisk business in many lines, even
old shoes. Most take goods on consignment and sell for a commission.
Another type, very rare so far, is the store specializing in merchandise from abroad. In Moscow there is a popular shop handling nothing
but East German products and one almost as popular handling nothing
but Czechoslovak products.

Another type of store, about which very little information has
been released officially and the Soviet Government is quite sensitive,
is that which serves resident foreigners, such as business executives,

salesmen, engineers, journalists, and diplomats, and a small number
of privileged Russians, especially those who can travel abroad.
Some of these stores sell for hard foreign currency and some for
ruble coupons, which are issued by the Soviet Bank for Foreign Trade
in exchange for hard foreign currency. The advantages in such stores
are the price savings, often as high as three-fourths off, and the
impressive assortment and depth of stock of Soviet and Western
durables and nondurables.

In the central business districts of many cities and in resort
areas there are stores featuring luxury items, gifts, and handicrafts,
and selling only for hard foreign currencies. Soviet citizens are not
allowed to buy there, and one who wanders in is usually asked to
leave promptly. Most items in such shops are priced at a significant
discount below what a Soviet citizen would have to pay. For example,
several popular brands of Soviet-made candies are discounted by 84
percent, some phonograph records by 50 percent, and two popular
brands of refrigerator by 66 percent and 52 percent, respectively,
while scarce Soviet automobiles are offered at discounts of 50 to 75
percent. Hard currency stores are often placed in or adjacent to
principal hotels, a fact that helps account for their limited notoriety.
Trade officials do not expect to sell large numbers of durables to
tourists for export, but they sell significant numbers to tourists who
present them as gifts to relatives and friends who are Soviet citizens.
The trade hierarchy occasionally advertises abroad to Russian
émigrés to solicit their mail orders for gifts to relatives living in
the U.S.S.R.

Another development is ordering in advance, usually by telephone,
and later picking up the goods, a technique which permits some
smoothing out of peaks in shopper traffic and a major saving of time
for the consumer. As of 1968, 7,000 stores provided this service.
One consumer quoted in Izvestia stated that he became a customer
of a store which adopted telephone order service specifically because
of that policy and that he was "never an admirer" of the shop before
that time. He went on to note that, prior to the telephone service,
he took 40 to 50 minutes in a store, and then, because of congestion
and lines, came out with only half of what he went in for.[99] However,
expansion of this practice will probably be slow. For one thing,
telephone ownership is extremely low. Moreover, there seems to be
little enthusiasm among managers for the practice. It should be
noted that the term "advance ordering" is sometimes also used to
refer to purchase transactions made before the goods arrive at the
store.

Associated with advance ordering but extremely uncommon is
home delivery. Recently two republic-level deputies wrote the
U.S.S.R. Minister of Trade a public letter which was critical and yet

aimed at better management and service to the consumer. The men were concerned with advance ordering and home delivery.

Much is unclear about these forms of trade. It is unclear, for example, who is charged with introducing them, where they are advisable and for which goods they must become widespread. Is this the task of every store? If not, then which specifically?

We think that we should not rely solely on initiative from below. Specialized, economically-accountable stores—or sections of these stores—for taking and filling advance orders and special stores for home delivery at the customer's request should obviously be opened in all cities and densely populated points. And it is necessary to work out some kind of normative—one such store with such-and-such a staff, with such-and-such means of transport, for a population of so many thousands. In other words, the task must be made more specific. It is not our aim to determine the selection of goods, but we could perhaps begin with something small—home delivery of orders for milk products, baked goods and vegetables.[100]

In January 1972, a resolution was passed by the Party Central Committee and the U.S.S.R. Council of Ministers favoring advance ordering and home delivery and ordering expansion of both by the trade officials.

Planned in-store display and use of show windows along the street are still not common, although for several years central government agencies have distributed a few manuals on merchandising in general and display in particular. This modest use results from lack of facilities and materials with which to work, lack of skill, lack of initiative, and sometimes, perhaps, the perceived lack of real need. Large downtown stores and large stores on arterial streets tend to use many show windows and exercise care with them. Contrary to the practice prevailing before the 1960s, stores seldom display goods which they are not offering for sale inside. When the goods are not for sale, they are usually so marked.

NOTES

1. V. Bulatov, "How to Run the Municipal Economy," Izvestia February 10, 1972, p. 2. CDSP, 24 (March 8, 1972), 12-13.
2. Lancelot Lawton, Economic History of Soviet Russia, 1 (London: Macmillan, n. d. [apparently about 1929]), 267.

3. See V. N. Bandera, "The New Economic Policy (NEP) as an Economic System," Journal of Political Economy, 71 (June 1963), 265-79; and Alec Nove, An Economic History of the U.S.S.R. (London: Allen Lane Penguin Press, 1969), pp. 83-159.

4. Leonard E. Hubbard, Soviet Trade and Distribution (London: Macmillan, 1938), pp. 9-17.

5. "Figures and Facts," Sovetskaya Torgovlya, no. 4 (April 1970), pp. 58-63. JPRS, 50700; TOUTAS, 130.

6. "Report of the U.S.S.R. Central Statistical Administration: First Stage of the Five-Year Plan—The Results of the Fulfillment of the State Plan for the Development of the U.S.S.R. National Economy in 1971," Pravda, January 23, 1972, pp. 1-2. CDSP, 24 (February 16, 1972), 10-16, at 15.

7. N. K. Baibakov, "On the State Plan for the Development of the U.S.S.R. National Economy in 1971," Pravda, December 9, 1970, pp. 1-3. CDSP, 22 (January 5, 1971), 8-16, at 14.

8. "Report of the U.S.S.R. Central Statistical Administration: On Results of the Fulfillment of the State Plan for the Development of the U.S.S.R. National Economy in 1972," Pravda January 30, 1973, pp. 1-3, and Izvestia, January 30, 1973, pp. 1-3. CSDP, 25 February 28, 1973), 7-14, 24, at 14.

9. A. N. Kosygin, "On the State Five-Year Plan for the Development of the U.S.S.R. National Economy in 1972," Pravda, November 25, 1971, pp. 1-4. CDSP, 23 (December 21, 1971), 12-24, at 13.

10. V. Nikitin, "A Scientific Basis for Retail Goods Turnover," Sovetskaya Torgovlya, no. 6 (1969), 15-17. JPRS, 48430, TOUTAS 32.

11. Ibid.

12. Ibid.

13. Naum Jasny, "Interpreting Soviet Statistics: Penny Plain, Twopence Coloured," Soviet Survey, no. 26 (October-December 1958), 9-14. Reproduced in Alex Inkeles and Kent Geiger, eds., Soviet Society: A Book of Readings (Boston: Houghton Mifflin, 1961), pp. 302-07, at 304.

14. K. Zigangirov, Ekonomicheskaya Gazeta, no. 22 (May 1970), 17. JPRS, 50795; TOUTAS, 135.

15. Roger Skurski, "The Factor Proportions Problem in Soviet Internal Trade," Soviet Studies, 23 (January 1972), 450-64. Also see Richard Moorsteen and Raymond Powell, The Soviet Capital Stock, 1928-1962 (Homewood, Ill.: Richard D. Irwin, 1966); and Abraham S. Becker, Richard Moorsteen, and Raymond Powell, The Soviet Capital Stock: Revisions and Extensions, 1961-1967 (New Haven: Yale University Press, 1968).

16. V. Kuzin, "How Trade is Developing: Convenient and Advantageous for All," Pravda, June 11, 1970, p. 3. CDSP, 22 (July 7, 1970), 21-22.

17. "Figures and Facts."

18. V. Shimansky, "Technology in the Store," Pravda, February 14, 1973, p. 3. CDSP 25 (March 14, 1973), 16-17.

19. See N. Tregubov, "How Trade Should Develop: Profitable to the Customer and the Store," Pravda, January 8, 1972, p. 3. CDSP, 24 (February 2, 1972), 28-29.

20. P. Popov et al, "The Path to the Customer," Izvestia, December 2, 1972, p. 2. CDSP, 24 (December 27, 1972), 10-11.

21. See "Architectural Premieres: Shapes of Renewal," Izvestia February 15, 1972, p. 5. CDSP, 24 (March 15, 1972), 20-21.

22. S. Matveyev, "Problems of Urban Transport," Trud, August 31, 1972, p. 2. CDSP, 25 (February 7, 1973), 17.

23. A. Segedinov, "Underground Urban Development," Stroitel'-stvo i Arkhitektura Moskvy, no. 5 (1971), 13-15. JPRS, 53584; TOU-TAS, 256.

24. Ibid.

25. "Moscow: Heart of My Homeland: Stages of an Experiment on the South Side," Izvestia, February 1, 1972, p. 6. CDSP, 24 (March 1, 1972), 7-8.

26. Philip Hanson, "Soviet Retailing and Wholesaling," Soviet Studies, 16 (October 1964), 186-208, at 201.

27. "New Shopping Centers," Stroitelnaya Gazeta, March 15, 1970, p. 1. JPRS, 50411; TOUTAS, 115.

28. G. N. Ragozhin and I. B. Lipatova, "Drawing up Comprehensive General Plans for Rural Communities," Stroitel'stvo i Arkhitektur no. 6 (1971), 20-22. JPRS, 53919; TOUTAS, 270.

29. P. Luk'yanov, "Revaluation of Fixed Assets," Sovetskaya Torgovlya, July 17, 1971, p. 3. JPRS, 53842; TOUTAS, 267.

30. M. Stepichev and V. Yegorov, "Demands Are High: We Sum up the Discussion of 'Man and the Service Sector,'" Pravda, January 15, 1972, p. 3. CDSP, 24 (February 9, 1972), 26-27.

31. "On Certain Measures to Improve Trade and Its Technical Equipment," Pravda, January 30, 1972, p. 1. CDSP, 24 (February 23, 1972), 13-14.

32. V. Mikhailov, "Level of Production and Level of Services: Busiest Hours Without Queues," Izvestia, September 5, 1970, p. 2. CDSP, 22 (October 6, 1970), 19-20.

33. A. I. Struyev, "Self-Service Is in the Customer's Interest," Pravda, December 15, 1971, p. 3. CDSP, 23 (January 11, 1972), 14.

34. A. Valeyev and M. Latypov, "How Is the Introduction of New Trade Methods Proceeding?," Izvestia, October 15, 1971, p. 3. CDSP, 23 (November 9, 1971), 32-33.

35. "May the Capital Be a Model City," Moskovskaya Pravda, July 10, 1971, pp. 1-3. JPRS, 53732; Political and Social Affairs, 166.

36. Kuzin, "How Trade Is Developing."

37. Ibid. Also O. Velikoretsky, "Under One Roof," Pravda, February 26, 1973, p. 2. CDSP, 25 (March 14, 1973), 17.

38. "May the Capital Be a Model City."

39. Ye. Rozanova, "The Capital Prepares for the Lenin Jubilee, Izvestia, December 4, 1968, p. 3. CDSP, 20 (December 25, 1968), 27.

40. Yu. Yaralov, "Window on the Future: Up-to-Date and Gold-Domed," Izvestia, January 1, 1971, p. 3. CDSP, 23 (February 2, 1971), 23.

41. "On Certain Measures to Improve Trade and Its Technical Equipment."

42. "Editorial: Reserves of Trade," Pravda, August 4, 1970, p. 1. CDSP, 22 (September 1, 1970), 14-15.

43. Valeyev and Latypov, "How Is the Introduction of New Trade Methods Proceeding?"

44. Shimansky, "Technology in the Store."

45. "Figures and Facts."

46. Kuzin, "How Trade Is Developing."

47. Ibid.

48. "Editorial: Reserves of Trade."

49. "Today Is Trade Workers' Day: In the Customer's Interest," Pravda, July 23, 1967, p. 1. CDSP, 19 (August 19, 1967), 28-29.

50. Ibid.

51. Ya. Orlov, "Experiment in Progress," Pravda, November 23, 1969, p. 3. CDSP, 21 (December 17, 1969), 31-32.

52. "Figures and Facts."

53. Struyev, "Self-Service Is in the Customer's Interest."

54. Ibid.

55. Ibid.

56. Valeyev and Latypov, "How Is the Introduction of New Trade Methods Proceeding?"

57. Struyev, "Self-Service Is in the Customer's Interest."

58. "Answers to Deputies' Questions: How Is the Introduction of New Trade Methods Proceeding?," Izvestia, December 24, 1971, pp. 1, 3. CDSP, 23 (January 18, 1972), 19-20.

59. Ibid.

60. T. Vasilenko, "Soviets and Level of Trade: The Gain from a Minute Saved," Izvestia, September 4, 1971, p. 3. CDSP, 22 (October 6, 1970), 19.

61. G. Ustinov, "Not an Exception, But a Rule," Izvestia, October 17, 1969, p. 3.

62. N. Klepikov, "The Psychology of Trade," Pravda, January 24, 1968, p. 3. CDSP, 20 (February 14, 1968), 26.

63. Ibid.

64. Stepichev and Yegorov, "Demands Are High."

65. "Editorial: Young Cadres for the Service Sector," Pravda, January 17, 1972, p. 1. CDSP, 24 (February 16, 1972), 31.

66. Kuzin, "How Trade is Developing."

67. Tregubov, "How Trade Should Develop."

68. Ye. Kanevsky, "Aspect of a Trade in the 1970's: Most Conspicuous," Izvestia, December 1, 1971, p. 3. CDSP, 23 (December 28, 1971), 29.

69. Ibid. Also Stepichev and Yegorov, "Demands Are High."

70. Kanevsky, "Aspect of a Trade."

71. For example, see "Izvestia Legal Service: Pensioner in the Service Sector," Izvestia, March 24, 1972, p. 4. CDSP, 24 (April 19, 1972), 23.

72. V. Varavka, "The Difficulties of Salespeople," Ekonomicheskaya Gazeta, no. 19 (May 1970), 17. JPRS, 50808; TOUTAS, 136.

73. Ekonomicheskaya Gazeta, no. 39, 1969; no. 40, 1969; no. 1, 1970; no. 6, 1970; P. Mikhailov, Izvestia, February 13, 1963, p. 3; N. Klepikov, Izvestia, April 28, 1965, p. 3.

74. Varavka, "The Difficulties of Salespeople."

75. N. Tregubov and G. Belkin, "Economic Experiment in Trade," Ekonomicheskaya Gazeta, no. 18 (May 1970), 17. JPRS, 50745; TOUTAS, 132.

76. "An Experiment at Five Stores," Izvestia, November 15, 1972, p. 3. CDSP, 24 (December 13, 1972), 7-8.

77. Tregubov, "How Trade Should Develop."

78. A. Nikitin, "Notes About the Customer and the Service He Receives: Service as a Two-Way Street," Izvestia, December 31, 1971, p. 5. CDSP, 23 (January 25, 1972), 26.

79. Klepikov, "The Psychology of Trade."

80. For example, see Varavka, "The Difficulties of Salespeople."

81. G. Tipukhyan and G. Novikov, "Mail Order Trade Today and Tomorrow," Sovetskaya Torgovlya, no. 5 (1969), 22-25. JPRS, 48369; TOUTAS, 30.

82. See V. Shmyganovsky, "Facts and Details: The Post Office's Age of Automation," Izvestia, December 18, 1971, p. 5. CDSP, 23 (January 18, 1972), 19.

83. B. Kotelnikov and A. Popov, "Package for You," Pravda, June 14, 1967, p. 3. CDSP, 19 (July 5, 1967), 24.

84. Tipukhyan and Novikov, "Mail Order Trade Today and Tomorrow."

85. M. Matrosov, "The Store, the Plan and Direct Ties," Pravda, July 12, 1968, p. 3. CDSP, 20 (July 31, 1968), 30-31.

86. Jere L. Felker, Soviet Economic Controversies: The Emerging Marketing Concept and Changes in Planning, 1960-1965 (Cambridge, Mass.: MIT Press, 1966), p. 153.

87. Philip Hanson, The Consumer in the Soviet Economy (Evanston: Northwestern University Press, 1968), pp. 124, 127.

88. Felker, Soviet Economic Controversies, p. 153; and Izvestia, Oct. 3, 1962, p. 3.

89. A Malkov, "Problems of the Rural Market," Ekonomicheskaya Gazeta, no. 41 (October 1971), 17. CDSP, 23 (December 14, 1971), 9-10.

90. Ibid.

91. P. Novoselov and S. Mezhiborskaya, "What Is New in Trade Credit," Den'gi i Kredit, no. 6 (1971), 20-27. JPRS, 53842; TOUTAS, 267.

92. Leonard Goldberg, Crediting According to Turnover: A Method of Financial Control of the Soviet Firm (Seattle: College of Business Administration, University of Washington, 1965), pp. 3-5.

93. Novoselov and Mezhiborskaya, "What Is New in Trade Credit."

94. See I. Borzhanskaia, "On the Development of Social Principles in the Activity of the State Bank," Den'gi i Kredit, no. 8 (1965), 40. Cited in George Garvy, Money, Banking, and Credit in Eastern Europe (New York: Federal Reserve Bank of New York, 1966), p. 127.

95. Novoselov and Mezhiborskaya, "What Is New in Trade Credit."

96. Yu. Zvyagin, "Curtsey Number 199," Izvestia, November 30, 1972, p. 6. CDSP, 24 (December 27, 1972), 20.

97. N. Gladkov, "Unheeded Warning Signs," Pravda, September 7, 1970, p. 4. CDSP, 22 (October 6, 1970), 20.

98. Felker, Soviet Economic Controversies, p. 135.

99. Ustinov, "Not the Exception, but the Rule."

100. Valeyev and Latypov, "How Is the Introduction of New Trade Methods Proceeding?"

3

THE SOVIET PEOPLE

POPULATION

After China and India, the Soviet Union had the third largest population in the world—241.7 million people—at the time of the latest census in January 1970. This was a 15.8 percent increase over the previous census in 1959, which recorded 208.8 million. Using 1970 borders on as consistent a basis as possible for each census, the population at the end of 1950 was 181.8 million; at the beginning of 1939 it was 193.1 million; and at the end of 1926 it was 167.7 million.[1] The largest and most important metropolitan areas are Moscow and Leningrad, which had 1970 populations of 7,061,000 and 3,950,000, respectively. Persons of working age, measured in the U.S.S.R. as ages 16-59 for men and 16-54 for women, accounted for 57.4 percent of the population in 1959 and 54.9 percent in 1970. The elderly as a percentage of the population grew from 12.2 to 15.0 in the same period. The corresponding percentages for persons under 16 were 30.4 and 30.1.[2] The statistically calculated life expectancy at birth around January 1970 is 69.7 years.[3]

Two factors in Soviet population structure stand out above the rest. The most noteworthy was the heavy loss of life during World War II. Estimates vary, but the loss was probably about 20 million, heavily concentrated among males. In 1970 in the age groups mainly affected, there were only 631 men for every 1,000 women in the category 45-49, 607 in the category 50-54, and 552 in the category 55-59. The effect of that war becomes vivid if one divides the population into two parts: below 44, and 44 or over. For the younger group there were, in 1970, 1,002 men for every 1,000 women. For the older group the figure was only 547.[4] This sex disproportionality has, of course, interfered drastically with normal family formation and structure.

The loss of population and attendant sex disproportionality has brought forth for many years a government program to encourage a high birth rate. Women who have given birth to and reared at least seven children become members of the Maternal Glory Order, while those who have given birth to and reared at least ten are awarded the title of Heroine Mother. Although this program has not been halted, it now lacks a sense of direction. The birth rate responded to patriotic cries in the years following World War II. During the 1960s, however, the birth rate declined every year for 10 consecutive years. It went up slightly in 1970.

A second and highly perplexing factor for the Soviet government and society is that the ratio of natural increase varies widely by ethnic group. Some Asian groups[5] have growth rates more than three times as high as some Slavic groups. The Uzbeks increased to 9,195,000 in 1970, a gain of 52.9 percent in the intercensus period. All in all, the share of the Russians, Belorussians, and Ukrainians in the population fell from about 76.2 percent in 1959 to about 70.4 percent in 1970. If the trend continues, their share will go down to 62-64 percent by 1980. Moreover, nearly all of the other European groups in the population exhibit a rate of natural increase lower than the national average. All rather small, these slow-growth groups include the Lithuanians, Latvians, Estonians, Germans, and Jews. Noting that the rate of natural increase in the 1960s was determined almost entirely by the birth rate, two Soviet demographers have urged that each Five-Year Plan have a specific section on the desired complex of birth rates.[6] It is not prudent or politic for demographers and other social scientists to refer openly to the differentials among ethnic types. However, the Moscow University Center for the Study of Population Problems and other institutions apparently are well aware of the data, the issues, and the implications for the evolution of Soviet society.

About 56 percent (136 million) of the population was urban in 1970, versus 48 percent in 1959, 32 percent in 1939, and 18 percent in 1913. The large absolute increase in urban population between 1959 and 1970, about 36 million, came from three sources. Natural increase in urban areas provided 14.6 million, while migration provided more than 16 million and reclassification of growing rural communities into urban status provided about 5 million. The rural population had a natural increase of about 18 million during the intercensus period but showed a decline of about 3 million. The 1970 rural count was 105.7 million, versus 108.8 million in 1959. The urban-rural data are potentially misleading in that the definition of "rural" varies among the Soviet republics. Moreover, the cutting points between rural and urban categories are higher than in the United States. In addition, some

Soviet communities that are populous enough to be classified as urban are not, because of a preponderance of agricultural workers.

THE RUSSIAN CHARACTER AND MIND

Although it is occasionally considered foolhardy to try to characterize a nation or a culture,[7] such attempts should prove useful in gaining some understanding of the U.S.S.R. The Russian "national" character and the Russian mind have been explored in several worthwhile works, mostly by Westerners. The people of Great Russia, who constitute about half of the population, have received much of the scholarly interest. In essence, much of the work revolves around the characters of the pre-1917 era, the post-1917 but pre-industrial era, and the contemporary era, the differentials, and the change process.

The Russians have a Byzantine heritage of great importance. Byzantine civilization itself was an amalgam of Hellenistic, Roman, and Christian traditions. Ironically, Byzantium thrust northward in the late 10th century and embraced Russia shortly before it lost Asia Minor to Islam. This politico-religious embrace brought the pagan Slav tribes into the Western world, although the Scandinavians had given them a glimpse a few decades before. It is a moot point how Russian cultural-economic history would have differed if the conversion to Christianity had come from Rome. It is possible that the now centuries-old Russian separatism from the rest of the Western world would not have developed. Be that as it may, Byzantium was the gateway through which Russia tentatively linked up with, but did not fully join, medieval Europe.

Several other formative stages may be identified. The Mongols were in control from about 1240 to 1480 and left an indelible stamp. Then the nobles and aristocrats of Muscovy emerged in the 16th century, combining nationalism and religion. They pressed the theme of "Moscow the Third Rome." The mantle of religious purity had passed from Rome to Byzantium (Constantinople), then from Moslem-occupied Byzantium to Moscow, they claimed. The Communist leaders of the Soviet state have capitalized on the somewhat mystical leadership role of Moscow in modern Russian cultural history. Russians are, so to speak, a chosen people. Next there was the ecclesiastical schism of the Old Believers in the middle of the 17th century, when the Russian Orthodox Church was being influenced by Western thought and practice. In the first quarter of the 18th century Peter the Great established many Western changes, including a new respect for technology. In the middle of the 19th century Tsar Alexander II introduced liberal reforms, including the emancipation of the serfs. And finally, one recognizes, of course, the Revolution of 1917 and the ensuing civil war.

Russia's separatism from the West, and indeed from the East, has not necessarily meant cultural or intellectual independence. As a matter of fact, analysis of Russian literature suggests that the Russians swung back and forth between a Slavophilia and a virtual Slavophobia, and that both contenders were powerful persuasive forces. Russian philosopher and essayist Peter Yakovlevich Chaadayev wrote deprecatingly:

> Even in the all-inclusive scientific world, our history is not connected with anything, doesn't explain anything, doesn't prove anything. If the hordes of barbarians who convulsed the world had not crossed the country in which we live before swooping down on the Occident, we could hardly have filled one chapter of world history. In order to be noticed we had to expand from the Bering Straits to the Oder.[8]

On the other hand, the same writer felt compelled to say, ". . . we are appointed, by the very nature of things, to serve as a real jury for the many suits which are being argued before the great tribunals of the human spirit and of human society.[9]

Nikolai Danilevsky bitingly stated:

> The struggle against the Germano-Roman world (without which Slav independence is impossible) will help to eradicate the cancer of imitativeness and the servile attitude towards the West, which through unfavorable conditions has eaten its way into the Slav body and soul.[10]

Poet and philosopher Vladimir Solovev perhaps typified the reaction against Slavophilia: "The Russian people were like a man who has contact only with inferior people and thereby gains an exaggerated opinion of himself."[11]

Dimitri Obolensky has warned that Russia was never a self-contained unit and that "we cannot understand her history in terms of cultural self-sufficiency."[12] Russia was not of the West, although it is tempting to think of it as a backwater of the Western tradition. Vera Micheles Dean points to this as one of the most persistent of the nonfactual assumptions about that country.[13] Russia was not of the West, or the East, and yet was not independent. One might think of her as something of a European periphery buffeted frequently and at length by crosscurrents. At best it has held an enigmatic position

in European politico-cultural-intellectual history. Berdyaev concludes
that

> There has been a vast elemental strength in the Russian
> people combined with a comparatively weak sense of
> form. The Russians have not been in any special sense
> a people of culture, as the peoples of Western Europe
> have been, they have rather been a people of revelation
> and inspiration. . . . Never has Russia been bourgeois.[14]

To examine more specifically the psychological makeup of the
Russians, one must turn mainly to the work of Benedict, Gorer, Rickman, Dicks, and the Inkeles-Hanfmann-Beier team and associates.
The research of anthropologist Ruth Benedict was based on the construct of the apparent communication accomplished by the cultural
techniques being analyzed. She was impressed by the extraordinarily
tight swaddling of Russian infants right up to the time of her work in
1949; by the use of stiff, horizontal moving of the infant instead of
rocking in the arms; and by the adult assumption of the inherent vio-
lence of a baby. As for adults, she was impressed by the need for
"pouring out the soul" and yet, in the same individual, an acute need
for privacy and personal inviolability. Benedict stressed the basic
Russian conviction that "strong feeling has positive value. Personal
outbreaks . . . were characteristic of all classes."[15] She concluded
that Russian poetry and folk songs create no role for mother love
and that motherhood is diffused. The Russian mother "is not specifically a maternal figure; she is quite sure of her sex without having
to produce children to prove that she is female—as the man also is
sure of his sex."[16] Margaret Mead was associated in this work. In
a comment on Benedict's article, she drew attention to the general
theoretical ground plan whereby a culture, such as the Russian, trans-
mits messages to the next generation.[17]

Out of the extensive research project that Benedict organized
in 1947 at Columbia University there also came a controversial book
by Gorer and Rickman.[18] The contribution of Rickman, a psychiatrist
who practiced medicine in the U.S.S.R. for two years, is principally
a set of provocative case studies. After sifting and evaluating much
confusing and incomplete evidence from many sources, the book concludes that there are two quite different Russias, that of the elites
and that of the masses. In generalizing about the masses, these
writers emphasize acute emotionalism, oscillation of emotional drives,
resentment of and hostility toward those who behave differently, and
an ability to merge self and ego into a peer "soul-collective" that
governs behavior.

As part of the work of the Harvard Project on the Soviet Social System, a program of clinical psychological research was carried out.[19] However, the subject group was disproportionately young, male, well-educated, and advantageously placed occupationally and politically. Methodology included intensive interviewing and an elaborate battery of projective tests. Inkeles, Hanfmann, and Beier contend that, while all persons manifest the same basic needs, some universal needs take on greater strength or central importance in organization of personality and become typical of the majority of a particular group. These researchers conclude that a need for affiliation is the strongest and most pervasive quality of the Russian personality. In addition, there is a need for dependence, which the research of Dicks also identified strongly.[20] This dependence applied not only to peers and parents but to formal authority figures as well.

The Inkeles team reports that the great emphasis on achievement found in the American control group in the study was absent in the Russian group. The American need for approval and for autonomy showed up weakly among the Russians. Russians showed high awareness of impulses, a predisposition to give in to impulse, and relied far less than Americans on impulse control to be generated and managed from within. Rather, they felt a need for such guidance to come from peer groups or from formal authority. Dicks agrees and calls it a desire for a "moral corset." The Inkeles team reports a conscious preoccupation with the polarities of trust versus mistrust in relations with others, and optimisim versus pessimism. It also found an ambivalence between activity and passivity. Thus there is support for Dick's conclusion that "the outstanding trait of the Russian personality is the contradictoriness—its ambivalence."

The Inkeles team concludes that the dilemmas of intimacy versus isolation and autonomy versus belongingness characteristic of Americans were not important for Russians. The Russians exhibited rather high and secure self-esteem and were little disposed to self-examination and doubt of self. More so than Americans, Russians felt guilty or ashamed when they believed they had deviated from moral or interpersonal behavior norms. Compared with Americans, Russians showed a higher degree of expressiveness and emotional aliveness, more hostile feelings, and much higher frequencies of fear and depression. More so than Americans, Russians saw other persons not only as social types but also as individuals with unique sets of characteristics. Russians exhibited more perceptiveness of an individual's motivational characteristics. However, with regard to problems involving social organization, Russians viewed things broadly and sweepingly, generalizing with little, and rather vague, detail. Russians appeared to "feel their way through such situations rather than rigorously to think them through, tending to get into a spirit of grandiose planning but without attention to necessary details." In conative functioning the Russians demonstrated passive accommodation, did not persevere systematically even in adaptive courses of action, and showed little precision or orderliness. Nevertheless, on occasion they showed great bursts of activity. Thus they exhibited a bimodality of assertiveness-passivity in contrast with Americans' steady, consistent patterns of strivings. With regard to authority, Russians expected paternalism that might and should include firm guidance, superordinate planning, and, if necessary, control of thought and belief.

Soviet farmers have tended to be a grave problem for Communist planners and leaders. The problem involves not only productivity and meeting national needs for commodities but, equally important, a philosophical difference in what rural people aspire to and what Communist theorists believe they should aspire to. Moreover, Communism was premised on the priority well-being of industrial workers, not farmers. Farmers were often considered petty bourgeoisie, along with merchants and individual artisans. Even in the current press, workers and peasants are normally referred to as "two different classes." Chairman Brezhnev frequently refers to three classes in Soviet society: workers, peasants, and intelligentsia.[21] Rather than idealizing the agricultural sector, as is done often in the West, many Soviet leaders and bureaucrats have vilified it. One may recall that the Communist Manifesto of 1848 referred disdainfully to the "idiocy of village life."

The Russian peasants, serfs prior to 1861, have been looked on with contempt by most of their educated and well-to-do countrymen, whether in Tsarist or Communist days. The able, aggressive Kulaks (literally "fists") among the peasants were hated and were eventually eliminated by the Bolsheviks, not solely because of their capital. In Marx's era and today peasants are perceived as reactionary because they exhibit more individualism than do workers. This is still less than that shown by Western European peasants, of course. Vucinich explains that the Russian farmer has a "private-property mentality" and "petty bourgeois propensities" that are incompatible with principles of rural socialism.[22] With their central thesis of large-scale production, Marx and Lenin had no fundamental sympathy for or empathy with the man of the soil or with individualism. Nevertheless, Lenin and his followers were pragmatic enough to appease the peasantry when setting up the Bolshevik regime and for several years thereafter. Collectivization had to come much later. Stalin once told Winston Churchill that his struggle with the Russian peasants had been a more perilous and formidable undertaking than the battle of Stalingrad.[23]

Paradoxically, Russian farmers traditionally exhibited some aspects that one is tempted to term "early collectivism." Prior to

1917 many thousands of farms were owned by several peasant families
jointly under a system called obshchina. Households generally performed their own work but sometimes shared the work. Major decisions affecting the farm were jointly reached. This Russian institution influenced Marxist thinkers to some extent, and had an effect on
Mexico in the 1920s and 1930s, on modern Israel over most of its
life, and on India during the late 1940s and the 1950s.

In most of Russia each peasant family had the use of some of
the best and some of the worst land in the village unit. Land was
parceled out in strips periodically, such as every 12, or at most every
20, years, for the sake of equal treatment. There was some similarity
to Medieval Western Europe. Thus few personal claims to any piece
of land grew up. A planting plan and crop rotation plan were decided
on and followed by everyone, although each farmer had his own strips
of land to cultivate. Harvesting of private parcels and use of common
land were jointly planned.

The paradox may possibly be explained in that the communality
of the peasant extended at first to the patriarchal family of which he
was a member and simultaneously to the estate of which he was part.
Later, after emancipation, the communality extended to the volost, a
unit of several adjoining villages and their common forest and grazing
land. (The volost may have evolved into the raion, a basic unit of
Soviet administration.) The communality was never to a nation or an
entire culture, or even to a planning district, but to a close-knit
family and to a geographically compact land area peopled by only a
few families. The work concept was not identified with mass production. In all of this it is important to remember that the master was
almost always absent and, up to the time of Peter I, the master held
the serfs and the estate only for the term of his service to the government or at most for life. Day-to-day authority rested with the general
assembly of the village, composed of the heads of families and their
elected leader, the starosta. Conflicts between individuals were
settled by the starosta, while matters of concern to the whole village
were submitted to the general assembly. The village headman was
accountable to the absent landowner. Emancipation of the serfs removed the authority of most former masters but served to increase
the importance of the village assembly and the starosta. The latter
evolved into the government's informal representative.

The village assembly has been succinctly described by psychiatrist John Rickman:

> The conduct of the village mir is comparable in the social
> and economic plane with Pentecost on the spiritual. There
> is first a discordance of individual opinion in which every-
> one expresses his personal views, sometimes stridently,

sometimes gently; the lack of unanimity to begin with is most striking and there is no sign of party organization. Then with an increasing number of silences (such as occur in groups of chattering people in any part of the world) defined courses of action are mentioned (the speaker claiming no prestige for voicing a policy and none being accorded him) and policy opinions are received with assent or else the hum of talk continues, meaning that opinion is not united. Once opinion is united there is a profound sense of satisfaction and of village solidarity, and the members of the village assembled at the mir disperse without a vote having been taken, with no committee formed and yet the feeling that each man knows what is expected of him.[24]

Gorer and Rickman note that the Russian peasants traditionally did not comprehend the idea of a majority vote. They call attention to Russian proverbs: "The mir is like a wave; one man's thought is everybody's thought"; "The mir's decision is God's decision"; and "The voice of the mir is the voice of God."[25]

A literary school of thought among some creative writers and thinkers has arisen in the contemporary Soviet Union that seems to consist of misgivings, nostalgia, protest, and even mysticism concerning rural man, his traditions, and the perceived struggle between rural and urban. It is perhaps exemplified by the words of poet V. Yakovchenko. After depicting the city and industrial life as "an evil genius" that "towers over all," he says:

Iron has found a tongue, a voice loud and sharp. Tear! Chop! Make holes, cut! That's the law. That's the right. Steel grows. Iron grows like giant grass. Stop! Fed by the age, you've grown above mankind. Never enough, never enough![26]

However, a historian has severely criticized this school of thought,[27] and editorials in Pravda have endorsed such criticism.

SOCIAL CLASS

Social class has always been part of Russian society. The complex structure was inextricably bound up with the elaborate system of direct and indirect service to the Tsars. After serfdom was abolished in 1861, it was mandatory that farmers migrating to the city carry passports identifying their humble origins and forever marking them as of the peasant class.

Instead of abolishing classes following the 1971 Revolution, the new Communist government officially defined social strata, made this hierarchy part of the legal system, and dispensed buying privileges according to this new set of rules. For several years the stringent product rationing system severely discriminated against professional and managerial people and their families. Ironically, today it is those very people for whom some products and brands are specifically marketed. Ostensibly these products are for all, but the obvious differences in buying power and patterns of access to the stores establish that such goods are for select target markets. The expanding interest in a relatively conspicuous consumption of fine consumer goods and services is a reflection of the passage of time since the Bolshevik Revolution. Formerly the unbridled zeal of that revolution demanded the destruction of the consumption and behavior standards held by the conquered upper and upper-middle classes. An example of the new wave is the publication of several etiquette books, the first since the Tsarist years. Another example is that older teen-agers in the elites and middle class, after years of asking, now find some youthful apparel designed explicitly for them, even though there is no compelling physical size rationale for such production deviation. It should be noted also that the inheritance laws of the U.S.S.R. permit passing on small estates, contrary to pure Marxist thought.

In view of her generally liberal convictions, Barbara Ward's conclusions on the subject are certainly notable:

> Certainly, we have seen in actual Communist societies that those who control power—the bureaucrats, the organization men—secure for themselves social differences, both in wealth and opportunity, which are at least equivalent to the kind of class distinctions we have in the West. Indeed, they may in some areas be wider since the base of society is still so desperately low. To have command of a car in a society where there are virtually no cars confers greater privilege than does the manager's Cadillac in the West. The gap between top executive and floor-cleaner is almost certainly larger in Soviet society because the whole community has not yet reached the affluence of mass consumption.[28]

Lenin assumed that rationalization and routinization of large-scale manufacturing and agriculture would furnish the basis for social equalization.[29] However, Inkeles points out:

Soviet experience indicates that the very fact of modern large-scale production—involving extreme division of labor, precise differentiation of function, emphasis on technical competence, and elaborate hierarchies of authority and responsibility—provides a natural basis for the development of distinct social groups.

It requires only the appearance of distinctive patterns of speech, manners, and dress, differential patterns of association, and social group consciousness, to lay the foundation of a system of stratification based on social-class groupings. . . . As stratification has become institutionalized there has been a noticeable tendency for social mobility to decline. . . .[30]

Field and Anderson constructed four family types existent in the U.S.S.R. The bountiful-neglectful type belongs to the power elite and upper ranks of the intelligentsia. Its children deride physical work and dislike any work at all and constitute a leisure subclass of sorts. Every string is pulled in their favor.[31] The overprotective family is in the middle intelligentsia. From the Soviet viewpoint, it turns out spoiled and misguided children who are not hooligans or lawbreakers but who are oriented toward private emotional ties and egotism. They put the economic and social life of the country second when it should always be first. The under-supportive family is frequently found in the lower socioeconomic groups and is characterized by little if any supervision of children. Drunkenness of the father is common. Fourth is the Soviet ideal family, which effectively integrates family warmth with socially approved external attitudes and relationships.

There is abundant evidence that the admiration of manual labor and aspiration for a career of labor have declined markedly. For example, the chief executive of one major industrial firm has stated that the "pyramid of preferences" of youth is the reverse of the "pyramids of requirements" of the economy.[32] Bemoaning the decline of esteem for labor, a Hero of Socialist Labor has said:

Many of us remember how a senior machine operator, an experienced craftsman, would lead a son or grandson by the hand to his working spot and train and teach him. But now I can't recall a father or older brother inviting an adolescent to work at his own plant.[33]

All of this has bred a preoccupation with credentials attesting to the completion of study programs. One occasionally hears of

diploma mills, fraudulent technical schools, and forged diplomas.[34]
The problems of access to a limited range of educational opportunities,
differential access, and adequate training are especially severe a-
mong rural youth.[35] An executive has stated, "The selection of children for the special schools [academic schools] is, more often than
not, based not on their gifts, but on the ambition of some parents."[36]
As far as higher education is concerned, Nove points out that the
children of university graduates tend to become university students.
"Higher education has become the way forward for the vast majority
of those who wish to become anybody in the U.S.S.R., whether in the
intellectual, governmental or party spheres."[37]

    Valid and reliable data on income patterns in the Soviet Union
are quite scarce. Yet it is clear that many persons receive compensation as much as four or five times as large as that of many other
persons. Most production workers are governed by a national remuneration policy which sets up a six-category scale. The worker is placed
in one of the categories on the basis of his skills and the complexity
of his work. The categories have fixed ratio relationships. Using
category one as 1.00, the higher ratios are usually 1.13, 1.29, 1.48,
1.72, and 2.00. Thus the most skilled worker receives wages twice
as high as the unskilled in category one in a given industry. However,
the absolute level of wages differs from one type of industry to another.[38] In addition, there are geographical differentials, which are
applied not only to basic wages but also to productivity bonuses that
may be earned. Professional, managerial, and technical personnel
tend to earn considerably more than workers; but this is not uni-
versally so. Among such people, some Western norms fail to apply.
For example, physicians and dentists are usually paid less than university professors. Enterprises are divided by size of output and
number of workers, and executives of the largest are entitled to
salaries three times as high as those of the smallest.[39] Further
diversity is introduced by two facts: First, peasants on collective
farms are expected to derive much of their effective income from the
extra work of tending their small private investments in crops and
animals, as are a good many suburbanites. Second, different persons
have access to different qualities of services, such as housing, recreation, and transportation.

> . . . the initial revolutionary equalitarianism was short-
> lived and . . . since the thirties the Soviet regime has
> stressed differential earnings as incentives to higher
> production. In addition, it has favored some segments
> of the population, such as artists and scientists, with
> unusually large earnings.[40]

Managers and professionals have been scolded for their in-grained habit of holding professional meetings and conventions in resort areas—at public expense, of course.[41] Earlier a Council of Ministers decree cautioned against excessive expenses on business trips.[42]

Among Soviet academicians there is a growing consciousness of socioeconomic class structure, market segmentation, and materials related to this subject. There has not been an impressive body of literature in the past, however. A few economists have touched on demand considerations having to do with such matters as age, na-tionality composition, taste, and climatic conditions.[43] The pioneering work of academician V. Siniutin is worth noting. He has pointed to the need for emphasis on various sociological and recurring economic factors. For example, he notes the importance to the national economy and to national demand of considering the aggregate change in income in each of the several socioeconomic groups in the population, the competition for state and cooperative stores in the form of the kolkhoz marketplaces for particular goods, impending market saturation for some products, and short-run and long-run changes in the age, sex, and social makeup of the population.[44] What has been done in the past on "social structure and social interconnections and processes" has been done by cultural anthropologists and conducted principally among ethnic minorities in rural and semirural areas. But now soci-ologists are showing considerable interest and are beginning to in-vestigate "contemporary culture and life styles in highly developed societies" in the U.S.S.R.[45]

The aggregate is increasingly being looked on as a combination of many parts, as evidenced by a research monograph published by a Russian sociologist on the subject of leisure. Because this idea is still novel to most of the Soviet public, the highly influential Litera-turnaya Gazeta (Literary Gazette), in commenting on the monograph and its constructs, took care to explain and defend the concept of segmentation:

> . . . unevenness or, to put it differently, inequality in the distribution of leisure can be reduced neither to individual differences of taste nor to different levels of income.
>
> There are certain social groups with a different structure of free time or, to use the language of soci-ology, a different posture in the sphere of leisure. And by no means do these groups fully coincide with social-economic classes or social-occupational categories: One has to visualize society in a somewhat different cross section when the differences in the cultures of various groups of the population take the foreground. The point

lies not only in whether the level is high or low but also in the different types of culture (a more specialized term to designate such phenomena is subculture: One speaks of youth, urban, etc. subcultures within the framework of a single society and a single culture).

This inequality cannot be regarded as a "deviation" from a certain abstract ideal of universal leveling. It would be even more absurd to demand the elimination of such inequality.[46]

Even the sine qua non of the U.S.S.R. is probably due for dissection. Russian historian I. E. Vorozheikin criticized his colleagues for "omissions" and "shortcomings" in overgeneralizing about the working class rather than studying each of the groups which, taken together, form the working class.[47]

Armstrong notes the rising educational level of the Communist Party elite.[48] Kassoff sees the emergence of a "more or less benevolent authoritarianism in the social and economic systems."[49] The latter argues that industrialism, along with its necessary accompaniments of technology, mass education, urbanization, physical distribution, and communication, is a major source for fundamental social change in the U.S.S.R.

Slowly increasing pluralism is the root cause of much of the emerging segmentation of the market. Stewart notes that, while all interest groups are officially illegitimate, they form anyway and successfully offset their official illegitimacy by careful professions of loyalty to the regime.[50] Lodge presents the growing political influences of specialist-elite groups, such as the legal profession and the economic and/or managerial elites, and the slowly decreasing influence of the Party elite. The explanation apparently lies in the expertise of specialist-elite groups and the compelling need for such expertise. Patterns of values become less ideological and more instrumental. According to this researcher, Russians put increasing weight on such matters as economic achievement, improvements in the material standard of living, and scientific advancement. And, it can be argued, the aggregate gain can surely justify some gain for those groups of individuals at various hierarchical levels who caused the gain to come about.[51] Bauer, Inkeles, and Kluckholn contend that political idealists are on the way out and that system-oriented conformists and opportunistic careerists who seek material advantages and prestige are taking over, for they are "less likely to disturb the smooth functioning of an orderly society."[52]

Karl Marx saw the family primarily as an institution for the purpose of holding and transmitting property and thus as thoroughly corrupt. Although Lenin apparently did not believe it was necessary to destroy the traditional family in Russia, the combined effects of ideology, prolonged civil war, starvation, and migration in search of food drastically changed for a time the woman's role in the family, her sex life, and her place in society. During the 1920s and until the late 1930s, free love was state policy; and marriage, when it was contracted at all, merely required a few minutes to register. Divorce was almost instantaneous. Abortion was customary until a 1936 change in the law. Children were generally perceived as potential wards of society. As Dunham puts it, it was an era of "sex-is-joy" and "de-poetization of love."[53] However, by 1940 the Soviet government intervened, whether because of some deep-seated streak of public opinion, some instinct of family preservation, the outbreak of World War II, or a need for an increase of population, and the free love era ended. The stable nuclear family was established as the desired norm. The pendulum swung, and a quasi puritanism was imposed that to a great extent prevails today.

Except for Moslems, most women of suitable age and health in the U.S.S.R. hold jobs. The great pillar of Soviet ideology, Friedrich Engels, taught that "the first condition for the liberation of the wife is to bring the whole female sex back into public industry."[54] Lenin saw in the public nursery the key to liberating women, fundamentally changing their life style, and bringing them into the labor force. The controversial writing team of Sidney and Beatrice Webb put it this way:

> This was one of the ideas on which Lenin most strongly insisted. He described the creche, in setting free the mother from the burden of a constant care of the young children, and thus enabling her to earn an independent livelihood, as being the "germ cell of the communist society."[55]

Despite Lenin's views, the number of places currently available in state kindergartens and creches exceeds demand. Many working mothers depend on a "babushka," a grandmother or other elderly female household member, for child care. "Pioneer Palaces" provide some after-school activities for school-age youngsters, members of the group known as Young Pioneers.

The intense drive for heavy industrialization, beginning in 1929 with the First Five-year Plan, absolutely required womanpower.[56]

This factor was compounded by the requirements to settle new frontier areas of the nation, to which males were normally sent first, and, much more important, by the heavy loss of men during World War II. Thus women not only indirectly exercise control over income but bring in nearly half the income in an extremely large but unmeasured proportion of Soviet households.

In addition, many women who are spinsters are employed. The population imbalance between the sexes, a result of World War II, has not had time to phase out. It must be noted, however, that employed women are underrepresented among the highly skilled workers.[57] And only 20.2 percent of the Communist Party members are women.[58] Thus fewer women than men possess entry into most positions of prominence.

In a 1940 study Inkeles and Bauer concluded that, primarily, it has been direct and sometimes dire economic need that explains the very high proportion of Soviet women who are employed, and that they would have much preferred to remain at home. A sense of independence and an interest in a career were important to married women only among the wives of professional and white collar men, they concluded. These researchers went on to predict that ". . . an improvement of the standard of living, in particular an increase in the value of real wages, might lead to a much greater withdrawal from the labor force of women from manual class families."[59] It would appear that these predictions have not been borne out, despite a substantial improvement in the standard of living over the last three decades. In 1940 women made up 52.1 percent of the population and 39 percent of the wage and salary earners, while in 1970 they made up 53.9 percent of the population and 50.5 percent of the wage and salary earners.[60]

Attitudes and value systems of local officials may have had some part in preventing this prediction from coming true. One housewife and mother of three children, one of them a preschooler, has publicly complained of systematic harassment by local leaders who insist that she take employment, even though the family is content with the blue collar husband's earnings. Local officials have termed her a "parasite" and have illegally threatened her with criminal prosecution. A Pravda staff article grudgingly affirmed her right not to work but suggested that she work part-time. Despite the comments of the newspaper, the harassment of the woman continued.[61]

That the housewife remains the homemaker and the chief purchasing agent for the household is clear. David R. and Vera Mace conclude that "the average Soviet woman has been stuck with the double obligation of doing a full-time job and running a home as well."[62] Social psychologists Bauer and Wasiolek have created a sketch about what they call the "typical" Soviet housewife which purports to capture the essence of her life situation.[63] This sensitive portrait tells of

Tatyana, who works full-time as an office clerk and is a wife and mother of two. Her mother Anna lives with the family. After getting off work at five in the afternoon, Tatyana spends two hours in queue after queue, shopping for the food for the family dinner and milk for the infant, finding many things out of stock, making substitutions, and stumbling onto some items that are usually hard to locate. She starts in a cooperative store and ends in a kolkhoz marketplace, all the while envying those who can shop during the day. Waiting for her turn in the communal kitchen of her elevator-less apartment house, cooking, carrying the meal to her apartment, serving the family, cleaning up afterward, and then going to the laundry room to wash the clothes requires another four hours' work. While doing the laundry she learns, almost conspiratorially, from a friend who is employed in a store that a shipment of boys' shoes arrived that day and will be available for sale the next morning. This important fact means that Tatyana will have to arise at five, join a line in front of that store at six, and hold her place in line until 7:30, when Anna will replace her and Tatyana will go to her office. Thus another day in the life of a typical Soviet housewife.

The above portrait, prepared in 1955, is still essentially descriptive of the Soviet woman of the 1970s. However, many millions have been freed from the shared kitchen, and most urban women have gained a few of the home appliances that are common in the West. In the early and mid-1960s, when the supply of many household goods, especially appliances, was often acutely low, there was considerable thought and public dialogue concerning the desirability of establishing appliance pools to allow collective utilization of such items as refrigerators and vacuum cleaners.[64] However, it is difficult to see a clear, consistent distinction between this and the old multifamily kitchens which the housing authorities had been trying to minimize for a long time. Some of the extreme thinking called for the minimization of family housekeeping and the buildup of communal food service and cleaning service. Inherent in this dialogue was the old issue of the proper role and extent of nuclear family life in Soviet society. Also involved was the availability of the wife for a job. This dialogue on the appropriate equipment and services in the home recurs from time to time.

Certainly the small amount of household space and limited refrigeration inhibit storage of foods in convenient amounts and combinations. The virtual absence of partially prepared foods increases the housewife's work. However, the 1971-75 Five-Year Plan includes this provision: "To increase the production and improve the quality of semiprepared foods, concentrates, cooked foods, and other items, in order substantially to reduce outlays of time on the home preparation of food."[65]

There is no scientifically derived evidence on the manner in which the husband and wife in the Soviet Union share in the decision process as it concerns consumption. Despite shortages of goods, the priorities that consumers set are quite important. In addition, the supply of products and convenience of access to them are improving.

Among the Moslems, the major non-European minority in the U.S.S.R., the actual position of women is quite different from that professed Soviet ideology. Although there has been some decline, the family remains patriarchal and the wishes of the male head are paramount. Subordination of women is furthered by the practice of early marriage for girls, a large number of children, and the de-emphasis of female education. One sociological study found that in a major Moslem area only 2 percent of the girls finished high school.[66] The Minister of Education of the Uzbek Republic labeled the vocational training of Uzbek girls "a critical problem"[67] The percent of working women is clearly very low. The actual figures are not released by the government, an indication that the statistics paint a sad picture from the Soviet point of view. Polygamy continues to occur occasionally among men who can afford it, with only the first wife going through civil ceremonies and the others going through religious ceremonies. The typical Moslem woman still retains a distinctive costume, eats traditional foods, and lives in a home furnished according to Moslem rather than Russian custom. Despite Russian disapproval of these practices, tradition is slow to change because there is little inter-marriage with Russians and much de facto segregation. Russians and Moslems mingle in the big cities, but collective farms tend to be nearly all-Moslem or nearly all-Russian.

NOTES

1. J. A. Newth, "The 1970 Soviet Census," Soviet Studies, 24 (October 1972), 200-222, at 200.

2. Ibid., p. 210.

3. D. Peter Mazur, "Using Regression Models to Estimate the Expectation of Life for the U.S.S.R.," Journal of the American Statistical Association, 67 (March 1972), 31-36.

4. "Report by the U.S.S.R. Council of Ministers' Central Statistical Administration: The Population of Our Country," Pravda, April 17, 1971, pp. 1, 3. CDSP, 23 (May 18, 1971), 14-18.

5. For helpful marketing material on Soviet Moslems, see Thomas V. Greer, "Cross-Cultural Considerations in Consumer Behavior: The Case of the Consumer in the Soviet Union," in M. Venkatesan, ed., Proceedings of the Association for Consumer Research,

1972 (Iowa City, Iowa: Association for Consumer Research, 1972). This conference was held November 1972 at the University of Chicago. Also see Lawrence Krader, Peoples of Central Asia, 3rd edition (Bloomington and The Hague: Indiana University and Mouton, 1971); and the readings in Edward Allworth, ed., Soviet Nationality Problems (New York: Columbia University Press, 1971); Allworth, ed., Central Asia: A Century of Russian Rule (New York: Columbia University Press, 1967), and Erich Goldhagen, ed., Ethnic Minorities in the Soviet Union (New York: Praeger Publishers, 1968).

6. D. Valentei and G. Kiseleva, "Problems of Social Life: The Family, Children and Society," Pravda, October 5, 1969, p. 3. CDSP, 21 (October 29, 1969), 10-11.

7. See Alfred Lindesmith and A. L. Strauss, "A Critique of Culture-Personality Writings," American Sociological Review, 15 (1950), 587-600.

8. Peter Yakovlevich Chaadayev, "Letters on the Philosophy of History," in Hans Kohn, ed., The Mind of Modern Russia (New York: Harper & Row, 1955), pp. 38-46, at pp. 42-43.

9. Chaadayev, excerpts from letters to A. I. Turgenev, in Kohn, pp. 47-57, at p. 57.

10. Nikolai Danilevsky, excerpts from Russia and Europe, in Kohn, pp. 195-211, at p. 210.

11. Vladimir Solovev, essay, in Kohn, pp. 225-31, at p. 226.

12. Dimitri Obolensky, "Russia's Byzantine Heritage," Oxford Slavonic Papers, 1 (1950), 37-63.

13. Vera Micheles Dean, The Nature of the Non-Western World (New York: Mentor Books, 1963), p. 26.

14. N. Berdyaev, The Russian Idea (London: Geoffrey Bles, 1947), pp. 2-3.

15. Ruth Benedict, "Child Rearing in Certain European Countries," American Journal of Orthopsychiatry, 19 (April 1949), 342-50.

16. Ibid.

17. Margaret Mead, "Discussion," American Journal of Orthopsychiatry, 19 (April 1949), 349-50.

18. Geoffrey Gorer and John Rickman, The People of Great Russia: A Psychological Study (New York: Norton, 1962; first published London: Cresset Press, 1949). The methodology is explained in Margaret Mead and Rhoda Metraux, eds., The Study of Cultures at a Distance (Chicago: University of Chicago Press, 1953).

19. Alex Inkeles, Eugenia Hanfmann, and Helen Beier, "Modal Personality and Adjustment to the Soviet Socio-Political System," Human Relations, 11 (1958), 3-22.

20. Henry V. Dicks, "Observations on Contemporary Russian Behavior," Human Relations, 5 (1952), 111-74.

21. For example, L. I. Brezhnev, "The 24th Congress of the Communist Party of the Soviet Union: The Report of the C.P.S.U. Central Committee to the 24th Congress of the Communist Party of the Soviet Union," Pravda, March 31, 1971, pp. 2-10. CDSP, 23 (May 4, 1971), 1-12, 37, at 1.

22. Alexander S. Vucinich, Soviet Economic Institutions: The Social Structure of Production Units (Stanford, Calif.: Stanford University Press, 1952), p. 85.

23. David Mitrany, Marx Against the Peasant: A Study in Social Dogmatism (New York: Collier, 1961), p. 184.

24. Gorer and Rickman, The People of Great Russia, p. 233.

25. Ibid., p. 135.

26. A. Yakovlev, "Against Antihistoricism," Literaturnaya Gazeta, no. 46, November 15, 1972, pp. 4-5. CDSP, 24 (December 20, 1972), 1-7, at 4.

27. Ibid.

28. Barbara Ward, The Rich Nations and the Poor Nations (New York: Norton, 1962), pp. 67-68.

29. V. I. Lenin, State and Revolution (New York: International Publishers, 1935), pp. 75-78.

30. Alex Inkeles, "Social Stratification and Mobility in the Soviet Union: 1940-1950," American Sociological Review, 15 (1950), 465-79.

31. Mark G. Field and David E. Anderson, "Family and Socialization: Some General Considerations," in Allen Kassoff, ed., Prospects for Soviet Society (New York: Praeger, 1968), pp. 386-417.

32. G. Kulagin, "The School of Labor," Pravda, June 18, 1971, p. 3. CDSP, 23 (July 13, 1971), 9.

33. Stepan Toporkov, "Worker Is a Proud Title—Diligence, Creative Energy and Skill Adorn a Person," Izvestia, December 12, 1971, p. 1. CDSP, 23 (January 11, 1972), 27.

34. For example, see G. Yakovlev, "The Fruits of Education," Pravda, May 19, 1970, p. 2. CDSP, 22 (June 16, 1970), 20.

35. V. A. Zhamin and S. L. Kostanian, "Economic Problems Entailed in the Transition to Universal Secondary Education," in Economics and Education (Moscow: Znanie Publishing House, 1970), pp. 25-48. Excerpted in Soviet Education, 13 (May 1971), 5-37; "On the Agenda: The Rural General Education School," Uchitel'skaia Gazeta, August 6, 1970. Reproduced in Soviet Education, 13 (March-April 1971), 19-29; I. Adamsky, "Three Lessons in One Hour," Izvestia, January 26, 1972, p. 3. CDSP, 24 (March 1, 1972), 15-17.

36. G. Kulagin, "The School of Labor, Part II," Pravda, June 19, 1971, p. 3. CDSP, 23 (July 13, 1971), 9, 20.

37. Alec Nove, "History, Hierarchy and Nationalities: Some Observations on the Soviet Social Structure," Soviet Studies, 21 (July 1969), 71-92, at 80-81.

38. I. Lazarenko, Labour Remuneration, Labour Incentive Funds and Soviet Trade Unions (Moscow: Novosti Press Agency Publishing House, 1972), p. 17.

39. Ibid., p. 19

40. Alex Inkeles, "Social Stratification in the Modernization of Russia," in Cyril E. Black, ed., The Transformation of Russian Society (Cambridge: Harvard University Press, 1960), p. 345.

41. I. Kasyukov, "Expensive Amusements," Izvestia, September 21, 1969, p. 5. CDSP, 21 (October 15, 1969), 24.

42. Izvestia, April 4, 1959, and June 6, 1959.

43. See the references in William Moskoff, "The Soviet Hide-Leather-Footwear Sequence in the Post-Stalin Period," unpublished doctoral thesis, University of Wisconsin (Madison).

44. V. Siniutin, Ekonomicheskie Nauki, no. 5 (1963). Translated in Problems of Economics, 7, no. 3, (July 1964), 21-25.

45. Iu. V. Bromlei, "Major Trends in Ethnographic Research in the U.S.S.R.," Voprosy Istorii, No. 1 (1968), 37-56. Translated in Soviet Anthropology and Archeology, 8 (Summer 1969), 3-42. See also Alexander Matejko, "Sociologists in Between," Studies in Comparative Communism, 5 (Summer-Autumn 1972), 277-304; Paul Lazarsfeld, "Sociology," in Main Trends of Research in Social and Human Sciences (Paris and The Hague: UNESCO and Mouton, 1970), pp. 94-103, and Bogdan Denitch, "Sociology in Eastern Europe: Trends and Prospects," Slavic Review, 30 (June 1971), 317-39.

46. "A Study of How Different Social Groups Use Leisure," Literaturnaya Gazeta, January 17, 1968, pp. 12-13. CDSP, 20 (February 14, 1968), 12-13.

47. I. E. Vorozheikin, "Major Changes in the Study of the History of the Soviet Working Class," Voprosy Istorii, No. 8 (1968), 153-63. Translated in Soviet Studies in History, 8 (Fall 1969), 91-116.

48. John A. Armstrong, The Soviet Bureaucratic Elite (New York: Praeger, 1959).

49. Allen Kassoff, "The Future of Soviet Society," in Allen Kassoff, ed., Prospects for Soviet Society, pp. 497-506.

50. Philip D. Stewart, "Soviet Interest Groups and the Policy Process: The Repeal of Production Education," World Politics, 22 (October 1969), 29-50.

51. Milton C. Lodge, Soviet Elite Attitudes Since Stalin (Columbus, Ohio: Merrill, 1969).

52. Raymond A. Bauer, Alex Inkeles, and Clyde Kluckhohn, How the Soviet System Works: Cultural, Psychological and Social Themes (New York: Vintage, 1961).

53. Vera S. Dunham, "Sex in the Soviet Union," The Russian Review, 10 (1951), 199-209. Additional helpful material on the evolution of women's economic and social role can be found in Susan M.

Kingsbury and Mildred Fairchild, Factory, Family and Woman in the Soviet Union (New York: G. P. Putnam's Sons, 1935).

54. Friedrich Engels, The Origins of the Family, Private Property and the State, as quoted in Alex Inkeles and Raymond A. Bauer, The Soviet Citizen (Cambridge, Mass.: Harvard University Press, 1961), p. 203.

55. Sidney and Beatrice Webb, Soviet Communism: A New Civilization?, 2 (New York: Charles Scribner's Sons, 1938), p. 824.

56. For detailed material on the woman in the Soviet economy, see Norton Dodge, Women in the Soviet Union (Baltimore: John Hopkins Press, 1966).

57. A. Kharchev, "Growing Sociological Research on Marriage and the Family," Zhurnalist, no. 11 (November 1972), 58-61. CDSP, 25 (March 21, 1973), 18.

58. "The C.P.S.U. in Figures," Partiinaya Zhizn, no. 10 (May 1965), 8-17. CDSP, 17 (August 11, 1965), 14-18.

59. Inkeles and Bauer, The Soviet Citizen, pp. 206-07.

60. "Women in the USSR: Statistical Data," Vestnik Statistiki, no. 1 (1971), 1-17. Translated in Soviet Sociology, 11 (Summer 1972), 57-86.

61. "Classified as a Parasite by Way of Prevention," Pravda, June 20, 1972, p. 3. CDSP, 24 (July 17, 1972), 23-24.

62. David R. and Vera Mace, The Soviet Family (Garden City, New York: Doubleday, 1963), p. 103.

63. Raymond A. Bauer and Edward Wasiolek, Nine Soviet Portraits (Cambridge, Mass.: M.I.T. Press, 1955), pp. 76-90.

64. See the Soviet references in Robert A. Feldmesser's chapter "Stratification and Communism," in Allen Kassoff, ed., Prospects for Soviet Society, pp. 359-85, at 373.

65. "Directives of the 24th C.P.S.U. Congress for the Five-Year Plan for the Development of the U.S.S.R. National Economy in 1971-1975," Pravda, April 11, 1971, pp. 1-7. CDSP, 23 (June 8, 1971), 15-26, at 17.

66. Alexandre Bennigsen and Chantal Lemercier-Quelquejay, Islam in the Soviet Union (New York: Praeger, 1967).

67. S. Shermukhamedov, "The Student Chooses an Occupation," Pravda, January 18, 1972, p. 3. CDSP, 24 (February 16, 1972), 34-35.

4

**ADVERTISING
AND
COMMUNICATIONS**

STRUCTURE AND BACKGROUND

In this chapter both communications and advertising are examined. These two sets of activities and their interaction may strike the Westerner as somewhat strange. Perhaps the most intriguing of all economic and social developments in the Soviet Union is advertising, in that Communists traditionally perceived this process as a total social waste, an intrinsically hideous means of forcing goods on consumers who did not want them. To be sure, advertising is employed on a small scale, but it represents an extremely significant break with orthodox Communist thought. In addition, despite the absence of hard data, advertising is apparently growing.

Government advertising agencies have been set up to handle work for clients. The only agency that serves foreign clients desiring to promote goods in the U.S.S.R. is Vneshtorgreklama (All-Union Foreign Trade Advertising Agency), established in 1964 in Moscow. This agency, which employed about 180 and had billings of about U.S. $12 million in 1969,[1] solicits and creates foreign advertising for placement in Soviet magazines, trade journals, and other media. In addition, it publishes for Soviet consumption Foreign Firms Offer and Bulletin of Foreign Commercial Information, which have circulations of about 5,000 and 3,000, respectively. It publishes Soviet Export to benefit Soviet producers in foreign markets. Vneshtorgreklama once had a monopoly over Soviet organizations desiring to promote products and services in other nations, but ministries can now independently place advertising abroad for themselves or subordinate institutions. Aeroflot and Intourist have chosen not to use Vneshtorgreklama. Some republics and cities in the U.S.S.R. have established advertising services. For example, the Ministry of Trade of the Ukraine maintains a chain of 40 small advertising agencies with headquarters in Kiev. However, their best-equipped and most modern advertising production facilities are in Kharkov. The All-Union Organization of Cooperatives also has an advertising agency. The agencies charge fees and commissions for their work. None offers marketing research services, but limited services of this sort will probably develop in the next few years. However, it must be recognized that there will be ideological obstacles in the way of good research.

There has been considerable disagreement on the appropriate organization structure for advertising agencies. Various persons have favored a geographical basis, while others have urged organizing around ethnic groups. Whether to maintain separate advertising agencies for the cooperative store system has also been controversial. Some people favor a centralized, integrated superagency for the whole economy. An opponent, the Deputy Minister of Trade in the Estonian Republic, believes that centralization and integration mean standardization and thus monotony. On the other hand, two economists asserted that advertising can be correctly organized only if a special central organization having jurisdiction over the entire nation is set up. They claimed that the net additional cost would be less than supposed, for the central organization would liquidate the many small and "amateurish" agencies. Another proponent, the influential Assistant Chairman of the U.S.S.R. State Committee for Material and Technical Supply, has stated that specialization in advertising and provision of appropriate new equipment are both deterred by the large number of organizations in the field of advertising and the lack of coordination or even communication among them.[2]

A central but not powerful or integrated organization, the All-Union Commercial Advertising Association, was set up in Moscow in 1965 by the U.S.S.R. Ministry of Trade. Two Soviet contributors to Pravda ("Truth"), the official Communist Party daily newspaper, recently commented, not unkindly, that they had assumed the All-Union Commercial Advertising Association

> . . . would turn into something like an advertising research and methodological center for the country. . . . The people on Tschaikovsky Street are working hard but uncertainly, because they have not been spoiled by attention to their association and to advertising in general.[3]

Planning is fuzzy and lines of authority, control, and communication are blurred in the Soviet apparatus for advertising. For instance, there was a major duplication of effort for the tea industry:

> The All-Union Commercial Advertising Association worked out an advertising campaign, a film script was

written, and spot announcements were prepared. Much thought was put into this and a great deal of money was spent. But it turned out that the tea growers of Georgia had simultaneously drawn up their own plan, which was conducted in Moscow under the heading of Georgian Tea Week. We have no coordinating center that would put advertising on a strictly scientific basis, develop socio-logical research to study the effects of advertising on the consumer and assume the job of publishing special literature on methodology.[4]

In all fairness, one must note that the All-Union Commercial Advertising Association does prepare some materials for practitioners and students of advertising. One of the most pressing but not methodo-logically insurmountable research needs that the Association could handle is to relate advertising rates of the media to their circulation and importance within a given category. Attempts to relate rates to advertising effectiveness must wait until later.

The small scale of even the All-Union Association in Moscow was demonstrated when a client, Red Dawn Knitwear, on its own initiative wished to spend the equivalent of U.S. $555,000 on pamphlets, catalog, greeting cards, and package design. "The Association was thrown into confusion, for it was very difficult to fill such a large order with the materials and equipment available."[5]

In order to gain more sympathy, support, and general legitimiz-ation in the artistic community and the intelligentsia at large, appeals have been made to Soviet artists and creative writers of all kinds to participate in preparation of advertising. They have been reminded that Vladimir Mayakovsky, one of Russia's most celebrated poets, once created "vivid verses" for the GUM department store and for many newspaper advertisements for various products.[6]

Amtorg Trading Corporation, a Soviet enterprise incorporated under U.S. laws, acts as agent for most of the foreign trade organiza-tions of the U.S.S.R. in transacting business with the United States. Amtorg broke with tradition by placing a large advertisement in the New York Times in 1967 soliciting inquiries for various Soviet trade organizations. It listed, described, pictured the trademark, and gave the addresses of 35 organizations that one could contact. The concept and the flavor of the copy in this celebrated message are encapsulated in the following excerpt:

Despite ideological differences, firms from many countries are engaged in successful business transactions with Soviet foreign trade organizations who are also ready to strike up relations with you.[7]

Despite the low-key, low-pressure tone that prevails in most Soviet advertising, it is necessary to note that it suffers from the limited credibility of Soviet communications media in general. Several worthwhile works have explored the mass media credibility problem.[8] Among them, Bauer and Gleicher concluded in the middle 1950s that word-of-mouth communication was the primary source of information because it was thought to be more trustworthy than the official information in the media.[9] This point is doubly vexing to the sender of information, regardless of the degree of influence the sender hopes the message has, for Russia has had an unusual cultural tradition on the subject of truth, as discussed in Chapter 3.

Through training, practice, and expectation, Soviet journalists are psychologically oriented toward documenting and encouraging the ultimate success of centrally planned change, whether it be clearly formalized or still hazy and internally inconsistent in detail. For example, the demographer D. Valentei recently urged "the use of the press, radio, television and the arts in forming demographic behavior along lines that are recognized as advisable at the present stage of the development of society and are conditioned by the moral and ethical norms of our life."[10] He was referring to desirable family size and differential birth rates by ethnic type.

However, the slowness of Soviet communications media and the limited detail with which they report and interpret news and current events is well known. Kommunist, the official theoretical periodical of the Communist Party Central Committee, has criticized Soviet communications as follows:

> . . . at times both in some of our newspapers and in radio, there is often little information and few commentaries and details which would help in understanding current policy. To withhold one or another event, not illuminating it from the position of socialist ideology in our time . . . is to give "freedom of action" to the falsification of bourgeois propagandists.
>
> . . . it is important not only to explain the different facts correctly, but to do this at the right time. One has to admit that the bourgeois information agencies have reached a high degree of operation . . . but we, at times, are late. This means that the false version spreads around the world faster than the true and more precise one. . . . Under present conditions the spread of information and its effectiveness become the most important sphere of ideological struggle and therefore any complacency is inadmissable.[11]

The communications media can take some consolation in the fact that there are apparent contradictions in Lenin's beliefs and advice. On the one hand, he said the Soviet Union is strong "when the masses know everything, can judge about everything and approach anything consciously."[12] On the other hand, one of his most famous statements was that "A newspaper is not only a collective propagandist and collective agitator; it is also a collective organizer." This second view has tended to prevail and has been applied to all media. In line with this thinking, the Communist Party must confirm the appointment of editors to all newspapers not managed directly by it. Moreover, professional journalists are seldom promoted to editor, for they are not as reliable as the career Party men who are so appointed.

Diversity of languages in the U.S.S.R. complicates the editorial operations of communications media and their advertising. Russian is the first language of only about 58 percent of the population, versus about 59 percent in the 1959 census.[13] Although the use of Russian as a second language is growing and a few non-Russians are adopting it as a first language, the population whose first language is Russian is growing at a slower pace than the rest of the population. For this reason and to meet demands for ethnic identification, the Soviets put out hundreds of periodicals and operate dozens of television and radio stations in languages other than Russian.[14] However, it is clear that the various language groups are not represented by media in proportion to their sizes.

RATIONALE FOR ADVERTISING

The manner in which advertising is used in the U.S.S.R. is reasonably indicative of, and largely in agreement with, the theoretical rationale that has been developing for the advertising process. One common use is in the sale of unacceptably large inventories, sometimes in conjunction with hierarchically approved and highly selective price reductions. Another is in selling obsolescent goods, with obsolescence in certain cases being the reason for the unsatisfactorily large size of the inventory. Still another common use is with goods that are seasonally produced, especially if they are perishable. However, there is some advertising that attempts to benefit a given industry, which may be made up of a few or many different enterprises. There is also some advertising that benefits a single manufacturer. Some advertising attempts to introduce new brands or services, while some tells of design changes in old, familiar brands. There is advertising that attempts to build consumer patronage for one store over another. The modest rivalry among department stores in large metropolitan areas is perhaps the best known. There is advertising abroad to benefit Soviet exports and related services in general, to benefit specific industries and brands in the export market, and to attract tourists to the Soviet Union. There is also public service advertising. There is the classified advertising for personal services and the large secondhand market. In addition, there is the omnipresent use of advertising to remind people of the Five-Year Plan, the role of the advertiser in that plan and in the total life of the society and economy, and the mutual obligation of the advertiser and the advertising audience to cooperate in achieving national, republic, and local goals.

Although there is an element of competition in the advertising process in the U.S.S.R., the Soviet theoretician's defense of advertising is that such a process is not competitive in essence, that either in discrete segments or in the aggregate it exerts an active influence on demand in fulfilling the economic plans of the government. It aids in redirecting and reallocating demand. This line of argument adds that Communist advertising serves the interests of the community as a whole rather than merely the interests of an individual firm, and that it educates the consumer in terms of tastes, functional information, and awareness of purchase alternatives. Soviet writers do not say so, but it appears that a quiet but pervasive background function of advertising is to help people recall that their material standard of living has been rising and that it is planned to rise much higher.

In examining the rationale for advertising it would be helpful to extract key thoughts from several Soviet writings on advertising through the years. In 1956 S. V. Serebriakov, a Soviet authority on distribution, explained that "the gradual widening of knowledge of buyers about goods by means of advertising works a positive influence on the simplification of merchandising."[15] Ilf and Petrov declared:

> The American does not have to think about anything; the huge commercial concerns think for him. . . . Drink Coca-Cola. . . . Coca-Cola is good for the manufacturer and the country! Capitalist advertising, persistent, sensational, capable of deafening the consumer, seeks only to sell goods, to force them on the buyer by any means. Soviet commercial advertising pursues entirely different aims.[16]

Sovetskaya Kultura, official organ of the Ministry of Culture, stated that Soviet advertising had five purposes: (1) to educate public taste; (2) to develop demand; (3) to help consumers quickly find what they want to buy; (4) to help them buy it easily; and (5) to tell them the price.[17] Anastas I. Mikoyan, well-known member of the Presidium of the U.S.S.R. Supreme Soviet, declared:

The task of Soviet advertising is to give people exact
information about the goods that are on sale, to help to
create new demands, to cultivate new tastes and requirements, to promote the sale of new kinds of goods and to
explain their uses to the consumer.[18]

The reasoning exhibited by M. Argunov in Sovetskaya Torgovlya
("Soviet Trade"). monthly magazine of the U.S.S.R. Ministry of Trade,
is helpful in pinning down the rationale for advertising. Building on
a case example of Textile Store Number 12 in Novosibirsk, which
successfully utilized a coordinated advertising campaign in newspapers,
radio, television, and handbills, Argunov stated the following:

I would like to recommend that all directors of trade
establishments really publicize their goods, help customers select the things they want, find new ways and
means of showing goods to the best advantage, and under-
take coordinated advertising campaigns.
    All this will not only help to fulfill the plan for
selling goods and increase the quality of merchandising,
but will also have an effect on correct formulation of
consumer demand.
    We should spare no effort in the organization of
good advertising. Neither should we economize on
advertising, because expenditures for it are repaid a
hundredfold.[19]

A 1967 article in Literaturnaya Gazeta ("Literary Gazette")
stated:

If in the U.S. advertising serves first of all the idea of
profit, it must become in our country the educator of the
consumer, it must instill proper tastes, it must take part
in the struggle for a better quality of produce. In this
respect huge, breathtakingly interesting prospects are
being opened.
    Nevertheless we cannot ignore the enormous
technical and organizational experience underlying the
advertising business in the U.S.A. We must without
hesitation take advantage of the best.[20]

The editors of Pravda acknowledged advertising's usefulness
to each enterprise in a 1969 statement:

The advertisement of consumer goods does not as yet
receive sufficient attention in our country and requires

active assistance in meeting the growing demands of the population. Under the new system of planning and economic incentive, when the index of the output sales is of greatest importance, well-placed advertising also promotes the successes of the enterprise.[21]

Izvestia asked for greater efforts to develop advertising into an independent industry. The newspaper stated: ". . . we have to admit that advertising is a prime mover of commerce, and in the conditions of economic reform in this country, is also a prime mover of production efforts."[22]

The editors of the influential Soviet journal Nauka i Tekhnika ("Science and Technology") took this position in 1969: "We feel that advertising can play a definite role in the further progress of science and technology and in organizing the information process."[23] The editors of that magazine invited the East German economist F. Tamme to explain the appropriate role of advertising, especially in industrial marketing:

> The good name of a factory emblem is achieved only as a result of effective concern for it. The positive opinion about the enterprise among the public or the potential customers cannot be achieved immediately without preparations. Advertising and public information are important means for the socialist running of an economy. They are interrelated and for this reason should be carried out together.
>
> [   ]
>
> More and more new articles in ever increasing quantities come on the market. For selling them it is essential to have stable markets. But these do not form by themselves. Moreover, the articles are becoming more and more complicated. The development of computer technology, automation, and so forth leads to the production of articles which are so complicated that the potential customers view these instruments and machines very frequently as a "black box" about which they know chiefly the readings on the input and the output and not what occurs inside. For this reason, along with the ordinary characteristics of consumer value, advertising should provide a solution to the problems which arise in using the commodities. Thus, it is essential to satisfy the growing demand of the customers for information. Advertising information should also be oriented at the subjective market factors, and here sociological and

psychological arguments intervene in the process of communications.[24]

Two *Pravda* staff journalists declared in 1971:

The time is long since past when advertising was regarded as something that was not really necessary. . . . Advertising informs, invites and advises. [For example] It helps the personnel working in everyday services and trade to find clients and customers.[25]

They went on to insist that advertising is not a survival of capitalism. They stressed the necessity of guarding against deceptive and misleading advertising, which can occur even in the Soviet system, and illustrated with a restaurant and a dry cleaner whose print promotion they considered unethical.

That there may be a long-run trend in the U.S.S.R. toward a rationale for advertising as being equally, properly, and simultaneously microeconomic and macroeconomic gains some support from the quotations presented above and from statements of a prominent Soviet advertising executive in 1972. After terming advertising a "powerful accelerator of the development of industry and trade," he found it advisable to explain the following:

It is incorrect to think of advertising as solely a directional, local tactic to provide information on goods and services. Every year it is becoming more and more an effective way to promote our life style and achievements. To a certain extent, therefore, it performs a social function. . . .

Good advertising not only creates favorable conditions for a product or service, but also molds rational needs on the part of the consumer.[26]

THE MEDIA

Newspapers

While the structure of the newspaper industry in a Western nation is essentially haphazard—a response to changing economic opportunity—that of the Soviet Union is organized. The importance of the newspaper and its frequency of publication fit the level of the assigned jurisdiction. However, size of professional staff and average number of pages or columns published do not fit the generalization very well.

From the late 1920s until the end of the 1950s, it was almost taken for granted that the government would have to subsidize the newspapers. Since that time, expectations appear to have become more varied. Many lose money and continue to get heavy subsidies. The prices for all newspapers are kept low, for it is national policy to stimulate readership. Nevertheless, even two to five kopecks, the normal range of newspaper prices, can be large relative to take-home pay. No data are available on profitability of the whole industry, but it is known that several of the largest newspapers earn a profit. For example, Izvestia, the national government daily, earns a profit of about 12 percent on sales, while it spends 30 percent of its sales revenue for newsprint, 25 percent for circulation costs, 30 percent for mechanical expenses, and 3 percent for editorial and management costs.[27] Two Leningrad newspapers, Smena and Leningradskaya Pravda, have shown profits in some recent years.[28]

There were 8,754 newspapers published in 1968, of which about 4,800 were put out by factories, universities, large collective farms, and other institutions. Such newspapers are put out one to four times a month. Omitting these 4,800, the total circulation was almost 119 million in 1968. There were 392 newspapers that published at least five times a week[29] and thus could be considered dailies. The government claims that per issue circulation of all newspapers combined was about 140 million in 1970.[30] Several national newspapers are printed in Moscow and other cities almost simultaneously by means of phototelegraphy and matrices sent by air mail. Experiments are going on using satellites to transmit newspaper pages.[31]

Several national newspapers, some of them daily and some weekly, are extremely important. General mass-circulation newspapers are Izvestia, spokesman of the Council of Ministers, and Pravda, spokesman of the Communist Party Central Committee. Founded in 1912 by Lenin, Pravda has been called "Communism's olympian oracle."[32] Among national newspapers, Pravda and Izvestia are particularly powerful. They are authoritative, solemn, and heavy with rhetoric. Of them John Gunther once said ". . . of all dull things in the U.S.S.R. the dullest are the great newspapers."[33] The two newspapers are extremely useful indexes to Soviet behavior in what they say and how they say it, and in what they omit. However, it is probable that a large number of Soviet citizens buy Pravda for the sake of a appearances and that readership is lower than circulation implies. The 1970 average daily circulation of Pravda was 9.2 million, while that of Izvestia was 8.5 million.[34]

The other national newspapers are designed for specific segments of the total market. The daily Komsomolskaya Pravda is youth-oriented, and the twice-weekly Pionerskaya Pravda is children-oriented. The weekly Ekonomicheskaya Gazeta deals with business and economics. Sovetskaya Kultura and Literaturnaya Gazeta deal in communications, cultural matters, literature, and some aspects of sociology. The former speaks for the Ministry of Culture and the latter for the Union of Writers. Krasnaya Zvesda treats military affairs, Selskaya Zhizn covers agriculture, and Uchitelskaya Gazeta treats education. Formerly a Russian Republic daily, Sovetskaya Rossiya became national in 1966.

Each republic except the Russian Republic has at least one republic-level newspaper. Most have several. For example, the large Ukraine Republic has 18, but the small Armenian Republic has 13. They range from standard-size dailies to tabloid-size weeklies, but all have a small number of pages, typically four and rarely more than eight. A few republic newspapers, such as the Pravda Ukrainy of Kiev, have high circulation and can compete with the best-known national newspapers. Republic-level newspapers restrict their news coverage mostly to the republic.

Below the level of the republic, there are the oblast-, and then the raion- and city-level newspapers. About half of the oblast newspapers are dailies, while virtually no raion newspapers and only a few city newspapers are dailies. All three serve as important communications elements for local affairs and needs. Among the several hundred city newspapers are 16 city evening newspapers, exemplified by the popular Vechernyaya Moskva. This is an interesting instance of market segmentation. These newspapers are light and even humorous when compared with the typical ponderous newspaper in the U.S.S.R. These and all other Soviet newspapers devote most of their space to stories prepared several days or even several weeks in advance. A small fraction of space is reserved for spot news.

Print media, especially newspapers, are more important than other media, except the outdoor medium, in present-day advertising in the U.S.S.R. Newspapers carried no advertisements from 1917 until the mid-1920s, when Lenin's famous quasi-capitalist New Economic Policy once again allowed them. But the 1927 demise of NEP also killed print advertising, which was not to arise again for two decades. Advertisements are now found in newspapers and magazines for general circulation and for specialized groups. Yet the print media usually devote only a very small percentage of their space to advertising. Disdain of advertising is not a reason for this small space. The reasons are the following: (1) no well-established tradition of advertising; (2) an erratic relationship between cost and revenue; (3) a long-standing shortage of newsprint; (4) a tradition of extremely short newspapers and magazines, judged by Western standards; and (5) primacy of editorials, news, and political education materials. The most prestigious periodicals offer classified advertising but avoid display advertising.

Vechernyaya Moskva ("Evening Moscow"), which has published one advertising page each day, recently started an eight-page weekly supplement. The first issue, with a printing of 100,000 copies, carried advertisements for jams, baby foods, television sets, computers, a dry cleaner, parking lots, and cruises. Russia's low-key promotion is typified in an advertisement stating "Jam is a highly nourishing product." Moskovska Reklamin ("Moscow Advertiser") is a weekly devoted to advertisements, most of them classified. It is highly popular and is sold out within a few hours of publication.

Rates for Soviet advertisers are not made public, and rates charged foreign advertisers bear no relationship to circulation. The advertising line rate per column is U.S. $7.20 in Nedelia, Izvestia's popular Sunday supplement which has a circulation of over 2.5 million, and in Trud ("Work"), which has a circulation of over 3.5 million. However, the same rate applies in Vechernyaya Moskva and Moskovskaya Pravda, which have circulations of about 200,000 and 230,000 respectively. The rate in Vodny Transport ("Water Transport") is U.S. $4.47 for a circulation of about 100,000.[35] Segmentation by reader interest is, of course, a partial explanation for the rate structure.

Of the several foreign-language newspapers, one of the most intriguing is the English-language Moscow News. Founded by American leftist Anna Louise Strong in the early 1930s, it accepts advertising but has rather little. Most of its advertising is directed to visiting buyers from foreign industry and trade organizations. Surprisingly little information is included in these messages. For example, a display advertisement, in its entirety, stated:

> Join those many the world over who eagerly buy beautifully designed and serviceable cotton fabrics from V/O "Exportljon," Moscow. Printed or plain-dyed. In a wide variety of vivid colours and attractive modern patterns. Exclusively fast or extra-fast dyes. Our fabrics are sure to give good wear. . . . And a good deal of pleasure. Write for information to: V/O "Exportljon," 33, Architect Vlasov St., Moscow V-420, U.S.S.R. Phone: 128-07-86. Telex: 203, 204.[36]

A stylized drawing of a young woman accompanied the words and occupied one-third of the space. There was also a large amount of white space.

The innovative newspaper mentioned earlier, Vechernyaya Moskva, has formed a consumers' organization that also includes members from the journalism field, commerce, and industry. The organization's purpose is to solicit consumer opinion and evaluate products, and then to feed this information back to manufacturing enterprises. The first product type studied was bread, one of the most important staples in the starchy Soviet diet. The potential for product redesign and advertising is rather interesting. Unfortunately there is no research tradition among Soviet media, but it is to be hoped that this small attempt will grow. Under the economic incentives programs of the government, such an information service is feasible.

Outdoor Advertising

The outdoor medium vies with newspapers for number-one position in Soviet advertising, but data on use are not available. This medium includes wall newspapers, posters, billboards of various sizes, signs, and illuminated signs. The tens of thousands of wall newspapers are occasional series put out by groups, usually amateurs in clubs, collectives, and organizations of all kinds in order to promote themselves, disseminate news, solicit assistance, and support official causes. They are not published on a regular basis. This term does not encompass the regularly published newspapers that one sometimes, but not commonly, sees displayed.

Posters, most of which measure about two by three feet, are found almost everywhere. Often they are clustered for greater impact or to take advantage of high-traffic sites. One scholar reports that the rate for posters declines only slightly with volume.[37] For example, one poster for five days costs U.S. $.33, while 3,000 posters for five days cost U.S. $833, or just under U.S. $.28 per poster. Billboards are mostly in large cities and suburban areas. There are both ground-level and elevated billboards. Posters and billboards are generally used for government propaganda, public service advertising, and advertising for trade associations or entire industries, but occasionally to benefit a particular enterprise or brand and often to promote a specific entertainment event. For example, five such advertisements for five competing brands of refrigerator, each expounding the merits of the brand, were exhibited within two city blocks in Moscow.[38] In another example, the Vice-Chairman of the Board of the Union of Rural Consumers' Cooperatives reported that the use of a combination of posters and handbills assisted in raising sales of television sets in rural areas of Stavropol Territory by about 67 percent over a six-month period as compared with the same period one year earlier.[39] Most poster and billboard advertisements are subdued and promise little, but the author recalls one that urged people to drink more tea and declared that "Tea is very effective for rheumatism, hypertension, dysentery, and gum diseases."

The promotional aspects of a firm's name are receiving more attention now. Some manufacturing plants, stores, and service institutions are beginning to reject the insipid registration-type name, such as "Magazin Khoztovarov Number 5" (Housewares Store Number 5). Names are being adopted and promoted that use patriotic, historical, biographical, geographical, fantasy, or word-play themes. As innocuous as it may seem to Westerners, the term "Tik-Tak" that now appears on the facades of some clock and watch shops in several cities is seen as innovative and quite pleasant by many Russians.

Illuminated or neon signs are rapidly increasing in number. Reserved by American standards, the signs usually consist only of identifying names, are usually blue or white, and seldom blink. A feeling has emerged that neon signs are not only acceptable but merit a place in the planning of all new commercial districts and refurbishment of old ones. To that end, Izvestia takes the position that the participation of advertising specialists should be required in urban planning. The newspaper goes on to urge that the design and production facilities for what it terms "nocturnal finery" be expanded and modernized in the 130 cities where such work is done. Noting favorably that in the West about 70 shades of color are available, it recommends expansion of the color range and the use of colored tubing so that the advertising signs would have some impact during daylight hours.[40]

The Chief Artist of Kharkov, A. Vyatkin, has argued rather fancifully for greater use of outdoor advertising:

Who does not know how felicitous advertising enlivens a city's exterior? And, indeed, it may be the "zest" of an architectural ensemble. The quality of advertising has improved lately. More fluorescent apparatus is being produced, and advertising has become more dynamic. But it is still far from what modern cities need.

The more energetically we take up the organization of public services and amenities and the designing of cities, the sooner beauty will come to every street. And this will mean the fuller implementation of the idea of the Communist Party Program that "art will even more inspire labor, adorn life and ennoble man."[41]

A Pravda article echoed, "Posters, signs and showcases, as we know, make a city and its streets attractive."[42]

Direct Mail, Cinema, and Exhibitions

There is no information on domestic use of direct mail, but foreign advertisers have available the mailing services of

Vneshtorgreklama. This agency will send foreign direct mail pieces to various lists of officials deemed to be important in procurement decisions, arranged by occupation and/or type of industry. Ostlund notes that the advertiser receives neither a copy of the mailing list nor an audit statement to show that the claimed service was completed.[43] He notes further that inclusion of a coupon or similar device in the letter as a control that the advertising material has gone out, and to the appropriate recipients, is not foolproof, for all such coupons must be returned to Vneshtorgreklama. The agency then sends the follow-up material furnished by the foreign client for that purpose and informs him of the number of inquiries received. Cost for this direct mailing service is about U.S. $.50 per name, including postage and envelope but not enclosures. A subsequent mailing is performed at half price.

Many of the 175,000 movie theaters are available for commercial messages. Ostlund reports that the advetrising rates in the "central cinemas" in Moscow, Leningrad, Kiev, and the remaining republic capitals are identical, regardless of seating capacity. These theaters accept advertisements ranging from 15 seconds to 5 minutes in length. The domestic rate is unknown, but the rate for a foreign advertiser for one week ranges from U.S. $78 for 15 seconds to U.S. $889 for 5 minutes.[44]

A quasi-advertising medium, the exhibition is standard Soviet practice and is used for domestic and foreign goods. Some exhibitions are specifically set up according to agreements with foreign governments or foreign chambers of commerce, while some are periodic affairs. The first specialized exhibition of American goods ever held in the U.S.S.R. was conducted in 1972, when the products of 28 U.S. firms in the computer technology industry were displayed and demonstrated in Moscow. Cost for an exhibitor depends on his requirements for space and services. Often there are substantial amounts of propaganda, domestic or foreign, blended with the commercial promotion. In certain instances the Soviet and East European products displayed are not all readily available in quantity.

A few Soviet industries, such as the tea growers and processors of the Georgian Republic, finance and maintain separately housed permanent exhibitions. They include displays and literature that may be considered partly educational and partly promotional. Some industries and enterprises contribute displays, sometimes elaborate, to the giant "exhibitions of economic progress" found in all large cities.

Magazines

Soviet leaders and planners have not attached as much importance to magazines as to newspapers. The rationale for this fact is that most Soviet newspapers have the capacity and design for informing and influencing mass audiences, while most magazines have tended to appeal to specialized audiences. Of course this difference is not inevitable but is the result of many years of evolution. This creates an interesting potential for magazine advertising to carefully chosen market segments.

There are slightly over 5,000 magazines published. However, an American scholar concluded that, after subtracting periodicals dealing only in technical information, bulletins, collections of statistics, and scholarly journals, there were 1,135 "magazines" as of 1968. In that year they had an annual circulation of 1,692.5 million and a single-issue average circulation of 135,800. Growth has been substantial. The corresponding figures for 1965 were 1,044 magazines with 1,088.4 million annual circulation and 94,500 single-issue average circulation.[45] In 1960 the figures were 923,576.9 million, and 57,300; and in 1950 they were 430,136.7 million, and 27,700. Thus during the 1950s and 1960s the industry showed a net growth of about 39 magazines a year. During those years annual circulation exhibited a 12-fold increase, while single-issue average circulation quintupled. Eight magazines are published weekly, 49 two or three times a month, 752 monthly, 264 six to ten times a year, and 62 fewer than six times a year. Izvestia reported in 1971 that total per-issue circulation of magazines and magazine-type bulletins had reached 156 million.[46]

The best-known and largest-circulation magazines are published on a national basis. About 77 percent of the single-issue average circulation belongs to national magazines.[47] Besides mass appeal magazines, there are national magazines specializing in commerce, industrial affairs, technology, science, agriculture, family life, health, sports, humor, art, literature, politics, military affairs, and other fields. Several dozen magazines are published for children and teenagers. Every ethnic republic has several magazines, usually in the local language, that are quite important within that jurisdiction. A directory, Specialized Magazines in the U.S.S.R., is available to foreigners through Vneshtorgreklama.

Among the most popular national magazines are Krokodil, published three times a month, the weekly Ogonyek ("Little Flame"), and the monthly Zdorovye ("Health"). They have circulations of 5 million, 2 million, and 10 million, respectively. Cosmopolitans are likely to read Za Rubezhom ("Abroad"), a magazine of translations from the foreign press, while applied science enthusiasts are apt to read Nauka i Zhizn ("Science and Life").

A great many magazines are edited for the female reader. One of the influential periodicals is the monthly Sovetskaya Zhenschchina ("Soviet Woman"), which is distributed in the U.S.S.R. but concentrates on its circulation in over 100 foreign countries. It is translated into English, French, Spanish, German, Hungarian, Chinese, Japanese, Korean, and Hindi. Rabotnitsa ("Working Woman") and Krestyanka ("Peasant Woman"), with circulations of 11.2 million and 5 million, respectively, are distributed nationally. Each ethnic republic has one or more women's magazines, including Kirghizstan Ayaldary; the Ukrainian Radyanska Zhinka; the Armenian Aiastani Ashkhatavaru; the Georgian Sakartvelos Kali, Zanoni Tadzikistan, Azerbaijan Gadiny; the Uzbekistani Saodat; the Moldavian Femeya Moldovoi; Turkmenistan Ayallary; Kazakhstan Aieldery; the Lithuanian Taribine Moteris; and the Belorussian Rabotnitsa i Selyanka. Tiny Dagestan publishes women's magazines in six languages.

There are many scholarly, professional, and academic magazines. Examples are Sovetskoye Gosudarstvo i Pravo ("Soviet State and Law"), put out by the Academy of Sciences Law Institute, Partiinaya Zhizn ("Party Affairs"), Kommunist, and Voprosy Ekonomika ("Economic Problems").

Many magazines are edited for specific industries, such as V Mire Knig ("In the World of Books") for the book publishing industry, bookstore managers, and librarians. As with other media, their rates do not correlate with circulation. For example, a full-page black-and-white advertisement in Cristallography, which has a circulation of 1,800, costs U.S. $222. The same service in Radio, which claims a circulation of 480,000, costs $280.[48] In Liteznoe Proizvodstvo, which reaches 12,700 scientific research personnel, engineers, technicians, and master foundrymen, this service costs U.S. $220. The same rate applies to Kartofeli'i Ovoshchi, which has a circulation of 48,500 farm workers.[49] A small number of magazines, such as Ekonomika i Organizatsia Promyshlennovo Proizvodotva ("Economics and Organization of Industrial Production") are aimed at industrial executives and their professional staff. The editors of this periodical have criticized the slowness with which they get printing and distribution support.[50]

There is a cluster of magazines perpetuating the 19th-century Russian tradition of "tolstyye zhurnaly," or "thick journals." Among these periodicals are Oktyabr ("October") and the controversial, unorthodox Novy Mir ("New World"), Yunost ("Youth"), and Zvesda ("Star"). Meant for intellectuals of all ages, Novy Mir has been purged from time to time. It has aggressively brought to Russian intellectuals Pasternak, Ehrenburg, Dudintsev, Yashin, and others. Meant for older teen-agers and young adults, Yunost has been heavily criticized. For example, in 1971 Literaturnaya Gazeta reported an investigation of Yunost in which it was decided that this magazine erroneously was urban-oriented and was avoiding its responsibilities to present material on military service, collective farm life, and even the working-class youth of urban areas.[51]

108

Samizdat, the self-published underground press, is thriving. Some book-length works are, of course, circulated; but the bulk of the activity is in magazines and newspapers. Some emphasize news and politico-economic issues, while some specialize in belles lettres. Of late this illegal movement has spawned several "thick journals" that try to survey and integrate the entire spectrum of Russian or Soviet culture. It is intriguing to speculate how large the underground press would become if it had access to the resources that the advertising process could supply it. The underground press is usually typewritten but sometimes handwritten. Occasionally it benefits from illegal printing equipment.

Radio

A Soviet history of radio terms that nation the "mother of radio."[52] According to the Russians, their countryman A. S. Popov invented the radio receiver in 1895, the year in which Marconi conducted some of his experiments. However, the first radio station in the U.S.S.R. did not go into operation until 1922.

Although precise data are not available, it is clear that many more persons have access to radio than to television. In fact, almost everyone can be reached by radio. Soviet sources estimated that in 1968 there were 42 to 48 million receiver sets, over half of which could receive shortwave broadcasts, and about 39 million wired-in speakers.[53] In 1972 the chairman of the State Radio and Television Committee announced that there were over 50 million receivers and almost as many wired-in speakers.[54] In early years the wired-in speaker accounted for most radios, but about 1963 the receiving set caught up with it and now has a slight lead. Fortunately for the consumer, the government planners show a preference for the receiver over the speaker. This coincides with a reduction of cost in making radios. The 1975 goal is that 85 percent of families will own a receiver.

The incidence and composition of radio ownership in rural areas is a special case worthy of study. The majority of radios on farms are wired into a radio diffusion exchange located on the farm or a neighboring farm. This exchange picks up signals from nearby cities and sends them into the farmer's home. Many of the systems have no built-in selectivity for the listener, and none offered selectivity until the early 1960s. Farm managers may delete some programs and/or the advertising blocks, combine schedules of several stations to get what they regard as an optimum mix, and insert their own lectures, announcements, and instructions for the benefit of the farm residents.

Domestic radio broadcasts programs and advertising in 60 languages, but this figure is still only half of the 120 languages and major dialects spoken in the nation. Each ethnic area has one or more stations. Radio Moscow broadcasts in 57 languages every day for audiences in other countries. There has been an on-again, off-again battle of jamming by the Russians and the Americans of some of each other's international broadcasts. By unspoken agreement, the Soviets allow programs from the British Broadcasting Company and various Scandinavian organizations in return for those groups' not jamming the Soviet programs aimed back. Radio Free Europe and Radio Liberty have constituted a Soviet grievance for many years. In the late 1960s the Voice of America began jamming Soviet broadcasts to the East European countries.

As on television, advertising on Soviet radio is presented only in prime time. This is between seven and nine in the morning and five and eight in the evening. The commercial messages are in blocks at the convenience of the station, and no advertiser can choose his time or proximity to a certain program type. Very little has been done to measure radio audiences and listenership, an activity that would be of great benefit to programming as well as advertising.

The Chief Marketing Administration of the Ministry of the Radio Industry has shown considerable aggressiveness in distribution and merchandising. At the initiative of that office, the Ministry of Trade established Houses of Radio in four large cities to promote radio sets, tape recorders, and other audio equipment. Now the Ministry of Radio is agitating for better advertising and dissemination of more technical product information in these stores and for transferral of the stores to its jurisdiction in order to use them for test marketing.[55]

Television

The audience that potentially could be reached by the "blue screen," as the Russians sometimes call television, is growing rapidly. Nevertheless, as of 1972, official government data showed that about 30 percent of the population lived in areas that still could not receive a television signal.[56] Production of television sets in the decade 1960 through 1969 totaled 36.65 million and showed a growth trend throughout. Output was 5.7 million in 1968, 6.6 million in 1969, peaked at 6.7 million in 1970, declined to 5.8 million in 1971, and rose to 6 million in 1972.[57] According to the government, 51 percent of families owned a set at the end of 1970,[58] but many others had access through public and communal facilities for recreation. Ownership is much higher in large cities. The Five-Year

Plan goal for the end of 1975 is 72 percent ownership. Assuming a generous allowance for the replacement rate and no change in channel inventories, it is probable that the proportion of families owning a television set approached 61 percent by the end of 1972. In the geographical areas that could receive television, there were about 90 television sets per 100 families in 1972.[59] However, an unknown but very small fraction of this number was in group recreation facilities. Although production was increasing and prices were high relative to income, one had to wait several months in most cases for delivery of a set until 1969. As sets finally became plentiful, prices were cut significantly in 1970, 1971, and 1972.

It should be noted that television expansion receives the necessary resources and priorities in some economies because this medium of communications is sometimes thought to be particularly useful to the government in disseminating information and influencing attitudes. Two authorities on Soviet mass media disagree on this point in relation to the U.S.S.R. J. W. Markham believes that the Soviet leadership was quick to see its value as an instrument of mass propoganda and agitation.[60] On the other hand, M. W. Hopkins concludes that electronic media were assigned rather low priorities until the 1950s, in the case of radio, and the early 1960s, in the case of television.[61] As late as 1965, the Communist Party journal of theory, Kommunist, described television as still a novelty and stated that an "inertia of attitude" in favor of the press, moving pictures, and radio interfered with giving television the stature in propaganda it deserved.[62] Despite many pressing alternative needs for resources, experimental television was begun in the Soviet Union in the early 1930s, and regular television transmission was begun on a small scale in 1939 in Moscow and Leningrad and resumed in 1945, after World War II. Even before television sets were in good supply, they qualified for installment credit for the consumer. Felker reported in 1966 that 70 percent of television sets sold in the Russian Republic in 1964 were on the installment plan.[63] Despite scarcity of the product, the turnover tax levied on it was relatively low. In the late 1960s the practice of allowing suitable trade-ins was established. In the same period color was introduced. It has made little headway thus far, although studios have been reequipped in several major cities and a few hours of color are telecast each week.

The size of audiences for television is affected by two important forces, one making for smaller audiences and the other for larger. One is the pattern of out-of-the-home recreation that has been predominant because of extremely crowded and inadequate housing (and often, even today, the sharing of an apartment by a family and an unmarried person, or the sharing of kitchens and bathrooms). The other force in operation is the changed work schedule. Because most enterprises now observe a five-day week and most of them close on the weekend, the public facilities for recreation and entertainment are severely strained. This latter factor makes for an even larger television audience than might have been predicted several years ago.

Even so, the Russian may not find the television fare to his liking. Few are willing to say so. However, one author recently doubted in public whether he should buy a set because of alleged faults and dullness of programming, particularly the films on this medium.[64] American television executive Elmer W. Lower describes Soviet television as "heavy" and "dull."[65] The Soviet humor magazine misses few chances to label that country's television as "stodgy." A Soviet journalism professor claims, however, that increased television viewing decreases consumption of vodka and, for people in small towns and villages, provides a window on the world.[66] In further defense, the Westerner cannot fail to note that the coverage of sports is rather extensive and the educational mission accomplished with some flair.

The largest Soviet cities have several services, or channels, while most of the rest of the European Soviet Union has two services. Television coverage is spotty in Siberia and the Soviet Far East, and is limited to one service. Even if the 1975 goal is attained, 44 percent of the population of eastern Siberia will still be outside the reach of television.[67] The Five-Year Plan goal is to ensure reliable reception of at least two television channels in all the union republic capitals and all major industrial centers. Across the country there are 127 stations capable of originating programs. Many other facilities, although called stations, can do no more than rebroadcast.

Programming suffers from distance, lack of notification to the viewer, undependability of scheduling, and variation in languages. The distance across the country is so great that television executives must contend with 11 domestic time zones. Relay stations, cable, and satellites are all utilized. One critic states that Orbita, the television satellite system, amounts to the linking of space technology with scissors and paste, since the executives and technicians constantly come up with a miscellany of delays, gaps, substitutions, cancellations, filler material, and insufficient variety for those receiving Orbita programs.[68] Even within one time zone, a daily or weekly telecast varies considerably in the hour at which it is shown. One Soviet academician has urged fixed schedules for television programming, plus detailed listings and previews.[69] Programming is complicated also by variation in languages. Television is presented in minority languages in 14 cities scattered through the ethnic republics.

Soviet television is a member of Intervidenie, or Intervision, the East European counterpart of Eurovision. Although not a founding member, the U.S.S.R. has been active in the association for several years. At this time the arrangements are suitable for simultaneous programming and exchange of programs, but not for advertising messages. If the theoretically desirable national specialization of production and mutual dependence on imports that Comecon exposes actually came about, Intervision could be a useful means for providing informative and persuasive commercial messages across national boundaries. Occasionally the Soviets and Intervision exchange a program with Eurovision.

A typical television station runs some 11 to 14 hours a day, but a few run as much as 16 hours. An average station includes 15 to 30 minutes of advertising, presented in a few blocks at the convenience of the station but always during prime time, between 6 and 11 in the evening. A block of commercials varies from 5 to 15 minutes in length. The cost to a foreigner for one minute on Moscow, Leningrad, or Kiev television is U.S. $2,000,[70] a rate that fails to reflect the large potential differences in audience size. As in some West European countries, no advertiser in the U.S.S.R. can sponsor a program or choose the time when his message will be presented.

A few stations appear to be interested in more advertising because of the revenue opportunities it offers and, especially, the access to a source of funds over which the station might have a measure of independent control. At one time each television and radio set owner had to pay an annual license fee, but that has been replaced by a surcharge on sales of new sets. In 1968 this surcharge brought 274 million rubles directly into the broadcasting budget.[71] Government subsidies are also received.

Most electronic advertising is extremely low-key, often no more than a mere announcement. However, one message for a Soviet foot lotion stands out. This film uses the Atlantes, huge statues of mythological characters at the entrance of the Hermitage in Leningrad, as the introduction and backdrop. The narrator recounts the mythological story while the camera examines the details of the statues' anatomy. Then ten bottles of the product suddenly flash on the screen. A Pravda reviewer satirically noted how appropriate this was, since each statue has ten toes.[72]

NOTES

1. Gordon Wills and Roy Hayhurst, "Marketing in Socialist Societies," European Journal of Marketing, 5 (Spring 1971), 13-28, at 24.

2. I. Tokareva, "Pay Attention to the Needs of Advertising," Ekonomicheskaya Gazeta, no. 49 (1969), 17. JPRS, 50104; TOUTAS, 96.

3. V. Rusakova and G. Sudets, "Problems and Judgments: Let's Remember Advertising," Pravda, February 19, 1969, p. 3. CDSP, 21 (March 12, 1969), 24.

4. Ibid.

5. Ibid.

6. K. Michurin and P. Federov, "Trade and Advertising," Pravda, May 4, 1965, p. 2. CDSP, 17 (May 26, 1965), 32-33.

7. New York Times, January 16, 1967, p. 57.

8. See the following: Robert Conquest, ed., The Politics of Ideas in the U.S.S.R. (New York: Praeger Publishers, 1967); Alex Inkeles, Public Opinion in Soviet Russia: A Study in Mass Persuasion (Cambridge, Mass.: Harvard University Press, 1951); Alex Inkeles and Raymond A. Bauer, The Soviet Citizen: Daily Life in a Totalitarian Society (Cambridge, Mass.: Harvard University Press, 1959); Priscilla Johnson and Leopold Labedz, eds., Khrushchev and the Arts: The The Politics of Soviet Culture, 1962-1964 (Cambridge, Mass.: MIT Press, 1965); Peter H. Rossi and Raymond A. Bauer, "Some Patterns of Soviet Communications Behavior," Public Opinion Quarterly, 16 (Winter 1952-1953), 653-70; Merle Fainsod, How Russia Is Ruled (Cambridge, Mass.: Harvard University Press, 1953); Merle Fainsod, Smolensk Under Soviet Rule (New York: Vintage Books, 1963); A. Finn, Experiences of a Soviet Journalist (New York: East European Fund, 1954).

9. Raymond A. Bauer and David B. Gleicher, "Word-of-Mouth Communication in the Soviet Union," Public Opinion Quarterly, 17 (Fall 1953), 297-310.

10. D. Valentei, "Problems of Social Life: On Demographic Behavior," Pravda, August 16, 1972, p. 3. CDSP, 24 (September 13, 1972), 14.

11. Communist Affairs, 3 (May-June 1965), 17.

12. Ibid.

13. Calculated from data in "Report by the U.S.S.R. Council of Ministers' Central Statistical Administration: The Population of Our Country," Pravda, April 17, 1971, pp. 1, 3. CDSP, 23 (May 18, 1971), 14-18.

14. For a helpful cultural examination of one republic's media, see Karlen Mooradian, "The Press and the Sword: Armenian Journalism Since 1512," Journalism Quarterly, 42 (Winter 1970), 746-56. Also see "Russians Upgrade Regional Newspapers," Editor and Publisher, July 9, 1966, p. 32.

15. S. V. Serebriakov, as quoted in Lyman E. Ostlund, "Russian Advertising: A New Concept," Journal of Advertising Research,

13 (February 1973), 11-19. Other helpful background materials can be found in James W. Markham, "Is Advertising Important in the Soviet Economy?," Journal of Marketing, 28 (April 1964), 31-37: Carter R. Bryan, "Communist Advertising: Its Status and Functions," Journalism Quarterly, 39 (Autumn 1962), 500-06; Reed Moyer, "Marketing in the Iron Curtain Countries," Journal of Marketing, 30 (October 1966), 3-9; Marxhall I. Goldman, "Product Differentiation and Advertising: Some Lessons from Soviet Experience," Journal of Political Economy, 68 (August 1960), 346-57; Marshall I. Goldman, "New Perspective of Product Differentiation and Advertising: The Soviet View," Boston University Business Review, 8 (Spring 1962), 3-12; Barry M. Richman, "Soviet Management in Transition," M.S.U. Business Topics, 15 (Spring 1967), 26-42; G. Peter Lauter, "The Changing Role of Marketing in; the Eastern European Socialist Economies," Journal of Marketing, 35 (October 1971), 16-20; Felisksas Palubinskas, "The Growing Importance of Marketing in Soviet Russia," The Western Economic Journal, Summer 1965, pp. 274-87.

16. Quoted in Elizabeth Swayne, "Soviet Advertising: Communism Imitates Capitalism," in C. H. Sandage and Vernon Fryburger, eds., The Role of Advertising (Homewood, Ill.: Richard D. Irwin, 1960), pp. 93-103, at p. 94.

17. Quoted in Parade, February 8, 1959, p. 8.

18. Quoted in David Ogilvy, Confessions of an Advertising Man (New York: Atheneum, 1963), p. 150.

19. M. Argunov, "What Advertising Does," Sovetskaya Torgovlya, February 1966. Reprinted in Journal of Advertising Research, 6 (December 1966), 2-3.

20. V. Terestchenko, "Psychology and Advertising," Literaturnaya Gazeta, February 8, 1967, p. 67. Reprinted in Industrial Marketing, 52 (August 1967), 65-67.

21. Pravda, February 19, 1969, p. 3. CDSP, 21 (March 12, 1969), 24.

22. Quoted in Dusko Doder, "Soviets Realize Advertising Can Help Sell Goods," Baton Rouge (Louisiana) Sunday Advocate, April 6, 1969, p. 12-F.

23. F. Tamme, "The Socialist Nations and Advertising," Nauka i Tekhnika, no. 10 (1969), 8-10. JPRS, 50229, TOUTAS, 103, pp. 1-6.

24. Ibid.

25. L. Krainov and G. Petrov, "Man and the Service Sector: Advertising Creates Obligations," Pravda, November 15, 1971, p. 2. CDSP, 23 (December 14, 1971), 10, 19.

26. Ye. Kanevsky, "The Effect of Advertising," Pravda, April 1, 1972, p. 3. CDSP, 24 (April 26, 1972), 32.

27. Buren H. McCormack et al., A Study of the Printing and Publishing Business in the Soviet Union (New York: American

Newspaper Publishers Association, 1967), p. 47. For a concise history of Russian print journalism, see Jay Jenson and Richard Bayley, "Highlights of the Development of Russian Journalism, 1553-1917," Journalism Quarterly, 41 (Summer 1964), 403-15.

28. Mark W. Hopkins, Mass Media in the Soviet Union (New York: Pegasus, 1970), p. 184.

29. Ibid., p. 190.

30. L. I. Brezhnev, "The Report of the C.P.S.U. Central Committee to the 24th Congress of the Communist Party of the Soviet Union," Pravda, March 31, 1971, pp. 2-10. CDSP, 23 (May 4, 1971), 8.

31. Michael Yablokov, "The Newspaper and Distance," Zhurnalist, July 1970, pp. 44-45. CDSP, 22 (January 12, 1971), 25.

32. James W. Markham, Voices of the Red Giants: Communications in Russia and China (Ames: Iowa State University Press, 1967), p. 170.

33. John Gunther, Inside Russia Today (New York: Harper, 1958), p. 303.

34. Pravda, May 5, 1971, p. 1. CDSP, 23 (June 1, 1971), 37.

35. Ostlund, "Russian Advertising."

36. Moscow News, August 8, 1970, p. 14.

37. Ostlund, "Russian Advertising."

38. Jere L. Felker, Soviet Economic Controversies: The Emerging Marketing Concept and Changes in Planning, 1960-1965 (Cambridge, Mass.: MIT Press, 1966), p. 150.

39. A. Malkov, "Problems of the Rural Market," Ekonomicheskaya Gazeta, October 1971, p. 17. CDSP, 23 (December 14, 1971), 9-10.

40. "The City's Lights at Night," Izvestia, August 16, 1972, p. 3. CDSP, 24 (September 13, 1972), 23-24.

41. A. Vyatkin, "Discussing Problems of Urban Development: Beauty and the Cost Estimate," Izvestia, January 19, 1968, p. 3. CDSP, 20 (February 7, 1968), 29.

42. V. Rusakova and G. Sudets, "Problems and Judgments: Let's Remember Advertising," Pravda, February 19, 1969, p. 3. CDSP, 21 (March 12, 1969), 24.

43. Ostlund, "Russian Advertising."

44. Ibid.

45. Hopkins, Mass Media in the Soviet Union, pp. 224-27.

46. "The Soviet Press," Izvestia, May 5, 1971, p. 1. CDSP, 23 (June 1, 1971), 37.

47. Hopkins, Mass Media in the Soviet Union, pp. 230, 356.

48. Ostlund, "Russian Advertising."

49. Wills and Hayhurst, "Marketing in Socialist Societies," p. 28.

50. Pravda, October 10, 1972, p. 3. CDSP, 24 (November 8, 1972), 26.

51. "Follow the Main Line," Literaturnaya Gazeta, January 13, 1971, p. 3. CDSP, 23 (March 2, 1971), 19.

52. M. Gleizer, ed., Radio i televideniye v SSSR: 1917-1963 (Moscow: 1965), cited in Hopkins, Mass Media in the Soviet Union, p. 244.

53. Pravda, May 7, 1968, p. 3.

54. "Ceremony Dedicated to Radio Day," Pravda, May 7, 1972, p. 2. CDSP, 24 (May 31, 1972), 21.

55. V. Sokolov, "Plant, Store and Customer," Izvestia, November 25, 1972, p. 2. CDSP, 24 (December 20, 1972), 26-27.

56. "Ceremony Dedicated to Radio Day."

57. Developed from annual reports on the economy published every year in Pravda and Izvestia in January, February, or March.

58. Alexei Kosygin, "The 24th Congress of the Communist Party of the Soviet Union: The Directives of the 24th C.P.S.U. Congress for the Five-Year Plan for the Development of the U.S.S.R. National Economy in 1971-1973," Pravda, April 7, 1971, pp. 2-7. CDSP, 23 (May 18, 1971), 1-11, at 9.

59. "Ceremony Dedicated to Radio Day."

60. Markham, Voices of the Red Giants, p. 115.

61. Hopkins, Mass Media in the Soviet Union, p. 251.

62. Kommunist, no. 13 (September 1965), as quoted in Hopkins, Mass Media in the Soviet Union, p. 236.

63. Felker, Soviet Economic Controversies, p. 152.

64. V. Sukharevich, Literaturnaya Gazeta, no. 34 (1969), 8.

65. Elmer W. Lower, "Television, Soviet Style—1967," Television Quarterly, 6 (Summer 1967), 29-33.

66. G. Kuznetsov, "Television, My Friend, My Enemy," Trud, November 14, 1971, p. 3. CDSP, 23 (January 4, 1972), 30.

67. G. Ustinov, "Deputy's Instructions," Izvestia, November 13, 1971. CDSP, 23 (December 14, 1971), 26-27.

68. Yu. Koginov, "The Pluses and Minuses of Orbita," Pravda, February 8, 1970, p. 3. JPRS, 50183; TOUTAS, 100.

69. Kuznetsov, "Television, My Friend, My Enemy."

70. Ostlund, "Russian Advertising."

71. V. Nikitin, "A Scientific Basis for Retail Goods Turnover," Sovetskaya Torgovlya, no. 6 (1969), 15-17. JPRS, 48430; TOUTAS, 32.

72. Yu. Borin, "The Atlantes Switch Jobs," Pravda, September 9, 1970. CDSP, 22 (October 6, 1970), 36.

5

**PRICING AND
CHANNELS OF
DISTRIBUTION**

PRICING

The Nature of Soviet Pricing

In the minds of most Westerners, prices tend to be the result of the interplay of supply and demand. Thus they are mechanisms for the rationing of consumption, the stimulation or dampening of production, and the general allocation of resources. However, in the Soviet economy, prices for nearly all goods are planned more or less centrally, are infrequently changed, and do not necessarily or consistently reflect supply, demand, relative scarcity, or actual cost, although these tendencies of Western pricing can be identified in some Soviet pricing activities.

In an economy where there is consumers' sovereignty, the basic adjustment to disequilibrium in the market for a product is to adjust supply to demand. In the Soviet economy, where planners' sovereignty prevails, the basic mechanism of adjustment is to adjust demand to supply. When there is compelling evidence in the form of surpluses or shortages at the prevailing prices, planners may be able and willing over the long run to alter, chiefly through offsets, the product mix or composition of output lying within a given jurisdiction of planning authority. It does not appear that Soviet planners are unaware of or necessarily unconcerned about demand. Most of their retail-level prices, although rigid and long-term, may be thought of as rates oriented at least in principle toward an intended supply-demand equilibrium.

The views of V. Sitnin, the chairman of the State Committee on Prices, are noteworthy. One of the most influential persons in the process of price formation, he takes the position that prices should be basically of the cost-plus type but related to "normed costs." He notes that this would permit the prices to be used for a large number of economic calculations for which many are not now suitable. Prices of some goods would be set by the central government. In rejecting short-run market forces he says: "Market prices are, in our view, alien to our economy. . . . The balance between demand and supply is achieved by proportional development . . . and is the concern of the planning organs."[1] However, he favors more frequent revision of prices.[2]

E. G. Liberman, a major contributor to economic and managerial reforms of the 1960s, has taken a rather eclectic view of pricing. He is not convinced that the one best way has been found and he feels that much thought and research, both theoretical and applied, remains for scholars and practitioners. He believes in "an expediently constructed system of planned price formation." He takes pains to defend the core of thought in the so-called "optimal planning price" school, which is oriented more toward mathematics than ideology. As consumer-oriented as he is, Liberman nevertheless maintains that the degree of consumer satisfaction is not, and should not be, the central idea in pricing, since, in his estimation, this approach amounts to the theory of marginal utility. According to Liberman:

> It is entirely sufficient in optimal evaluations to maximize not the aggregate of individual, unmeasurable consumer "preferences" but rather the total consumption fund. But it is contemplated to determine the structure of the consumption fund in terms of items (resource vectors) on the basis of a well-organized assessment of consumer demand and to make corrections with regard to norms of need satisfaction. In this way we depart from subjective evaluations and attempt to take into account the collective experience of consumers.[3]

In order to hold the door open for future thought on pricing, Liberman warns: "Not every combination of different theories should be immediately classified as antiscientific eclecticism."[4]

One must not expect perfectly dependable generalizations in Soviet pricing practice. Alec Nove concluded: "It seems clear . . . that the practice of Soviet price determination is not easily reducible to any set of principles at all."[5] A Russian inspection executive in the coal industry, after tracing through the widely disparate prices and varying amounts of loss involved in the prices, attributed the particular prices mostly to long-standing traditional agreements. He concluded that "there is simply no principle for establishing prices."[6]

In that Soviet pricing practice does not necessarily reflect relative scarcity, prices are sometimes a hindrance rather than a help in
planning investment projects. On occasion such planners must use an
informal set of coefficients of scarcity. This is for the purpose of
correcting the prices of the various types of materials, some of which
are substitutes for each other, that might go into the investment. The
reasonable assumption is that abundant input materials should be used
when they are the technological equivalent of scarce input materials.
Otherwise planners would have little idea of how well resource allocation has been executed. The extent of use of planners' shadow prices
and the question of whether they are generated anew for each major
investment project are not answerable at this time.

The principal components of Soviet price are enterprise wholesale price, the turnover tax, the wholesale trade margin, and the retail trade margin. In addition, there are usually transportation charges. The retail price is normally about double the enterprise wholesale price. Besides these components there may be an industry wholesale price if the several production organizations making the same
generic product have a joint selling agency. This price would include
any cost and markup of the sales office. That some of these sales
offices exist is well established, but their number is not known. If a
sale is made to a state user rather than to the trade network, the turnover tax is usually, but not always, omitted. It is perhaps helpful and
convenient to the Westerner to think of Soviet pricing as being semi-
integrated in the channel of distribution.

The producer's wholesale price (enterprise wholesale price) is
usually determined by averaging the costs of the several enterprises
making the same generic product and then adding a defined ratio of
profit. Thus the "profitability" of the enterprises in a given industry
varies widely from heavy rates of loss to high rates of profit. If this
scatter is unacceptably great, settlement price accounts are occasionally used in industries that have joint sales offices. In this case
the sales office pays each factory its individually computed price and
sells to customers at the industry wholesale price, while the adjustment entries flow through the settlement accounts in the financial records. Although a money-losing factory may be subsidized year after
year, the politicians and planners do not like the situation. It is not
always the loss per se that is regretted, for the loss may be beyond
the control of the manager, such as the case where production equipment is obsolete. Most politicians and planners make a not unreasonable assumption that such subsidies on a continuing basis tend
to depress professional initiative and operating efficiency.

The planning for Soviet prices has become more complicated.
As concern for the ultimate consumer has grown, the variety and
quantity of goods have increased. Even before this movement had

any importance, the number of generic types of products necessary in a modern economy and the considerable variation within each generic type required the formulation of literally hundreds of thousands of prices. Today it may be necessary to determine several thousand prices for the goods of just one generic type.

Fundamental policy questions on prices are determined by the U.S.S.R. Council of Ministers and the Communist Party Central Committee.[7] Operating decisions of national scope are made by the State Committee on Prices of the U.S.S.R. State Planning Committee, the Ministry of Finance, the Ministry of Trade, and the industrial ministries. There is some decentralization of authority down to the republic-level Councils of Ministers and their appropriate subordinate units, especially the republic Planning Committees and the republic Ministries of Trade. In turn, some republics have delegated some authority to the oblast level and larger cities.

Although this limited decentralization can aid in relating demand and supply and gains the motivation of local trade officials and even some input from practicing managers, it apparently does not receive the professional attention by marketing researchers, economists, accountants,[8] and technicians that the intricacies and interconnections of the Soviet economy warrant. Republic-level control over retail prices is especially common in the case of local production with limited geographic dispersion of sales. In a revealing article, Pravda reported that the Azerbaidzhan Republic State Committee on Prices confirms requested prices chiefly on the basis of the prices for similar goods. Instead of physically inspecting the products, it relies on extremely brief written descriptions that include no information on quality. When the Khandar Production Combine requested a price of 10 rubles 50 kopecks for a children's tricycle, the republic-level Ministry of Trade recommended 50 kopecks less because the product was poorly made. However, the Price Committee, using the analogy method, set the price at 13 rubles.[9]

In 1969 Nove reported that subnational bodies appeared to control the prices of products aggregating about 45 percent of all retail trade, but this figure was only approximate.[10] Prior to the changes of the late 1950s, subnational entities apparently controlled the prices of products aggregating about 10 percent of all retail trade. Of course, this decentralization or any part of it can be withdrawn at any time. National planners retain direct price control over the most basic products and over many others that have a large amount of turnover tax in the price.

Some variation of price by geographic zones exists, even for some identical, nationally distributed products. Before World War II there were eight zones, but this was greatly simplified later. Much of this variation is attributable to nothing more than differences in transportation costs built into the price of some goods. Some variation is due to persistent local overages, the bureaucratic inability of the channels of distribution, and/or transport shortages in moving the goods and offering them for sale where they are needed, even if it is only 100 miles away. Sometimes, however, one sees instances of zonal pricing that suggest subsidy or penalty for a purpose, as in some agricultural development and frontier areas. The greatest source of geographic variation in price is the decentralization of substantial amounts of price-making authority to the republics and their subdivisions, as noted above. This is especially noteworthy for sales of consumer goods made by small local factories.

A small difference between some urban and rural prices exists today, but there are no data on their incidence or that would allow measurement of their effect. At one time rural residents had to pay surcharges that averaged 7 percent on the affected products. Enough products were affected that the average price level for rural consumers was 5 percent above that for urban consumers.[11] The premium was several times what could be explained by the transportation differentials. A Russian writer claims that the total extra costs of rural distribution, not just transport costs, were higher than the 7 percent for some goods and lower for some.[12] An American scholar concluded that the surcharge was an attempt to reduce rural demand and a form of rural taxation.[13] A partial realignment of urban and rural prices got under way in the late 1950s, and full realignment became an official national goal in 1965. During the 1966-70 Plan adjustments were made for several items, including knitwear, cotton apparel, sugar, and confectionery goods.[14]

There is a strong interest in forecasting prices, at least the wholesale level of prices. The Economic Research Institute of the U.S.S.R. State Planning Committee has prepared a forecast of wholesale price levels for 22 branches of the economy through 1980, and the Research Institute for Price Formation is preparing forecasts of wholesale prices for about 500 products. Republic-level activity is understandably sparse, but the Economics Institute of the Estonian Republic Academy of Sciences has begun some forecasting work. A Soviet economist has urged the inclusion of price forecasting in the regular activities of research institutes of the branches of the economy. He stated that this work is deterred by inadequate knowledge of the trends in some constituent costs, such as the materials input and the decreasing labor cost attributable to increasing automation. In addition, he urged the various research institutes dispersed throughout the economy to study the effects of scientific and technological progress on wage costs, labor productivity, and depreciation allowances in their areas of concern, since these factors bear directly on product cost and wholesale price.[15] It is likely that most of this price forecasting work is concerned with enterprise wholesale prices and with industry wholesale prices without inclusion of the turnover tax or any concern for the retail price level. This is because the political leaders may decide to decrease or increase substantially the tax on a particular type of product with little regard for cost and little historical trend toward the particular revision.

Pricing at the Retail Level

It has been a matter of some pride to Russian political leaders that most retail prices were quite stable over long periods of time, such as an entire five-year planning period. However, such a policy is apt to divorce prices from current conditions of production and perhaps from conditions of demand. Brzak and Marsikova note that price adjustments are possible, of course, but mainly through long-term general programs of adjustments rather than specific revisions. They describe this as very cumbersome and report a search for acceptable methods that would ensure not only periodic adjustment but continuing adjustment as well.[16] The lengthy time that wholesale prices of industry and of enterprises have tended to prevail has meant that when adjustments were finally made, some of them were rather large, typically much larger than changes at the retail level.

Several factors have perplexed executives in retailing. As the economy became more affluent, the need for markdowns to clear goods became more pressing. In 1961 the planners created a special fund "amounting to 0.4 percent of retail commodity circulation, out of which trade establishments may reduce the prices of the so-called non-marketable goods."[17] Retail markdowns are now becoming fairly common. However, they require authorization from higher trade officials and usually take a long time to be approved. A Moscow store manager has commented: "The trade network is usually late in cutting prices because of the complexities of making them. Therefore, they make very large price cuts in order to ensure at least some likelihood of sale."[18] He pointed out the desirability of having the option to make several small successive price reductions instead of one large reduction. This alternative is not feasible without quick action on requests to reduce prices. Sometimes the initiative for markdowns appears to come from the higher authorities. The percentage reduction and the duration of the offer are regulated from above. For some physically obsolete, badly shopworn, or esthetically unpleasing items, markdowns continue in effect indefinitely. Markdowns for end-of-season clearance appear to be less common, although there are no data to prove the point. There are some stores designated as "cut rate" that specialize in marked-down merchandise transferred from stores where it would not sell.

Inadequate retail markups on many goods are alleged frequently. Bakanov, Serebriakov, and Fefilov, economists specializing in distribution, state that the present system of markups has developed empirically for the most part and has inadequate theory or even factual verification behind it. The trade markup deviates substantially from the retailer's costs for most products. Loss producers include bread and other baked goods, sausage, eggs, fish, potatoes, vegetables, sugar, salt, flour, and macaroni products. These analysts warn that, when the retailer's costs exceed the markup, he resorts to cuts in other costs and customer service deteriorates.[19] Orlov reports that cotton goods, linen, soap, and other goods are sold at a loss to the retailer.[20] One store manager has urged that the markup, or trade discount, as it is often called, be differentiated more finely. It is not enough that fabrics, for example, carry a trade discount of 4 percent off the retail price. Harder-to-sell fabrics should carry a higher trade discount and vice versa.[21] Unauthorized upward deviations from list prices frequently occur, and the price discrepancy is often as much as 20 to 40 percent above the legal price.[22] It is alleged that the Ministry of Trade is lax and permissive regarding price monitoring and enforcement.[23] One Western scholar thinks insufficient distribution of official price lists is an important reason and takes note of a city that had 3,500 retail stores but only 40 price lists.[24]

Pricing New Products.* Policies on the prices for new products have discouraged innovation and even the introduction of products that are only partially new. Customer products made to special order, such as many types of machines, for which no price lists exist, are usually priced at cost plus about 5 percent. This has tended to put the customer in an adverse position.[25] For a new product that is meant for production, the price is usually set in relation to existing wholesale prices on similar or substitute products. Some slight addition may be allowed for a product that is adjudged quite superior to similar or substitute products. During the late 1950s and early 1960s regional economic councils set temporary prices for 6 to 12 months on new nonmajor products, using as a basis prices of similar products or cost plus about 5 percent.

Policies such as this do not cover costs of research and development, thus discouraging manufacturing plants from creating new goods. In 1963 the Council of Ministers began allowing the republics to assign temporary prices for new items in a limited number of types of goods if they were of improved quality and in high demand. The guideline was to set the temporary prices at a relatively high level. If demand

---

*See also "Technology and New Products" in Chapter 1.

dropped, prices would then be reduced.[26] A Soviet analyst agrees with the higher prices for new goods but contends that they must have a time limit if there is to be no discouragement of consumption.[27]

The State Prices Committee promulgated a new set of policies for new products in 1969.[28] When designers receive technical assignments, one of the fundamental parameters to be included in instructions is a ceiling price for the item. This ceiling price is calculated on the basis of probable costs to produce the item in its second year of series production.

The new set of policies enumerates three classifications of new products. The first is products designed to replace products previously in production or interchangeable with them. Wholesale prices for these new products are decided on the basis of prices in effect for base items, which typically means the old products, and the comparative advantages in use of the new expressed in aggregate savings to the economy. National gain is computed as the difference between the upper and lower limits of the projected prices. The upper limit is the price level where the old product and the new product are equally advantageous to the user. This normally implies the price of the old product; but if the price of the old product is apt to change during the research and development phase of the new product, this change must be forecasted. If the new product is applicable in several diverse situations and its output will be below total requirements, the upper limit on the price is calculated on the situation in which the least economic saving is to be realized. The lower limit of the price of the new product is the level at which production of the old and the new are equally advantageous to the maker. If the upper limit is more than 10 percent higher than the sum of the lower limit plus outlays on putting the item into production, 30 to 50 percent of the gain must accrue to the maker in the form of higher price. However, the new product cannot earn a rate of profit higher than a figure 50 percent greater than the normative for the given group of products.

There are two other classifications. A second category of new products is those of the same type as the old but distinguished by "different technical and economic parameters." One does not have to calculate economic gain for this type. The price depends on the costs to produce and, apparently, on the degree of improvement in basic parameters, such as capacity, speed, or power. A third category is composed of products that exhibit new principles and are being put into production in the U.S.S.R. for the first time. The only guideline known at this time for this category is that the profitability normative for the given branch of industry will apply, a guideline that is perhaps politically wise but technologically and managerially questionable.

It appears that the State Prices Committee is beginning to adopt several views. First, cost accounting for new products has been poor. A planned, more inclusive, and more sophisticated accounting must be practiced. Second, the price will not be satisfactory to the economy unless the new product characteristics, including quality, are spelled out in detail and enforced for the benefit of customers. Third, prices of new products should be tied to the desired trends of development in the economy, sectors of the economy, and specific industries. Fourth, in general price reductions as economic levers are not used enough. Fifth, price policy should consider the life cycle of the product. According to the Committee, it would be desirable if, in its later life, the product received a lower price, since the manufacturing costs are stable or have decreased. There should be a price disincentive at this point. The sets of graduated prices being studied offer considerable promise in relation to the product life cycle but will require much research if they are to be truly useful devices benefiting the economy as a whole and specific markets. Sixth, the producing enterprise should study the projected dynamics of prices, i.e., not merely adjustments in price for the present product but possible prices for successor products as well. Studying even the probable adjustments in price for the present product is relatively new work and responsibility for the enterprise, and probably will have to be shared with central planning agencies. The length of the product life cycle and the constituent phases are, of course, influenced by the resources and zeal poured into the research and development for the next generation of the product type. Thus the manager must not be surprised or disappointed if the price for product A-2 is cut because of the progress on prototypic models of product A-3, even while product A-1 still dominates in output.

The Turnover Tax

A major component of price is the turnover tax, which is imposed on nearly all consumer goods plus electricity, natural gas, and oil. This device produces a large fraction of the budgetary revenue of the national government. The government also takes the lion's share of each organization's profits, levies an individual income tax and social insurance taxes, and sometimes borrows. According to the Moscow Financial Institute,

> Turnover tax is a part of the value of the surplus product
> (net income) which is included in advance in the price of
> a commodity and passes into the budget of the socialist
> state via the price mechanism.29

Government income from this source is regular and rather stable and does not depend on the less than perfectly dependable results of the operations of production enterprises. All except the smallest organizations must pay their turnover tax to the government promptly. State wholesale houses pay daily, most organizations every 10 days, and very small organizations once a month.

Although the turnover tax remains extremely important to the government for revenue purposes, for allocating resources, and for redistributing funds, and is growing in absolute amount, it has declined in its share of the budget. It provided 62.1 percent of such revenue in 1947, 42.0 percent in 1959, and 38.6 percent in 1963.[30] At the same time, the relative importance of state deductions from enterprise profits has grown, and by the late 1960s they exceeded revenue from the turnover tax.[31]

Ever since the turnover tax was imposed in 1930 as an amalgamation of several taxes used throughout the 1920s, there has been disagreement as to its nature. Marxian theory decries excise, i.e., indirect, taxes. Soviet economists insist that the turnover tax is not an excise. Their officially sanctioned rationale, essentially, is that the turnover tax is not added to the price of the product, for the final price has already been determined at some economically justified level. The Soviet position is that, if the turnover tax were reduced, the price would be unaffected but the enterprise's profits account would be increased. Then the government would have to take a larger share of the profits account. In short, the turnover tax is a part of profit and thus an investable fund, according to the Russians. Most Westerners feel that the effect of the turnover tax is the same as a Western excise tax. It must be added also that some observers think that the turnover tax is to some degree nothing more than an offset to the state-subsidized underpricing of the capital goods that were utilized in making the consumer goods.[32]

There are a few admitted Soviet exceptions for the purposes of certain social objectives. The Russians include relatively high turnover tax as a constituent of the prices of liquor and tobacco products in order to discourage demand. Precious stones and jewelry also are taxed heavily as luxury items. The rather inelastic demand for some of these goods suggests that the turnover tax on them is little more than a revenue producer. Even on items unrelated to luxury or social avoidance, the turnover tax is sometimes very high, often 33 to 50 percent of the retail price. It is very low or non-existent on a few items, such as books and children's clothing. There may be a rather crude, inconsistent form of progressively graduated taxation at work. Bornstein believes that the turnover tax assists in making the distribution of real income less unequal than the distribution of money income.[33] However, comprehensive information on turnover taxes is not released by the government.

It is fairly clear that the price planners are simultaneously manipulating the probable state deductions from enterprise profits, the level of the turnover tax, and the retail price. It is also clear that the turnover tax acts as a cushion between households and producing enterprises. With this device the price planners can change selected retail prices without correspondingly changing the price of the producing enterprise. Or they can benefit the producer without raising the retail price.

Currently there are three basic methods of assessing the turnover tax. One Soviet economist states that, in simplified form, they are the following: a percentage of the retail price; a percentage of the difference between retail price (less trading margins and sales agency margins) and enterprise wholesale prices; and an absolute amount of money per unit of product. He argues that the most desirable is the second.[34] There is apparently wide variation in use of the methods, but the second is used more than the others. Examples of the first method are margarine, salt, macaroni products, crockery, rubber footwear, and electrical goods. Examples of the third method are cereal and oil products.[35] In all of this, one must recall that the purpose of the second approach is not to influence the decision on percentage of markup the retailer charges, for this is not the retailer's prerogative and has already been decided at a higher level. The turnover tax on particular goods, along with final retail price, is raised or lowered once in a while to absorb excess purchasing power, to reduce inventories, or to favor a particular group. Turnover tax data on specific products are almost never available, but the various brands within a generic type of product are apparently treated quite similarly.

Consistency with Marxian Theory of Value

According to orthodox Marxian theory, labor is the basis of all value. To Marx, value was "a mere congelation of homogeneous human labor," i.e., "crystals" of a "social substance."[36] Marx acknowledged the role of materials input and instruments of production and thought of them as embodied labor. In order to meet the problem of differential efficiency in production, Marx stated that the amount of value in a product was determined by the socially necessary labor time. An item produced less efficiently was not more valuable than one produced more efficiently. He accepted the costs of the functions of packaging, storage, and transport to the extent of the labor expended. He qualified this to exclude any socially unproductive execution of a function, such as storage of a product in order to realize more from its sale. Marx's beliefs about value included almost no place for the concepts of utility, even form utility. Yet he believed that an unwanted product did not constitute value.

Soviet politicians, planners, and economists have vigorously discussed and argued value theory per se and value theory as it relates to price formation, but most of this has been since the death of Stalin in 1953.[37] During much of Stalin's long administration price tended to exist independently of value. Thought on value was belittled. In 1952 Suslov ridiculed those who made a so-called fetish of Marx's law of value. Although leaders since Stalin have permitted the debates quite openly, the labor theory of value has not, of course, been implemented.

In looking at the various positions of Soviet thinkers on value and pricing, one is reminded, perhaps incongruously, of a group of bickering Western theologians. Some are dogmatic, while others are flexible. Some are concerned only with ends, while some others are concerned seemingly as much with means as ends. Some are concerned more with current relevance, while some are drawn to primordial purity. There is even a group that takes the position that value and prices are tools of efficiency in use, not rules to be manufactured from a theoretical economic doctrine.[38] It would be difficult enough to decide how to do what Marx wanted and to do it in ways Marx would find acceptable. But there is a severely confounding element in all of this: the fact that neither the intellectuals nor the practitioners really are sure just what Marx meant on the concepts of value and price. He refrained from details concerning the principles under which the authorities would set prices.[39] Thus, operationalizing his ideas is difficult and stimulates disagreement. Moreover, it is unclear whether he really intended a translation into money prices.

In practice there are several specific deviations from Marx's beliefs on cost recognition. Goldman has pointed out that Soviet recognition of advertising costs, even though these expenditures are low, violates the purity of the labor theory of value.[40] Soviet thinkers answer that their advertising is informative and thus adds to real value, but Goldman notes a trend toward competition in some of their advertising. He calls attention to other deviations, such as interest charges on working capital,[41] excessive storage time, and waste in running the trade bureaucracy, all of which affect price. There is also duplicatory cost resulting from irrational transportation. Margaret Miller states that there is no way that rent for land can be reconciled with Marxian theory.[42] Another major deviation lies in the fact that the turnover tax is levied on goods inconsistently. Therefore, it is reasonable to conclude that Soviet prices do not reflect value as Marx saw that concept. What Soviet prices do reflect, although quite tenuously, is some sort of undefined social utility measure of value.

The historical emphasis in Soviet handling of distribution channels has been largely that of minimizing the number of levels in the
channel and centralizing the controls over planning and operations,
although some ideological and managerial adjustments have occurred.
Soviet leaders have been guided by Lenin, who summed up his position
in this way:

> . . . the proletarian government must become a sharp,
> zealous, daring manager, a careful wholesale trader.43
>
> [   ]
>
> . . . the loss of time and labor on the delivery of
> goods to the consumer through an abyss of small middle-
> men who also are ignorant of the market conditions creates
> both superfluous shipping and excessive buying.44

It is convenient to think of Soviet channels as falling into two
types, those for consumer goods and those for producer goods. In
the producer-goods sector some products flow directly from one
manufacturer to another manufacturer, but most flow through supply
bases, i.e., industrial wholesale establishments. In the consumer
goods sector, the authority channel is from the producer to the wholesaler to the retailer, although sometimes an industry sales office
represents several producers of similar or interchangeable goods.
However, the physical movement of the goods often is direct from the
factory to the retail level. This is called direct-transit selling. Sometimes the direct-transit merchandise goes not to a retail shop but to
a warehouse serving several related shops located near each other.
This warehouse is not considered a wholesale base by the Russians,
although they believe that the work of this joint warehouse is still
technically within the sphere of wholesale activity. Channel arrangements even include room for direct-to-consumer selling. It is not
widely used in the economy, but door-to-door selling does occur
regularly in the sale of insurance, photographic services, and private
enterprise repair services.

Channels for Consumer Goods

Numerous reorganizations of Soviet wholesaling have taken
place through the years, but the effect has been largely to reallocate
power between the vertical and horizontal, i.e., between ministries
and other central government organizations, on the one hand, and
republics and regions, on the other. The basic physical functions of

130

wholesaling have continued. They consist largely of assembling, sorting, storing, forming assortments, filling orders, packing, and traffic. There has been little emphasis on active buying, selling, or marketing research, although interest in them is growing.

The shortage of space in warehouses of wholesale establishments has been severe for years. It forces most merchandise on to the retail level, which is acceptable if the total supply and composition of products is adequate. When the supply does not meet these criteria, the wholesale warehouse space shortage intensifies the tendency for merchandise to accumulate in some communities and stores and to disappear elsewhere. Much fluidity in the distribution process is lost.

From the early 1960s through the early 1970s there was continuous dialogue on the advisability of direct trade ties between large retailers and groups of small retailers, on the one hand, and manufacturing enterprises, on the other hand. Gradually the dialogue shifted to fairly widespread acceptance of the advisability of such relationships and a consideration of how to do it, under what circumstances, and how to prepare and enforce the delivery contract. Evsei Liberman stated in 1972 that direct contractual relations support the goal of accountability and provide a way to make the planning of the product mix more specific.[45] However, it is not known at this time what percentage of Soviet trade in consumer goods goes through direct contracts between retailing and production organizations.

Interest in these contracts is growing. A prominent trade executive announced that in 1970 there were 2,200 such contracts between Moscow retailers and industry, and that this grew to 2,900 by the beginning of 1971. These direct contracts furnished about 34 percent of the footwear, 54 percent of the knitwear, and 60 percent of the clothing for all Moscow stores. Of the 2,900 contracts, 560 provided a delivery periodicity. This executive stated that the number of contracts between Moscow retailers and the wholesale organizations had decreased by one-third but did not specify the base period.[46] An interesting possibility that direct trade ties may help to bring about is vertical cooperative advertising. Writing in Ekonomicheskaya Gazeta in 1971, the aggressive manager of a large department store highly recommended this promotional policy and suggested that either the manufacturer or the wholesaler pay about half of mutually beneficial advertising.[47]

The wholesale trade fair as an institutional type and as a manifestation of noncentral ties between business organizations is noteworthy. This institution, typified by the famous fairs of Nizhni Novgorod and Kiev in Tsarist days, was prominent in the historical development of Russian commerce.[48] It fell into ideological disrepute for a while but was reinstated in the 1960s. Many of the fairs try to cover in depth a fairly narrow line of merchandise types.

These fairs tend to be held once or twice a year. In attendance
are representatives of production organizations, wholesalers, and
some large retail concerns. In recent years the dates for holding the
fairs have tended to move to an earlier point in the year. This is
good, in that the wishes of trade organizations and their responses to
prototypic sample products can be registered earlier, while factory
production plans still have some fluidity. It is also bad, in that trade
organizations must project their needs farther into the future. Thus
trade organizations may be placing orders with manufacturing enterprises in May of one year for delivery throughout the next calendar
year. The fairs are plagued by the ingrained habit of manufacturers
of exhibiting sample merchandise much superior to that which they
later deliver.[49] The youth-oriented newspaper Komsomolskaya
Pravda has criticized the fact that wholesale trade fairs and professional and business conventions are often held in the most desirable
resort areas of the nation.[50] Two small-scale but useful adjuncts to
the wholesale trade fair are evolving. In a few lines of commerce
representatives of production, wholesaling, and retailing meet annually, at the beginning of the year, to discuss production plans, dis-
cover oversupply and impending oversupply, and attempt to forecast
shortages. These are not primarily sales meetings.[51] In addition,
a few large department stores occasionally hold open-house gather-
ings for product designers, production executives and engineers,
wholesale house managers, and others, in the hope that relationships
can be made more harmonious and consumer desires be put into the
channel.

That the manufacturers take advantage of trade organizations
and the ultimate consumer in various ways is clear. One obstacle
lies in the timing of orders, as indicated above. One economist has
urged the preparation and distribution of bulletins to assist trade
organizations. They would include information on manufacturers and
their product mix, scheduled capacity and planned changes in capacity,
reports on the percentage of demand that has been met, and descriptions of new products that are in development.[52]

Some actions of trade organizations contribute to the problem,
however. In a conciliatory gesture, the First Deputy Minister of
Trade of the Russian Republic admitted in 1971 that not all the errors
and blunders were attributable to production enterprises. Trade groups
made some too. However, he stated that it was impossible for trade
officials to see the complete market picture as far in advance as present channel arrangements necessitate, and that such buyers have no
legal right to change their orders later. He recommended that the
buyers be given the right to make appropriate adjustments of up to
15 percent of the amounts ordered.[53] In another conciliatory move,
the deputy head of trade for Leningrad explained that the absence of

certain merchandise from some stores did not necessarily mean that
the factories were at fault. Frequently the goods were in the wholesale warehouse. To reduce the severity of this problem, the Leningrad
wholesale establishments now publish a quarterly handbook listing
their inventory that is not considered scarce.[54] Obviously this is
only a partial solution. Another factor is that wholesaling officials
and higher-level trade executives often ignore the quantities requested
by retailers. Instead of retailer-interpreted demand, the usual or
traditional quantity governs the agreement that trade officials negoti-
ate with ministries and manufacturing plants. An example is a hard-
goods retailer, Store Number 3 in Ufa, which requested 2,500 washing
machines for 1971. The republic wholesale base sent this store over
6,000. At the same time it raised its aggregate order to the Ufa
Machinery Plant, maker of the appliances. The result was overstock-
ing at every level of the distribution channel.[55]

There is some confusion, bias, and laxity in enforcement in the
rules and policies governing the rights of trade organizations versus
the rights of production enterprises. The Civil Code gives wholesalers
and retailers six months in which to claim deficiencies in quality of
goods, while standards promulgated by the U.S.S.R. Council of Ministers on June 15, 1965, and April 25, 1966, for use in arbitration between trade and manufacturing organizations permit only four months.
On some factors, such as quality of the shipping container, the Council standards favor the manufacturer over the wholesaler and the
retailer. This discrepancy is especially noteworthy, in that disputes
of any seriousness usually go to arbitration.[56] The allowed protest
period for perishable foods is, understandably, only 24 hours. There
is evidence that the statute of limitations is enforced.[57] Liberman
complains that arbitration boards are lax about assuring timely payment of bills they have adjudged equitable.[58]

Fines deriving from disputes over assortment have been uncommon. According to one Russian commentator:

> Rarely do matters reach the point of economic sanctions
> for violation of the terms of delivery of goods: Fines do
> not increase deliveries, and you can't stock the shelves
> with them. . . .
> Thus, in real life a failure to fulfill an order in
> terms of assortment does not affect an [industrial] enter-
> prise's financial well-being. This is one of the major
> reasons for the incomplete satisfaction of demand.[59]

The standard answer of retailers and wholesalers is that there
is no point in making relations with the manufacturers any worse.[60]
Izvestia castigates this "granting of amnesty." Nevertheless, the

Assistant Director of the Moscow City Executive Committee's Chief
Trade Administration claims that both the incidence and the effectiveness of such fines are growing and notes that apparel manufacturers
are particularly bad offenders.[61]

Legal redress often is not sought, and it tends to be unsatisfactory when it is sought. Nevertheless, about 700,000 economic
disputes were submitted to the State Arbitration Commission in 1970
for hearings, up by one-third over 1965.[62] These disputes include
those between trade and production and those between production
enterprises. Several lawyers have deplored the widespread failure
to take legal action. Some have urged the raising of the present range
of damages, which is 3 to 8 percent of the value of the undelivered
goods properly ordered and supported by certificates of allocation,
where that is necessary. Others recommend that the value of the
undelivered products be applied as full credit toward the fulfillment
of the customer's plan. Some suggest that compensation for losses
should come directly out of the factory's material incentive fund, the
account from which bonuses and fringe benefits are paid. Some lawyers who are not very concerned with due process have recommended
that the fine be exacted by the State Bank as a transfer accounting
entry. They would leave it to the offending production enterprise to
seek arbitration afterward.[63] It is very likely that, if awards of
compensation to the aggrieved party were stressed instead of stressing
fines payable to the state budget, more customer firms would take legal
action.

Channels for Producer Goods

"Material-technical supply" plans are in preparation constantly.[64]
Perhaps the most important is the plan prepared annually by means
of a complex flow of ideas, proposals, tentative plans, counterplans,
appeals, modifications, and rejections among the State Planning Committee, enterprises and associations, ministries, territorial authorities, and other bodies. The official goal is to complete and disseminate the plan for the following year by October, but this is seldom
achieved. When completed, the plan has two basic parts. The first
part is the material balances presented as a statement of sources
and uses of commodities in physical units. The sources are broken
down into the major categories of opening inventory, current-period
production, and imports, while the uses are broken down into the
major categories of current-period consumption, inventories, and
exports. The second part of the material-technical supply plan consists of intended allocations of each product among well over 100
major administrative entities. These entities are mainly economic

ministries and other government bodies. Output and allocation of some important products is specifically approved by the U.S.S.R. Council of Ministers after the State Planning Committee submits its work. However, the number of such products declined markedly from the late 1950s to the late 1960s. The great bulk of products is planned without specific approval of the Council of Ministers.

After acknowledging indebtedness to the research of Wasily Leontief, Nikolai Fedoryenko notes the usefulness of the intersectoral balances data and input-output tables and coefficients prepared for the years 1959 and 1966 in planning production and the work of supplier categories.[65] However, Gertrude Schroeder concludes that these important tools are very little used in formulating the actual plans and that the work is done in a rather traditional manner.[66]

The specific reforms introduced in 1965 included the reestablishment of the industrial ministries that Khrushchev had abolished in 1957 in favor of regional economic councils, and a powerful new agency called the State Committee for Material-Technical Supply (Gossnab). Since that time there has been considerable bureaucratic competition between Gossnab and the ministries, although Gossnab appears to be in the ascendancy. The interface with each ministry seems to be a little different, and some relationships not very well defined. Gossnab apparently has much operating authority to see that certain goods in certain amounts arrive at certain factories at certain times and that others leave that factory. However, it seems also to have great staff authority to advise on industrial selling and purchasing, to monitor such activity, and to recommend enforcement of rules and contracts and sanctions, if its staff intervention is not sufficient. Gossnab has organized itself into operating units based on both geographic territories and product type. It appears that Gosplan continues to carry out the selling and procurement functions for a few products.

All the industrial ministries engage in important activities of an industrial marketing and purchasing nature. Each has one or more organizational units with a variant of the name Main Administration for Supply and Sales. Ministries must ask for, determine, and adjust the resource requirements of enterprises subordinate to them, redivide the allocation the ministry finally receives, monitor the sales and purchases of these enterprises, measure costs and efficiency in the enterprises, and control so as to reach targets while remaining inside the operating norms.

There is considerable belief in the U.S.S.R. that more attention should be given to the operation of networks of industrial wholesale houses that would sell to any enterprise, research institute, or design bureau whether it had an allocation certificate or not. Such establishments would tend to handle unspecialized items needed in diverse types of business, such as oil products, hardware, building materials, and general-use tools.[67] Some such organizations exist, and experiments are being conducted with others.

One of the activities of Gossnab's subordinate territorial bodies is to run a network of semiregulated wholesale establishments dealing in producer goods. They sell to customers who have allocation certificates and those who do not but make some distinctions by type of product from time to time. The number of such establishments grew from 119 in 1966 to over 600 in 1970, while their sales rose from 112 million rubles to 1.5 billion rubles. Existence of these establishments serves to furnish some much-needed breathing space in the tightly drawn allocations flowing through the channels of distribution. These wholesale houses get part of their goods from central Gossnab allocations but get most by negotiating directly with enterprises that have some uncommitted regular output or unplanned surplus output. These wholesale establishments take such goods from factories and sell them for a commission payable by those factories.[68] The relative freedom of such wholesale organizations is distressing to many traditional thinkers in the U.S.S.R., but the Council of Ministers has issued decrees supporting the manner in which this set of activities is proceeding and endorsing its expansion.

The reforms of the 1960s also treated the subject of direct contracts between production enterprises and their customers and suppliers. For decades there had been contracts, but they were mere formalities imposed by superior purchasing and sales organizations. Now the U.S.S.R. is moving slowly toward encouragement of these direct contracts, in the hope of attaining stable, long-lasting relationships that will build a mutual interest in the product and its timely delivery. Gossnab and the industrial ministries are doing this work in consultation with each other, but Gossnab appears to have the upper hand. Details of the contract, but not the major thrust, are left to the two concerned enterprises to formulate. Economist N. Y. Drogichinsky believes that direct contracts should be long-term and suggests five years, especially for the largest customers, a period of time that would be basically appropriate for the way the Soviet economy is planned. He stated in 1972 that only a small part of output was covered by direct contracts but that coverage should be maximized. Schroeder's research indicates that in 1970, direct contracts affected over 7,000 of the more than 50,000 industrial enterprises, and that in 1969 such contracts were particularly important in rolled metals, nonferrous metals, cement, paper and cardboard, chemicals, storage batteries, and motors for cranes.[69] Schroeder is quite pessimistic about all of this, for she perceives as less than optimal the specific dyads that are being named and states that planners above the enterprise level keep changing the contract.[70]

Decentralization of authority is made extremely difficult, in that the broad-brush changes made at the top of the hierarchy must be reflected in successively finer detail as one approaches the factory at the bottom. In addition, although law and regulations allow for arbitration and penalties for "violation of contract discipline" in producer goods as well as consumer goods, there is not much effect at this time. The penalties on any one supplier are not financially significant, responsibility for failure can often be transferred, and there is anxiety about worsening business relationships. Moreover, there is not much faith in the fairness and universality of rule enforcement and sanctions. This refers not only to spotty enforcement but also to selective yet systematic deterrents to enforcement. If two disagreeing production enterprises report to a common superior in the hierarchy, they stand little probability of gaining an arbitration hearing, for the behavioral climate disapproves of internal strife. If the dispute is with an entity of another authority jurisdiction, the probability is higher.[71] One must conclude that the direct contract in industry has a future, but it is a clouded future.

In the traditional and still prevalent situation in which a manufacturing plant is locked into the system of centrally determined allocations of materials balances, is there some way that the plant can obtain more than its authorization or obtain it faster than the planned schedule? First, it may find, that the semiregulated wholesale supply houses have the item, although that is unlikely. Second, some fortunate factories can make some items for themselves. This is especially true for enterprises possessing a variety of sophisticated equipment and having access to a design bureau. This tactic, of course, requires some input and thus may have some effect on the rest of the plant's work. There have been instances of illicitly using money from the material incentive fund to pay for overtime employment. Third, the industrial buyers sometimes scrutinize the market for producers that might not be subject to the same set of materials balances, i.e., that are under another administrative jurisdiction. These producers may have small overages or even small uncommitted regular output, a situation that occurs with some frequency among enterprises administered at the subrepublic level. A few products, such as some motors, wheels, pumps, hinges, and paints have rather diverse applicability, no matter what their source. Fourth, some plants use tolkachi (expediters), as discussed in Chapter 1, to prod the suppliers or to locate the plants mentioned above. Fifth, there is the black market, also discussed in Chapter 1. Sixth, the enterprise may attempt something closely related to the black market. It may conspire with retailers to divert selected goods, such as building materials, hardware, tools, paper, and office supplies, from store stocks to business use, with or without fraudulently filled-in sales receipts.

Soviet economic history has recorded more failures to achieve goals in agricultural production and marketing than in manufacturing, transportation, or trade. This results from several factors: inadequate investment; unrealistic planning; unfavorable weather; farmer resistance; and the low priority of agriculture relative to industry and transport in most planning periods. Khrushchev in particular was volatile in his handling of agriculture. His successors have been less changeable. Especially noteworthy is the fact that they have provided agriculture with state purchase targets at least two or three years in advance and have tended to make relatively few major changes in these figures. However, they too have found agriculture difficult to govern. That agriculture remains a problem area was illustrated in the necessity to import large quantities of grain from the West in the early and mid-1970s; the necessity to ration some foods, including potatoes and butter, in early 1973 in several large cities; and the replacement of the Minister of Agriculture in early 1973.

National agricultural procurement is planned by the Union-Republican Ministry on Procurements, once called the State Committee of Procurements, and by the Ministry of Agriculture. Plans are eventually broken down to the farm level. Bureaucratic error is apparently common, for there are frequent complaints of farms that receive purchase plans for items that they have never produced and that are not suitable for the specified farm, and complaints that the variety specified for a particular farm makes specialization impossible. The Ministry is heavily involved also in above-plan procurements. The extent of voluntarism in these above-plan procurements has varied considerably, depending on the power structure in the hierarchy. As of the 1970s it appears that above-plan procurements are extensively planned by central authorities and are not truly voluntary.

A network of agricultural wholesale procurement stations is maintained throughout the nation. Despite shortages of many items, a long-run problem has been that these procurement locations frequently turn down agricultural deliveries. Many reasons enter into this, such as poor timing, inadequate packing materials,[72] and inadequate storage; but bureaucratic confusion is an additional explanation. Other important factors are the unsettled question of the exact authority of product inspectors and irregularities in their standardization and grading of products.[73] It appears that this problem has lessened a bit in recent years; but it is still important, especially in perishable commodities. Complicated plans and organization structure, coupled with poor flow of information in the channels and among the farmers, transport, and storage authorities, makes selling and delivery difficult. As one farming executive said bitterly, "It's easier to grow the harvest than it is to sell it." He added that marketing his products became more complicated every year.[74] Moreover, some agricultural goods meant for the procurement network never reach it because of the acute shortage of trucks and the almost unbelievable conditions of rural roads.

Procurement prices have sometimes allowed large profits on particular items, but much of the time have allowed very thin profits— or losses. Subsidies have been common. A recurring factor has been that of territorial differentiation of procurement prices.[75] Moreover, most of the time the prices paid state farms have been different from those paid collective farms, a fact that is not meaningful unless one relates it to the differential amounts of investment the state puts into farming and supporting services. Payments to farms for above-plan procurements normally carry a premium, often as much as 50 percent. Prices are often differentiated also on the technological level of the farm and on its natural advantages, such as soil and water.

The agro-industrial complex is discussed with considerable enthusiasm today and already exists on a very small scale. The essence of this idea is that industrial methods should be increasingly used on farms, economies of scale should be exploited, and channels should be so arranged that the resources, plans, and output of specific specialized farms are linked to particular processing and manufacturing plants. Permanent arrangements for storage and transport during and following the activities of growing, processing, and manufacturing, plus contracts with wholesalers and large retailers, are also envisioned. It appears that much of the early work in implementing this concept is going into beef, lamb, pork, milk, poultry, and eggs[76] rather than industrial crops. Another relatively new concept is the inter-collective farm enterprise, which appears to be a variant of the agro-industrial complex. Under this concept several farms may send young animals to a feed-lot operation for fattening. Although it provides some needed specialization and scalar economies, it is perplexing in that authority and responsibility are not carefully delineated, especially as to time of slaughtering, sale of the output, prices, and time of payment. Ways of handling these matters vary from one jurisdiction to the next.[77]

Although farmers' marketplaces were a traditional feature of pre-Revolution Russian marketing, their continued existence is quite interesting. Usually called kolkhoz markets, they are outlets for (1) products which collective farms have left after meeting government delivery contracts and above-plan agreements and (2) products which residents of the collective farms raise on their small individual household plots and wish to sell. According to Soviet ideology there should be no need for this institution, and its continued existence is mildly embarrassing to some politicians and thinkers. Feelings are fairly well typified by this statement of a Soviet scholar:

> In the future, the communal sector is to be the only one and is to provide all the country's agricultural products. . . . Premature abandonment of farmers' private plots would mean a "leftist" leap across necessary stages of development. . . . It will be some time before we can do without collective farmers' private plots.[78]

Marketplaces are usually taken care of by local party functionaries and municipal trade authorities. Almost every town, except those on the settlement frontier, has at least one, while Moscow has 40.[79] Construction of new market facilities is geographically biased. The Ukraine, which is more ideologically disposed toward this institution, completed 10 new ones, with a total of 2,200 stalls, in 1969 and builds more new ones each year.[80] On the other hand, Soviet Central Asia discriminates against this institution, and local authorities there have assigned a significant fraction of the booths and other facilities to the state retail store network. According to the Russian Republic Ministry of Trade, the former practice of transferring into the local area budget about half of the service and rental fees that the farmers' marketplace collected has been prohibited. All such income is now supposed to go into administration and improvement of the marketplace. In addition, the restrictions against marketplaces at railroad stations and on river and lake piers have been lifted by the transport ministries.[81] So-called trade service bureaus exist in some of the marketplaces. Staffed by market personnel, they offer to take an animal carcass and pay the farmer 15 to 20 percent less than he would get if he sold it in individual cuts. It frees his time for alternative work.[82] It is widely believed that the hierarchies of the state and cooperative store networks oppose this practice. The cooperative stores also offer a trade plan, whereby they take the products and offer them for sale in the marketplace for a commission, often as high as 10 percent. They tend to ask slightly lower prices than the farmers who act as individuals but slightly higher prices than what the retail stores ask.

Prices fluctuate considerably in these marketplaces but generally are higher than government-set prices in retail stores because of the higher quality of the items and because government prices do not necessarily reflect scarcity. The government's toleration of the interplay of supply and demand in these marketplaces is an intriguing but very limited incidence of the Western-type free market. As a matter of fact, local officials occasionally intervene because of extremely high prices and impose temporary ceilings on selected goods.

For example, in 1969 ceilings of double the retail store price were used in Moscow and several other cities.[83] Whether intervention is desirable and justified is being argued at this time. It appears to conflict with the general tone and spirit of agricultural policy emanating from the top political leadership in recent years.

An example of this institution is the marketplace of Sochi, a city of about 65,000 on the eastern shore of the Black Sea. Located in the center of town, nestled among public buildings and adjoining a park, it is an L-shaped, open-air market with about 40 stalls made of concrete and wood, some of them canopied. It is meticulously clean and staffed almost entirely by women and elderly men. Because of the mild climate, it is in use constantly. Another example is the central market of Kiev, which occupies a large enclosed permanent building in the heart of the shopping district. It includes well over 300 stalls and also some limited preparation areas.

Some collective farms operate stalls in nearby marketplaces on almost a permanent basis. Some visit distant marketplaces from time to time. As an Izvestia staff columnist put it in describing a central Russian marketplace, "A robust fellow with a southern suntan at springtime demands an unimaginable price for his product. . . ."[84] Russian scholar N. Ya. Bromlei has calculated that "Profits from private plots constitute 30 to 50 percent of the actual earnings of a collective farmer."[85] Gosplan calculates that kolkhoz farmers received 41.3 percent of their total incomes from the private sector in 1965, but not all of this was through the marketplaces. The corresponding figures for 1970 and 1975 were anticipated to be 32 percent and 25 percent.[86] There are perhaps three keys to the forecasts. One is the plan to consolidate many tiny agricultural villages into larger communities. This plan will put the farmer at a greater distance from his main private holding. Another factor is that rural retail trade facilities are scheduled to improve, thus possibly permitting the farmer to deviate from his traditional self-sufficiency. Another is the improving payments by the collective to the farmer for his labor.

Kolkhoz marketplaces remain a sound institution, and their absolute volume of sales has been rather stable for many years. Nevertheless, their share of retail trade in the economy is slowly decreasing. They accounted for about 2.8 percent of total retail sales in the late 1960s, versus about 12 percent in the early 1950s. They are, naturally, a much more significant factor in the sale of foods. In a 1970 statement, the Ministry of Trade estimated that farmers' markets in 1968 conducted about 8.6 percent of the retail sales in the combined food categories in which they usually specialize (vegetables, fruits, eggs, milk, and potatoes).[87]

Economist V. Makarova reports that, as of 1970, the private
sector accounted for 65 percent of the potatoes, 53 percent of the eggs,
38 percent of the vegetables, 36 percent of the milk, 35 percent of the
meat, and 19 percent of the wool produced. Not all of this was marketed, of course. Much was consumed by the growers or bartered to
other growers. However, 19 percent of the eggs, 17 percent of the
meat, and 41 percent of the potatoes marketed were from the private
sector. The private sector in 1970 held 25.1 percent of the beef cattle,
20.8 percent of the sheep, 26 percent of the pigs, and 81.3 percent of
the goats, and used 2.94 percent of the plowland.[88]

NOTES

1. Ekonomicheskaya Gazeta, no. 6 (1968), 10-11.
2. V. Sitnin, "The Five-Year Plan and Price Formation," Izvestia, March 5, 1971, p. 3. CDSP, 23 (March 30, 1971), 5-6.
3. E. G. Liberman, Economic Methods and the Effectiveness of
Production (White Plains, N.Y.: International Arts and Sciences Press,
1971), p. 165. This book was first published in Moscow by Ekonomika
Publishing House in 1970.
4. Ibid., p. 172.
5. Alec Nove, The Soviet Economy (2d rev. ed.; New York:
Praeger Publishers, 1969), p. 149.
6. A. Chernets, "Coal Oddities," Izvestia, July 22, 1965, p. 3.
CDSP, 17 (August 11, 1965), 36-37.
7. For materials on pricing in connection with rationing from
1929 to 1936 and during and following World War II, see A. Baykov,
The Development of the Soviet Economic System (New York: Macmillan,
1947), pp. 236-39, 251-52; Nikolai A. Voznesensky, The Soviet Economy
During World War II (Washington, D.C.: Public Affairs Press, 1948);
and A. Arakelian, Industrial Management in the U.S.S.R. (Washington,
D.C.: Public Affairs Press, 1950).
8. On Soviet general accounting and cost accounting, see the
following: Robert H. Mills and Abbott L. Brown, "Soviet Economic
Developments and Accounting," Journal of Accountancy, 121 (June
1966), 40-46, reprinted in Kenneth B. Berg, G. G. Muelier, and Lauren
M. Walker, Readings in International Accounting (Boston: Houghton
Mifflin, 1969), pp. 113-23; Richard B. Purdue and E. De Maris, "Accounting in the U.S.S.R.," Journal of Accountancy, 108 (July 1959), 47-
57; Robert W. Campbell, "Soviet Accounting and Economic Decisions,"
in W. T. Baxter and Sidney Davidson, eds., Studies in Accounting
(Homewood, Ill.: Richard D. Irwin, 1962), pp. 357-58; Myron Sharpe,
ed., Planning, Profit and Incentives in the U.S.S.R. (White Plains,
N.Y.: International Arts and Sciences Press, 1966); Robert W.

142

Campbell, Accounting in Soviet Planning and Management (Cambridge, Mass.: Harvard University Press, 1963); David Granick, Management of the Industrial Firm in the U.S.S.R. (New York: Columbia University Press, 1954); David Granick, The Red Executive (Garden City, N.Y.: Doubleday, 1960); Joseph S. Berliner, Factory and Manager in the U.S.S.R. (Cambridge, Mass.: Harvard University Press, 1957); and Leonard D. Goldberg, Crediting According to Turnover (Seattle: College of Business, University of Washington, 1965).

9. A. Gamedov and L. Tairov, "The Little Gilded Glass," Pravda, June 15, 1972, p. 3. CDSP, 24 (July 12, 1972), 26.

10. Nove, The Soviet Economy, p. 152.

11. Sh. Turetski, as cited in Nove, The Soviet Economy, p. 152.

12. Ibid.

13. Marshall I. Goldman, Soviet Marketing: Distribution in a Controlled Economy (New York: Free Press of Glencoe, 1963), p. 92.

14. V. Sitnin, "The Five-Year Plan and Price Formation."

15. I. Babynin, "Problems of Prognostication," Ekonomicheskaya Gazeta, no. 51 (December 1970), 15. CDSP, 22 (January 26, 1971), 25.

16. V. Brzak and D. Marsikova, "New Methods of Management and Organization of Foreign Trade in Socialist Countries," Soviet and East European Foreign Trade, 6, no. 3-4 (Fall-Winter 1970), 214-67.

17. N. Kotelevsky, "The Role of Prices in Regulating Demand and Supply of Consumer Goods," Problems of Economics, 7, no. 3 (July 1964), 16-20, at 20. Also see Evan E. Anderson, "Soviet Retail Pricing," Journal of Retailing, 44 (Summer 1968), 61-69, at 67; and Reed Moyer, "Marketing in the Iron Curtain Countries," Journal of Marketing, 30 (October 1966), 3-9, at 8.

18. M. Iosolevich, "Goods with Buyer Appeal," Izvestia, February 26, 1972, p. 2. CDSP, 24 (March 22, 1972), 29.

19. M. Bakanov, S. Serebriakov, and A. Fefilov, "Profitability of Trade," Pravda, March 31, 1967, p. 2. CDSP, 19 (April 19, 1967), 36-37.

20. Ya. Orlov, "Experiment in Progress: Blank Spots in the Reform," Pravda, November 23, 1969, p. 3. CDSP, 21 (December 17, 1969), 31-32.

21. Iosolevich, "Goods with Buyer Appeal."

22. M. Shamenov, "'Sliding' Prices," Sovetskaya Kirghiziya, December 4, 1969, p. 3. JPRS, 50034; TOUTAS, 93.

23. Ibid.

24. Jere L. Felker, Soviet Economic Controversies: The Emerging Marketing Concept and Changes in Planning, 1960-1965 (Cambridge, Mass.: MIT Press, 1966), p. 118.

25. George R. Feiwel, The Soviet Quest for Economic Efficiency: Issues, Controversies, and Reforms (New York: Praeger Publishers, 1967), pp. 132-33.

26. Kotelevsky, "The Role of Prices," p. 17; and Felker, Soviet Economic Controversies, p. 117. "Discussion on Problems of Price Formation," Voprosy Ekonomiki, No. 7, 1963 (translation).

27. See. V. Chernysheva, Problems of Economics, 7 no. 4, (August 1964) 36-50; and Felker, Soviet Economic Controversies, pp. 127-28.

28. N. Orlov and I. Balabanov, "Prices for New Items," Ekonomicheskaya Gazeta, no. 31 (July 1969), 11. CDSP, 21 (October 15, 1969), 10-11; and L. Gusarov, "Price Is the Instrument of the Plan," Ekonomicheskaya Gazeta, no. 40 (October 1969), 5-6. CDSP, 21 (November 19, 1969), 15-17.

29. Moscow Financial Institute, Soviet Financial System (Moscow: Progress Publishers, 1966), p. 177.

30. Ibid., pp. 186-87.

31. P. Os'kin, "Certain Questions of Improving the Turnover Tax," Finansy SSSR, no. 5 (1971), 44-49. JPRS, 53728; TUEA, 274.

32. Philip Hanson, The Consumer in the Soviet Economy (Evanston: Northwestern University Press, 1968), p. 108.

33. Morris Bornstein, "The Soviet Price System," in Morris Bornstein and Daniel R. Fusfeld, eds., The Soviet Economy: A Book of Readings (Homewood, Ill.: Richard D. Irwin, 1962), pp. 112-44, at 119.

34. Os'kin, "Certain Questions."

35. Soviet Financial System, p. 192.

36. Karl Marx, Capital, vol. I. Reproduced in Robert Freedman, ed., Marx on Economics (New York: Harcourt, Brace & World, 1961), pp. 29-33, at p. 32.

37. For discussion of Soviet arguments during the 1940s, 1950s, and early 1960s, see Felker, Soviet Economic Controversies, pp. 120-29; Nove, The Soviet Economy, pp. 300-13; and P. J. D. Wiles, The Political Economy of Communism (Oxford: Basil Blackwell, 1964).

38. For example, see R. Campbell, "Marx, Kantorovich and Novozhilov: Stoimost Versus Reality," Slavic Review, 20 (October 1961), 402-18; Nove, The Soviet Economy, pp. 305-13; Michael Ellman, Soviet Planning Today: Proposals for an Optimally Functioning Economic System (Cambridge: Cambridge University Press, 1971), pp. 1-8, 28-52; and G. Sorokin, Planning in the U.S.S.R.: Problems of Theory and Organization (Moscow: Progress Publishers, 1967), pp. 41-56.

39. See Ronald L. Meek, Studies on the Labour Theory of Value (London: Lawrence & Wishart, 1956), p. 261.

40. Goldman, Soviet Marketing, p. 101.

41. Also see V. Pereslegin, Finance and Credit in the U.S.S.R. (Moscow: Progress Publishers, 1971), pp. 91-116.

42. Margaret Miller, Teresa M. Piotrowicz, Ljubo Sirc, and Henry Smith, Communist Economy Under Change (London: Andre Deutsch for Institute of Economic Affairs, 1963), p. 19.

43. As quoted in V. I. Gogol, "The Role of Wholesaling in the Distribution of Goods," from his book The Economics of Trade in the Soviet Union. A long passage from Gogol is reproduced in Robert Bartels, Comparative Marketing: Wholesaling in Fifteen Countries (Homewood, Ill.: Richard D. Irwin, 1963), pp. 227-50, see p. 234

44. Bartels, Comparative Marketing, p. 239.

45. E. G. Liberman, Economic Methods and the Effectiveness of Production, p. 14.

46. M. Karzanova, "Industry, Trade and the Contract," Izvestia, December 17, 1971, p. 3. CDSP, 23 (January 11, 1972), 13.

47. A. Shapovalov, Ekonomicheskaya Gazeta no. 30 (1971), 17.

48. See Leonard E. Hubbard, Soviet Trade and Distribution (London: Macmillan, 1938), p. 148; and Ronald F. Drew, "The Siberian Fair: 1600-1750," Slavonic and East European Review, 39 (June 1961), 422-39.

49. For example, see D. Frandetti, "Why Footwear Travels Around," Pravda, June 8, 1972, p. 3. CDSP, 24 (July 5, 1972), 27.

50. See Murray Seeger, "To the Beach, Expenses Paid," Washington Post, August 31, 1972, p. G-1.

51. I. Kashtelyan, "On the Path to the Consumer," Pravda, May 10, 1972, p. 3. CDSP, 24 (June 7, 1972), 30-31.

52. I. Mironenko, "Who Is the Primary Customer?," Pravda, June 24, 1972, p. 2. CDSP, 24 (July 17, 1972), 25-26.

53. V. Shimanskiy, "The Consumer—Trade—Production," Ekonomicheskaya Gazeta, no. 23 (June 1971), 15-16. JPRS, 53595; TOUTAS, 257.

54. Kashtelyan, "On the Path to the Consumer."

55. Mironenko, "Who Is the Primary Customer?"

56. N. Dumin, "Instructions on the Procedure for Receiving Products and Commodities Need Clarification," Sovetskaya Yustitsiya, no. 18 (September 1970), 16-17. JPRS, 51783; TUEA, 181.

57. B. Mochalov, "Higher Schools, Specialists and the Law," Izvestia, June 9, 1972, p. 3. CDSP, 24 (July 5, 1972), 32-33.

58. Liberman, Economic Methods, pp. 39-40.

59. Ya. Orlov, "Consumer Demand Is the Guideline—How to Develop Trade," Pravda, April 15, 1971, p. 3. CDSP, 23 (May 11, 1971), 43-44.

60. For example, see Izvestia, January 11, 1972, p. 1; January 13, 1972, p. 2; January 14, 1972, p. 4. CDSP, 24 (February 9, 1972), pp. 12-13; and Ekonomicheskaya Gazeta, no. 19 (May 1970), 17.

61. "Contractual Obligations," Izvestia, April 25, 1972, p. 3. CDSP, 24 (May 24, 1972), 24-25; Karzanova, "Industry, Trade and the Contract."

62. G. Ustinov, "The Important Role of Arbitration," Izvestia, November 27, 1971, p. 3. CDSP, 23 (December 28, 1971), 26-27.

63. "Contractual Obligations."

64. Helpful but sometimes rather critical descriptions of the planning process can be found in the following: W. Leontief, "The Fall and Rise of Soviet Economics," Foreign Affairs, 38 (January 1960), 261-72; Nove, The Soviet Economy, pp. 87-96; George R. Feiwel, The Soviet Quest for Economic Efficiency: Issues, Controversies, and Reforms (New York: Praeger Publishers, 1967), pp. 66-78; and Edward Ames, Soviet Economic Processes (Homewood, Ill.: Richard D. Irwin, 1965), pp. 72-75. Description of procurement at the enterprise level can be found in Dean G. Farrer, "Soviet Industrial Purchasing Agent," Journal of Purchasing, 5 (November 1969), 41-52

65. Nikolai Fedoryenko, "Economico-Mathematical Methods in Planning and Management," in Nikolai Fedoryenko et al., Soviet Economic Reform: Progress and Problems (Moscow: Progress Publishers, 1972), pp. 101-151, at pp. 109-11.

66. Gertrude Schroeder, "The 'Reform' of the Supply System in Soviet Industry," Soviet Studies, 24 (July 1972), 97-119, at 99-100.

67. See N. Y. Drogichinsky, "The Economic Reform in Action," in Fedoryenko et al., Soviet Economic Reform, pp. 188-228, at p. 216.

68. See Schroeder, "The 'Reform' of the Supply System," pp. 108-09.

69. Ibid., pp. 105-06.

70. Ibid., p. 106.

71. See G. Ivanov, "Why the Footwear Factory Did Not Fulfill Its Annual Assignment," Pravda, January 11, 1972, p. 2. CDSP, 24 (February 9, 1972), 4-5.

72. For example, see N. Laptev, "The Perfidious Apple Stem," Pravda, October 25, 1971, p. 4. CDSP, 23 (November 24, 1971), 25.

73. For example, see A. Yershov, "What the Inspector Can Do," Izvestia, February 23, 1972, p. 3. CDSP, 24 (March 22, 1972), 27-28.

74. G. Borisenko, "Where Should Fruit Be Marketed?," Pravda, July 21, 1965, p. 2. CDSP, 17 (August 11, 1965), 36.

75. See Keith Bush, "Soviet Agriculture in the 1970's," Studies on the Soviet Union, new series, 9, no. 3 (1971), 1-45.

76. For example, see Ye. Gregoryev and A. Karamyshev, "First Steps of the Animal-Husbandry Complexes," Pravda, February 22, 1972, p. 3. CDSP, 24 (March 22, 1972), 16-17.

77. See B. Pleshchkov, "Improve the Work of Inter-Collective Farm Enterprises," Pravda, October 31, 1972, p. 2. CDSP, 24 (November 29, 1972), 10-11.

78. V. A. Golikov, "On Certain Questions of C.P.S.U. Policy in the Area of Agriculture at the Present Stage," Voprosi Istorii KPSS, no. 7 (July 1972), 16-30. CDSP, 24 (November 29, 1972), 14.

79. V. Panov, Moskva, March 3, 1969, pp. 165-81. JPRS, 48336; TOUTAS, 29.

80. See N. Kuzmenkov, "The Kolkhoz Market Under the New Conditions," Sovetskaya Torgovlya, May 23, 1970, p. 3. JPRS, 50727; TOUTAS, 131.

81. "Let Collective Farm Markets Prosper," Izvestia, February 5, 1966, p. 4. CDSP, 18 (February 23, 1966), 26-27.

82. A. Nizhegorodov and M. Stoikevich, "Offered by the Market," Pravda, October 3, 1972, p. 6. CDSP, 24 (November 1, 1972), pp. 22-23; and "Editorial: The Collective Farm Market," Sovetskaya Torgovlya, September 9, 1972, p. 1. CDSP, 25 (April 4, 1973), 22.

83. Handelsblatt, June 19, 1969.

84. N. Koshelev, "The Collective-Farm Market," Izvestia, July 31, 1970, p. 3. CDSP, 22 (September 1, 1970), 14-15.

85. "The Standard of Living in the U.S.S.R.," Voprosy Istorii, no. 7 (1966), 13, as quoted in Simon Kabysh, "New Policy on the Private Plots," Studies on the Soviet Union, new series, 6, no. 1 (1966), 26-24, at 34. Also see Philip Grossman, "A Note on Agricultural Employment in the U.S.S.R.," Soviet Studies, 19 (January 1968), 398-404.

86. I. A. Gorlanov, in Bush, "Soviet Agriculture in the 1970's."

87. "Figures and Facts," Sovetskaya Torgovlya, no. 4 (April 1970), 58-63. JPRS, 50700; TOUTAS, 130.

88. V. Makarova, "The Combination of Communal and Private Sectors," Ekonomika Selskovo Khozyaistva, no. 6 (June 1972), 54-60. CDSP, 24 (November 29, 1972), 13-14.

6

**TRANSPORTATION
AND PHYSICAL
DISTRIBUTION**

TRANSPORTATION

The various resources of an economy and the markets for those resources are tied together by transportation and physical distribution. In an economy as large and complex as that of the U.S.S.R. there must be a rather sophisticated and intricate set of transportation networks. Physical size of the country is also a significant factor. The largest country in the world in area, the U.S.S.R. has about 8,599,000 square miles, or more than twice the area of the United States. It stretches almost 6,000 miles from east to west and over 2,800 miles from north to south. About two-thirds of its borders are water, but much of that is nonnavigable except in summer.[1]

Although Soviet transportation remains rather self-oriented, there are stirrings in the system that are somewhat encouraging to both the intermediate and the ultimate consumer. According to orthodox Communist doctrine, transportation is a necessary evil. The traffic that necessitates the existence of a transportation system should be more the recipient of influence—i.e., the object of cost-cutting, perfect time regularity, and demand diminution—than a factor of influence on the transport services and facilities provided. There has been no explicit "common carrier" concept in Soviet thought. Indeed, to profess such ideas would have been professionally dangerous. Even in Tsarist times, there was no great tradition of service, no competition among the rail companies, and almost no duplicate routes. In fact, about two-thirds of the rail system was government-owned and -operated even then.[2] Besides their commercial applications, the railroads were sometimes used by the Tsars as political tools and for expansion of Russian borders in Asia. Nevertheless, to the chagrin of some people and to the approval of others, the common carriers of today do not intervene to any great extent in the affairs of shippers and consignees. However, at least the railroads apparently believe in the theoretical desirability of such authority.

Railroads

The Soviet Union has been a railroad economy, but the dominance of the rails has been declining markedly since the early 1960s. This mode of transport accounted for about 80 percent of intercity domestic freight, measured in ton-kilometers, in 1928, rose through the late 1930s to 87 percent in 1940, reached an all-time high of 91 percent in 1945, and remained around 89 percent until the early 1960s.[3] Prior to the early 1960s there was only infinitesimally small intercity freight movement by truck. Since that time the planners and political leaders have put increasing amounts of resources into highways, city streets, and trucks, as well as into pipelines. Railroad freight still shows absolute growth, and the 1971-75 Plan specifies a growth of 22 percent in ton-kilometers. Precise data on the relative decline of the railways are not available at this time. Indeed, the data are inconsistent. Premier Kosygin and the official reports of the 24th Congress of the Communist Party have used a figure of about two-thirds to describe the share of the market the railways now command.[4] Exactly what is included in the data base from which that figure was derived is unknown. Perhaps the most bothersome question concerns the amount of freight hauled in trucks not operated by common carriers.

Although the U.S.S.R. had over 83,500 miles of railroad route at the end of 1970 and ranks second in the world after the United States, the geographical coverage remains thin. Moreover, 45 to 50 percent of the rail route system accounts for 85 percent of the freight turnover.[5] Approximately 80 percent of Soviet track is of 5-foot gauge, a result of the advice many years ago of an American consultant, George W. Whistler, father of the painter James McNeill Whistler. He reasoned that this figure was more satisfying than the popular 4 feet, 8.5 inches and that the Russian projects would be isolated tracks, not parts of a giant future system.[6] The other 20 percent of the tracks have gauges of 2 feet, 6 inches; 1 foot, 11.675 inches; and 3 feet, 6 inches. The most narrow gauge is found in some of the new agricultural lands. The Soviet rails match in gauge only with Finland among the nation's European neighbors.

The Soviet Union is one of the few countries with an active railroad expansion program. Every year at least a few hundred miles of route is added and some double-tracking done. This is in addition to sizable efforts at building and improving yards, sidings, spurs, control equipment, and other facilities. Second track totaled about 22,600 miles at the end of 1970.

Rail links to Soviet Central Asia and their role in regional economic development have been controversial for many years but have received heavy investment.[7] One of the most important projects completed in the 1966-70 Five-Year Plan was the Gurzov to Astrakhan route along the north shore of the Caspian Sea. This 207-mile connection shortened the distance from the Central Asian republics and Kazakhstan to the Caucasus and southern Russia by 400 miles and also relieved the pressure on the southern Urals lines. Two of the major projects of the 1961-65 Plan affected these same regions. In an effort to connect Soviet Central Asia and the Caucasus, a railway ferry service was established on the Caspian Sea between Baku and Krasnovodsk. In addition, a 78-mile route from Samarkand to Karshi was built.

Major new routes scheduled for the 1971-75 period include completion of the 430-mile railway from Tyumen to Surgut on the Ob River, begun under the 1966-70 Plan in order to link new oil fields in western Siberia with the existing rail network. Other important projects are completion of the Khrebtovaya-Ust-Ilim railway in eastern Siberia and the 250-mile connection between Beineu and Kungrad, which will significantly shorten the distance between the western part of Soviet Central Asia and the European part of the nation. New routes totaling nearly 3,500 miles in length are planned for the 1971-75 period versus 2,300 miles in the 1966-70 period. Second tracks are scheduled for several heavily used lines, including Leningrad-Murmansk, Karaganda-Tashkent, Tselinograd-Barnaul, and Moscow-Kazan-Sverdlovsk. Second tracks totaling 4,300 to 4,900 miles will be laid, versus only 1,200 miles in the 1966-70 period.[8] One Soviet transportation specialist argues, however, that construction of 15,500 miles of second track is needed during the 1970s to cope with traffic forecasted for 1980.[9] The proportion of second track to total mileage was almost constant during the 1960s.[10]

The rails of the western half of the U.S.S.R. converge near Taishet; and from that linking point east to a point near the Pacific littoral there is only one line, the fabled Trans-Siberian. Opened in 1916, it is now completely double-tracked. Because of economic needs in Siberia and because the route runs very close to the Chinese border in several places, a somewhat parallel rail route to the north is planned, parts of which may be under construction. The Trans-Siberian line, Turkestan-Siberian line, South Siberian line, and others have fostered corridor-type market development not unlike that of the early western United States. However, in the Soviet Union since 1917 the primary intention of railroad construction has tended not to be general economic development of a territory. It has been specific:

for example, the exploitation of particular mineral deposits, the cultivation of the soils of a particular valley, or access to a certain site for a hydroelectric station. In addition, there has been an occasional construction project that appeared to be militarily or at least geopolitically inspired.

There was a massive effort throughout the 1960s to convert railroads to electric and diesel traction. By the end of 1970 the length so converted totaled 68,000 miles. In 1970 electric and diesel locomotives accounted for 96.5 percent of all ton-kilometers of freight moved.[11] This represented a complete reversal in two decades, for in 1950 steam locomotives accounted for 95 percent of the freight ton-kilometers handled.[12] Lenin and others had urged conversion from the very beginning; but through the years internal politics, technological conservatism, finances, and initially badly designed diesel locomotives[13] had held back the changeover. In 1941 there were only 1,159 miles of electrified line. About 3,600 miles of line will be electrified during the 1971-75 period.

Rolling stock will be increased by 425,000 freight cars during the 1971-75 Plan, a figure about 65 percent higher than the increase registered during the 1966-70 period. There is a renewed emphasis on larger-capacity freight cars and all-metal construction. In all likelihood, however, the need for diverse types of specialized cars will not be met; and probably many defective and inadequate cars will not be replaced. In one celebrated case, the use of unsuitable cars has meant the waste of an average of 50 carloads of iron ore a day between the Mikhailovka Ore Combine and its metallurgical plant customers.[14]

Operating characteristics are interesting. Differentiation of train speed has been slight. Providing fast freight services significantly interferes with constancy of speed, a factor necessary to reach the overriding objective of Soviet railways to maximize the line capacity. The time and distance between trains on a given line are short by American standards. However, the All-Union Railway Transport Research Institute and other organizations are aware of the need for fast freight service and have conducted some experiments with it in recent years. Perhaps just as great a need is research on reduction of demurrage.[15] Nevertheless, one cannot fail to be impressed by the amount of freight movement the Russians are able to extract from their limited facilities.

Motor Transport

Except for a few areas such as Transcaucasia, the U.S.S.R. has not relied heavily on motor transport in the past. However, recent

Five-Year Plans have attempted to relieve the pressure on railways by increasing the reliance on highways. In addition, one would expect that as consumer goods output grows and the planners and executives give more attention to variety in such goods, the need for the normal operating characteristics of motor freight will also grow. A large increase in common carrier motor freight, especially of the short-haul type, is scheduled for the 1971-75 period. It was originally intended that common-carrier truck freight, measured in ton-kilo-meters, would increase 60 percent during the 1971-75 period, versus an increase of 22 percent on the railways.[16] However, in 1972 the 1975 goal was scaled down to 338 billion ton-kilometers, which would represent a 53 percent rise over 1970.[17] The growth was 54 percent between 1965 and 1970 and 45 percent between 1960 and 1965.[18]

Deputy Minister of Foreign Trade Nikolai Smelyakov, who has spent much time researching and observing in the United States, has been one of the leading proponents of motor freight and highway expansion. He has said:

> All expenses, no matter how great, will be compensated a hundred times over. It is no accident that American advertisements depict roads with dollars moving along down them—symbols of the advantages and profitability to be derived from their construction. . . . The economic importance of highways can hardly be over-estimated.[19]

Data on roads and trucks and their use are helpful and allow identification of general conditions and trends; but one must be cautious, for the data are inconsistent and are sometimes based on varying definitions. As of 1971 there were 1.3 million kilometers in the non-city road network, of which 511,000 kilometers, or 37 percent, were hard-surfaced. An unknown but small fraction of this was of concrete or asphalt. The 1966-70 Eighth Five-Year Plan added 132,600 kilometers of hard-surfaced roads, while the Ninth Plan specifies additions of 110,000 to 130,000 kilometers of such roads.[20] Over 5 billion rubles were spent on road construction during the 1966-70 period. However, the building of roads is limited by several factors. Climate and terrain militate against highway construction and maintenance and motor freight in large parts of the nation where the winter is long, snow drifts accumulate, and poorly drained soils and permafrost conditions create heaving and buckling of surfaces. Moreover, there are the factors of undependable equipment and the practice of usually performing only one daily shift of work even in good weather.[21] Competition for the scarce road construction funds is vigorous. There are five principal categories of use that are competing for the authorizations and funds: established agricultural areas; underdeveloped and new agricultural areas; districts undergoing industrialization; corridors between major metropolitan areas; and expressways near and around large cities.

The great bulk of hard-surfaced roads is in the European part of the country. However, major projects for the 1971-75 period whose construction will continue into the 1976-80 period include a highway from Moscow all the way to the Soviet Far East and a large road project in certain Uzbekistani areas that lack railways. Bridge construction is, of course, in competition with roadways. In remote parts of Siberia, the Arctic North, and the Far East, traffic even on good roads often must use ferries for passage across rivers. In winter the ice becomes a temporary bridge.

In recent years there have been countless complaints and suggestions about improving road construction, but most of the thinking falls into certain patterns. One is merely to solve the shortage of asphalt. Another is that road construction organizations be restructured, perhaps combined, and be assigned appropriate specialists and equipment. Another is to increase bank credit for farms that do not currently have funds but reasonably expect to generate them in the future and want roads now. Still another is amending and standardizing the widely varying percentage of their incomes that trucking lines pay out for road construction and maintenance. This figure is said to be 4 percent in the Ukraine but only 2 percent in the Russian Republic.[22]

Few city streets were designed to accommodate the heavy truck traffic and local passenger car traffic that will develop in the years ahead. In fact, only about 60 percent of the streets are hard-surfaced in several major cities, such as Gorky, Donetsk, Kuibyshev, and Novosibirsk; and the buses can move through them now at only five to six miles an hour.[23] Many communities are formulating ambitious, but as yet unfinanced, plans for expressway systems. The grandest scheme is that of Moscow Province, which specifies a 372-mile-long set of six expressways, in places eight lanes wide in each direction. They would radiate in all directions from Moscow's already completed 67-mile-long outer beltway. Surveying work was begun in 1972.[24]

Production of trucks has been increasing but lags far behind the need. The planned 1975 output in units is to be about 50 percent gre greater than 1970.[25] One of the largest projects of the decade is the Kama Automotive Works at Naberezhniye Chelny, which will produce about 150,000 high-load-capacity trucks annually plus an unspecified number of trailers.[26] Six new enterprises will supply it with components. The absolute output of light-load trucks, much in demand by factories and trade enterprises, as well as that of trailers and vehicles suitable for extremely cold climates, is being increased steadily; but the percentage of production devoted to high-capacity vehicles is rising. The Ministry of the Motor Vehicle Industry announced that at the end of the 1961-65 Plan the mean average load capacity of trucks produced was 3.76 tons, but in 1970 it was 4.5 tons. In 1975 it is scheduled to be 5.0 tons.[27]

The operations of truck fleets are a perennial subject of complaint and investigation. Great amounts of time are lost through illogical routes, mechanical breakdowns, lengthy loading and unloading work, and erroneous dispatching instructions.[28] Empty and near-empty trucks are so common that load inspection stations on the highways have been given the authority to order drivers to stop and pick up additional cargo, even if it is several miles off the route. Sometimes this policy can have adverse results. In one celebrated case a factory-owned truck that set out to pick up motors that had arrived by air freight was side-dispatched by a highway load inspector. Finally, after nearly 24 hours, the truck arrived back at its calculator plant home to find production had had to stop.[29] Moreover, problems of servicing and repairing trucks are quite severe.[30] On the other hand, the Ministry of the Motor Vehicle Industry claims that aggregate ton-kilometer costs dropped from 6.1 to 5.3 kopecks between 1965 and 1970 and should drop to 4.8 kopecks in 1975. This reduction has been occurring, however, because of the changing design characteristics of the vehicle stock itself.[31] In addition, there is growing concern about and some progress in safety consciousness, safety devices, driving rules, traffic regulation enforcement, and the notoriously poor services along the highways.

There is considerable disagreement on how large and how important common-carrier motor freight should be relative to the motor freight carried on by enterprises. The dispersion of trucks and related repair equipment is illustrated by Khabarovsk Territory, where each of about 2,000 enterprises belonging to 22 different ministries and departments possesses from one to 20 trucks.[32] In Belorussia, the network of rural cooperative stores has acquired and operates more than 1,000 tractor-trailers to transport their merchandise.[33] Proponents of common carriers point to cargo consolidation and avoidance of empty runs. The Deputy Minister of Motor Transport for the Russian Republic asserts that common carriers use 15 to 20 percent less fuel and lubricants.[34] Among proponents there is a vigorous argument as to the optimum size for common carriers.[35]

Pipelines

Until the late 1950s pipelines played little part in Soviet transportation. This fact is explained principally in that production of oil and gas was not large and the production was geographically scattered. Small fields need only small-diameter pipe, and small-diameter pipe offers no cost savings over rail and barge movement. What is more, the relatively small number of trucks, cars, and farm vehicles did not exert much demand pressure on production and distribution of petroleum-based products. However, between 1950 and 1955, the volume carried by the pipelines, measured in billions of short ton-miles, almost tripled. Then between 1955 and 1960 the volume more than tripled again and reached the fairly important level of 35.1 billion short ton-miles.[36] There was further growth during the 1960s. As of 1967 there were 18,600 miles of pipeline for oil and 29,100 for natural gas.[37]

The 1971-75 Five-Year Plan includes a 50 percent increase in the volume of natural gas and 100 percent increase in the volume of oil carried by the pipelines.[38] Progress on actual construction of sections of new lines in recent years has been quite substantial, including the oil pipeline across Siberia to the Pacific.[39] Pipelines for oil and gas have been built to Eastern, Central, and even Western Europe; and considerable amounts of the industry and utilities of the East European nations are tied to Soviet fuels. The ease with which the U.S.S.R. has sold its long-term contracts for gas in Central and Western Europe will tempt it to construct additional lines and offer gas at much higher prices in the future. Moscow has been willing to take steel pipe in payment for some of the gas and thus has continued to enlarge the gas network at home. In addition, construction is going forward to connect the network of Iran with that of the Soviet Union for exports of Iranian gas.[40] Thus the Soviet Union may become a sizable intermediary in the gas business. Even if the Iranian gas is used in the U.S.S.R., it will free other gas for export to European nations.

Although 20 percent of the Soviet fuel balance is now supplied by natural gas and about one-third of all dwelling units use this fuel, official growth goals have not been met in recent years. Moreover, the gas system suffers from too many branch lines, poor welding of the pipe, and defective pumping stations and compressors. Many industrial users do not have a continuous supply.[41] According to the Minister of the Petroleum Industry, enormous quantities of natural gas have been wasted in the fields because of poor collection and transportation facilities. In addition, he has noted the need for integrated development of several oil fields in widely varying locations because of the age and limited additional life of the important Urals and Volga oil regions.[42] In line with this, research, development, and field testing of large pipe, up to eight feet in diameter, and pipe suitable for the harsh regions of the Far North are scheduled for the 1971-75 Plan.[43]

Nature did not favor the Soviet economy in placement of navigable rivers and their directions of flow—predominantly southeast in the European portion and north in the Asian portion—in that the system does not correlate particularly well with the most important flows of traffic produced by resource location and population concentration. Another negative fact is that most rivers are ice-bound at least four to five months a year. There are ambitious engineering proposals to divert water from and/or change the direction of flow of some northern rivers, for the purposes of better water transportation and provision of water for irrigation and industry.[44] One massive plan being actively researched would move four times the volume of water involved in the well-known Feather River Project in California.[45] The 1971-75 Five-Year Plan specifies an increase of 24 percent in freight carried by inland waterways.

Inland waterways are used mainly for moving building materials, timber, oil, ores, and metals. Measured in ton-kilometers, the rivers of the Volga Basin carry about 60 percent of all river-borne freight. However, in recent years two dams on the Volga that have created large lakes have also created problems. Their shallow waters become so choppy during the frequent windstorms that barges lose significant amounts of time in waiting,[46] and they have lengthened the previous 4-month-long average frozen period on the Volga by about 12 days. Even Moscow has become a river port, for it is on the Moscow River, which connects by way of the Oka to the Volga system. Also of importance are the Northern Dvina-Neva system in the northwest, the Dnieper in the Ukraine and Belorussia, and the Don. In Siberia the Lena, Yenisei, and the Ob, with its tributary the Irtysh, have considerable potential. Timber, oil, and building materials predominate in their present use. In the Far East the Amur carries grain, timber, and manufactured goods. In Central Asia the undependable Amu Darya is used principally for cotton, wool, and manufactured goods. The Caspian Sea, actually a very large lake, carries considerable traffic, including oil north from Baku and then up the Volga. However, its depth has fallen more than 10 feet in recent years, causing severe dislocation of port facilities and encouraging choppiness from the many windstorms.

Large amounts have been spent on about 9,300 miles of canals to connect rivers. Perhaps the most famous, the 62-mile-long Volga-Don Canal, was a pet project of Stalin and was opened in 1952. However, it has not provided the impetus to inland water transport that was forecasted. Other major canals include the White Sea-Baltic, the Lenin Volga-Baltic Waterway, the Dnieper-Bug, the Northern Dvina Waterway, and the Moscow Canal. The Soviet government has repeatedly urged interconnection of the rivers, canals, and lakes of Eastern and Western Europe with its own. In 1971 a connection with Iran was established whereby small ships are routed from the Mediterranean through the Black Sea, the Don and Volga River systems, and the Caspian Sea to northern Iranian ports. Recently a ship with a displacement of 3,000 tons carried products from Spain, France, Italy, and Romania to the Iranian port of Pahlavi.[47] Others go from the Mediterranean into central Russia. The reduction or elimination of transshipments is an attractive factor, but ships and cargoes are necessarily small. One Soviet shipping executive has already pointed out some cases in which this service is unnecessarily and uneconomically used.[48]

Although the waterway network is the most extensive in the world, the routes are circuitous and the distances, time factor, and climate discouraging. Despite the many river linkages, most traffic remains of the short-haul variety. However, containerization is rather well established and utilized in rail-barge interchange.

Maritime Transportation

The Soviet maritime service has been growing as its American counterpart has been declining.[49] At the beginning of the 1970s the Soviet merchant fleet was the world's seventh largest, while that of the United States was the fifth largest, measured in deadweight tonnage. Despite new U.S. legislation on shipbuilding and the merchant fleet, the Soviet fleet stands an excellent chance of equaling the American by the end of the decade. Year after year the Soviet growth is over half of the aggregate growth for the world's 12 largest fleets. The U.S.S.R. has a long-established shipbuilding industry, but it buys more from Poland and East Germany than it constructs itself. Finland and Yugoslavia are also major sources. The 1971-75 Ninth Five-Year Plan specifies a 40 percent increase in maritime freight over 1970. This increase is large but well below the 70 percent rise that occurred between 1965 and 1970.[50]

Before World War II, 90 percent of the Soviet Union's foreign trade, of which there was little, went by sea. Today, despite developing a major and modern merchant fleet and improving the ports, much of this trade goes overland. This is, of course, mainly because of Comecon trade arrangements with the East European economies.

There are some problems in Soviet maritime transportation, one of them rather basic. As a Soviet economist stated, "Apart from unfavorable natural and geographic conditions, the great distances that industrial regions, especially in the North, are from sea lanes has an effect in our country."[51] The typical Soviet tanker is a little

smaller and significantly slower (13 versus 15 knots average) than
its American counterpart, although it is much newer (8 versus 19
years average age) than the American. The typical Soviet freighter
is much smaller and a little slower 13 versus 14 knots average), although it too is much newer (13 versus 22 years average age).[52] In
addition, cargo volume performance by the fleet has been below
planned levels in several recent years. Moreover, labor productivity
in the merchant marine has risen less than that in some other modes
of transportation in several recent years. Maritime containerization
is a distinctly troublesome point. Soviet writer V. Novikov stated:
"Soviet shipping authorities must take radical measures even now in
order to avoid bringing up the rear in 'containerization' in the im-
mediate future."[53] In addition, there are well-reasoned managerial
complaints of unnecessarily expensive and low-quality fuels for the
ships.[54] Moreover, there is no legal code or set of comprehensive
statutes regulating Soviet carrier liability to other Soviet organizations.[55]

However, much progress is being made. The Soviet merchant
marine is acquiring many ships of new design, among them the Mir
series of supertankers. The first of the series launched has a deadweight of 150,000 tons, can go 22,000 nautical miles without replen-
ishment of any kind, and moves at 16.5 nautical miles per hour. These
vessels are three times as large as present Soviet tankers (the Sofia
series), but the crew is only 34 to 36.[56] Prospects for the future of
the maritime service are bright also in that significant amounts of
space are being sold to non-Communist shippers and the routes followed are becoming worldwide. For example, in the late 1960s the
merchant fleets of the U.S.S.R., Poland, and East Germany merged
some of their services to and from West Africa and the east coast
of South America in order to gain efficiencies, generally compete
better in those corridors, and hopefully get better treatment from
the shipping conferences of those regions. One combined regional
fleet, the Baltamerika Line, provides a minimum of five trips a
month to the east coast of South America and five trips a month from
that area to Northern and Eastern Europe. The Soviet Union and the
Comecon nations cooperate with each other through the Bureau for
Coordination of the Chartering of Ships and the International Shipowners Association.[57] In Western and Northern Europe the Soviet
fleet, operating independently of its allies, makes regular and frequent
calls at such ports as Hamburg, Rotterdam, Antwerp, Le Havre, and
Bilbao. Moreover, before the 1971-75 Five-Year Plan is finished,
the Ministry of the Merchant Marine in Moscow plans to have in
operation a computer center that will give detailed data almost
instantly on the location, route, and cargo of all Soviet vessels and
cross-tabulations of such data.

Most of the seacoast of the U.S.S.R. is icebound three-quarters of the year. A recurring theme in Russian history is getting and maintaining ice-free outlets to the seas of the world. Today the nation has several ice-free ports on the Baltic, Murmansk on the Barents Sea (because of the influence of the Gulf Stream), and, of course, several Black Sea ports. On the Pacific are Vladivostok, Nakhodka, Korsakov, and others; but they are occasionally closed by ice for short periods. Commerce through Vladivostok has been limited for military security reasons. Thus harbor investments are increasingly being shifted to other Pacific coast cities.

Growth of Soviet interest in the Pacific Basin and especially in the Asian nations forming the western rim of that vast region is exhibited in an as yet unnamed port now under construction on Wrangel Bay. Japanese firms will supply machinery, equipment, and building materials for piers and jetties to handle coal, wood chips, and containers. The Japanese are considering the cost-speed factors of overland shipment, using Soviet ports on the Pacific, through the U.S.S.R. to East and West European markets.

Coastal shipping service is quite limited because of the climate and the discontinuous coastline. There is a noteworthy amount on the Black Sea. The Northern Sea Route through the Arctic is now open its full length several months a year because of large icebreakers, including the atomic-powered Lenin.[58] Starting in the 1972-73 winter season, year-round navigation was established in a 1,300-mile section from Murmansk to Dudinka, which lies near the mouth of the Yenesei.[59] The objective commercial potential of the Northern Sea Route is debatable; but there is a historical, emotional commitment to this development. There are military aspects as well.

Air Freight

Although little information has been released on Soviet air freight, it is clear that it is growing. One Soviet economic geographer claims that his country already occupies first place in volume of such cargo.[60] It is known that air freight is used extensively for instruments and scientific apparatus and often for pharmaceuticals, replacement parts, and fresh fruits and vegetables. For example, one group of farms near Krasnodar sent 500 tons of strawberries, two or three tons at a time, by air freight to Leningrad and Moscow in one month. However, much of the financial advantage to the economy of using this mode of transport was canceled, in that the farms used passenger flights and sent their own employees along to take care of the shipments. Aeroflot absorbed the round-trip fares for all such attendants.[61]

It is possible to carry anything by air if it has relatively high unit value, but in the remote areas of new settlement some goods not of high unit value are occasionally flown in because of the slowness and other disadvantages of alternative modes of transportation. After analyzing the needs of the far northern districts, the Novosibirsk Institute of Cooperative Trade recommended regular use of air cargo for the more valuable and perishable products and urged the Ministry of Civil Aviation to reduce rates for such areas.[62] A transport publication, Gudok, has reported that experimental design bureaus in the Siberian cities of Irkutsk and Bratsk are working on dirigibles meant for regular freight service.[63] In presenting the 1971-75 Five-Year Plan, Premier Kosygin stated: "Considerably more use will be made of aircraft . . . for freight carriage to areas remote from other means of communication."[64] Two new airplanes have interesting prospects for this type of transport. The Tupolev 144 supersonic transport, already advertised in the American professional magazine Aviation Week, shows considerable promise for both domestic and overseas air cargo service. The Ilyushin 76 transport, which began flight tests in 1971, was designed specifically for mass cargo, including large containers. Designed to use dirt fields as well as airports, it has a speed of about 550 miles per hour.[65]

PHYSICAL HANDLING AND WAREHOUSING

The U.S.S.R. shares a common Western problem. It wishes to minimize storage and waste of goods and yet avoid frequent small shipments. At the same time the economy has an extreme shortage of warehouse space, loading and unloading equipment and related apparatus, and appropriate packing materials. (Also see "Channels of Distribution" in Chapter 5.) This fact is particularly troublesome in the agricultural sector, because of perishability, seasonality, and the occasional lack of agreement between agricultural organizations and urban procurement offices. Inventory control practices are backward; but officials are cognizant of the deficiency, and a few pilot computer installations are already functioning. Handling and storage problems, combined with slowness of transport, contribute greatly to the traditional and continuing substitution of one product for another in industry and trade and in agricultural enterprises' substitution of a derivative product for the original. An example of the latter is butter for milk.

Government leaders have called attention to the need for a sharp reduction in losses in all stages of production and marketing and the attendant requirement for more storage capacity and improved storage facilities.[66] The need for additional refrigerated warehousing has been stated over and over. Some urban planners and economists have urged that warehouses in cities be placed underground.[67]

Since they have extremely little equipment for lifting and hauling, most warehouses and factories employ large numbers of persons to do such work manually. One staff member of the Academy of Sciences Institute of Economics has estimated that one-sixth of industrial workers are engaged in physical handling and that about 85 percent of them perform this work without aid of any mechanical device.[68] One plant in Yerevan that makes only a few hundred loading machines a year has 30,000 sales orders waiting in its files.[69] A contributing factor in the problem of loading and unloading is that most railroad cars and trucks have been of simple basic types not necessarily related to the needs of shippers. In addition, although industrial enterprises have about 70,000 miles of spur track,[70] it is still too little. Many industrial shipments, even some of considerable bulk, must be loaded or unloaded at railway stations.

The editors of Izvestia have stated that, although work methods in actual manufacturing are well advanced, the whole complex of handling and storage in all stages of the channels of distribution has been neglected. They note that even in machine-building plants, a supposedly sophisticated type of business, one-fifth of the workers are in physical handling and very often have no mechanized assistance.[71] One of this periodical's staff writers has recommended the creation of a national agency to research, plan, and standardize warehouse management and equipment.[72] Most managers who have equipment such as forklifts and stacking cranes have had to build them on their own premises.

There has been a continuing dialogue on the slowness with which containerization of freight has been developing.[73] However, it is scheduled to double during the 1971-75 Five-Year Plan.[74] In 1972 the All-Union Association for Containerized and Packaged Shipping was created within the Ministry of Transportation for the purpose of planning and organizing the use of containers and pallets, while scientific research on the subject was entrusted to the State Planning Committee's Institute of Comprehensive Transport Problems.[75]

NOTES

1. See A. Lavrishchev, Economic Geography of the U.S.S.R. (Moscow: Progress Publishers, 1969), p. 156.

2. Walter M. W. Splawn, Government Ownership and Operation of Railroads (New York: Macmillan, 1928), p. 109. Also see Samuel O. Dunn, Government Ownership of Railways (New York: D. Appleton,

1913), p. 34; and Harold Kellock, Railway Age, January 1, 1927, p. 163.

3. See Ernest W. Williams, Jr., Freight Transportation in the Soviet Union (Princeton, N. J.: Princeton University Press, 1962), p. 14.

4. Documents of the 24th Congress of the Communist Party of the Soviet Union (Moscow: Novosti Publishing House, 1971), p. 168.

5. G. Shakhunyants, "The Reliability of the Tracks," Gudok, June 23, 1971, pp. 2-3. JPRS, 53584; TOUTAS, 256.

6. William R. Siddall, "Railroad Gauges and Spatial Inter-action," The Geographical Review, 59 (January 1969), 29-57.

7. See Robert N. Taaffe, Rail Transportation and the Economic Development of Soviet Central Asia (Chicago: University of Chicago Press, 1960).

8. See Ye. F. Kozhevnikov and Yu. Kazuin, "Long Distances Are Being Shortened," Pravda, June 1, 1971, p. 2. JPRS, 53513; TOUTAS, 254.

9. I. Ionnisyan, "Second Tracks: Stage by Stage," Gudok, January 27, 1970, p. 2. JPRS, 50034; TOUTAS, 93.

10. Ibid.

11. Documents of the 24th Congress of the Communist Party, p. 169.

12. Holland Hunter, Soviet Transport Experience: Its Lessons for Other Countries (Washington, D.C.: The Brookings Institution, 1968), p. 61.

13. See J. N. Westwood, A History of Russian Railways (London: George Allen & Unwin, 1964), pp. 273-75. Also see James H. Blackman, Transport Development and Locomotive Technology in the Soviet Union (Columbia, S.C.: College of Business Administration, University of South Carolina, 1957); and C. D. Buford, "Russia: Distribution Without Competition," Distribution Age, January 1961, pp. 38-40, 62-63.

14. V. Parfenov, "'Sieve' on Wheels," Pravda, October 10, 1969, p. 2. CDSP, 21 (November 5, 1969), 23.

15. For example, see K. Glazov, "Idle Again," Pravda, June 1, 1972, p. 3. CDSP, 24 (June 28, 1972), 34; V. Leonov, "Arithmetic of Shipments," Izvestia, December 14, 1972, p. 2. CDSP, 24 (January 10, 1973), 18-19; and L. Karpov, "Problems and Judgments: Intensity of the Plan," Pravda, June 10, 1970, p. 3. CDSP, 22 (July 7, 1970), 8, 23.

16. Documents of the 24th Congress of the Communist Party, pp. 168-69.

17. "Motor Vehicle Transport," Ekonomicheskaya Gazeta, no. 39, September 1972, p. 1. CDSP, 25 (February 7, 1973), 17.

18. Ibid.

19. N. Smelyakov, "An Expensive Road Is the Cheapest," Literaturnaya Gazeta, no. 11 (1966), 14. CDSP, 19 (April 26, 1967), 8-9.

20. "Motor Vehicles Await Roads," Izvestia, December 12,
1971, p. 3. CDSP, 23 (January 11, 1972), 15.

21. "Russian Republic's Main Routes—Report from the Kremlin,"
Izvestia, June 30, 1972, p. 1. CDSP, 24 (July 26, 1972), 29-30.

22. "The Rural Road Is a Public Artery," Izvestia, May 11,
1972, p. 2. CDSP, 24 (June 7, 1972), 29-30.

23. S. Matveyev, "Problems of Urban Transport," Trud, August
31, 1972, p. 2. CDSP, 25 (February 7, 1973), 17.

24. "Expressways for the Moscow Area," Pravda, July 26,
1972, p. 2. CDSP, 24 (August 23, 1972), 24.

25. Documents of the 24th Congress of the Communist Party,
p. 264.

26. Ibid.

27. N. M. Potapov, "New Phase in the Development of the
Branch," Za Rulem, June 1971, pp. 1-3. JPRS, 53511.

28. For example, see A. Glushchenko, "The Truck Goes out on
a Run," Pravda, July 9, 1968, p. 2. CDSP, 20 (July 31, 1968), 29.

29. A. Morozov, "Obstacle Course," Izvestia, April 27, 1972,
p. 2. CDSP, 24 (May 24, 1972), 30.

30. For example, see N. Govorushchenko, "The Motor Vehicle
Must Have Excellent Service," Pravda, December 17, 1971, p. 2.
CDSP, 23 (January 11, 1972), 14.

31. Potapov, "New Phase in the Development of the Branch."

32. M. Malakhiyev, "Coefficient of Dispersion," Izvestia,
November 16, 1972, p. 3. CDSP, 24 (December 13, 1972), 23-24.

33. V. Schlemin, "Central Union of Cooperative Societies
Convenes," Sovetskaya Torgovlya, May 20, 1969, p. 2. JPRS, 48369;
TOUTAS, 30.

34. Malakhiyev, "Coefficient of Dispersion."

35. For example, see "Trucks and Freight," Izvestia, October
13, 1968, p. 2. CDSP, 20 (October 30, 1968), 25.

36. The raw data can be found in Williams, Freight Transportation in the Soviet Union, p. 14.

37. Lavrishchev, Economic Geography of the U.S.S.R., pp. 364-
68.

38. Alexei Kosygin, Directives of the Five-Year Economic
Development Plan of the U.S.S.R. for 1971-1975 (Moscow: Novosti
Publising House, 1971), p. 45.

39. For example, see F. Chursin, "Medvezhye-Urals Pipeline
Goes into Operation," Pravda, April 29, 1972, p. 1. CDSP, 24 (May
24, 1972), 25; and V. Sukhanov, "Across Siberia to the Ocean," Izvestia, June 8, 1972, p. 1. CDSP, 24 (July 5, 1972), 26.

40. Kommunist Tadzhikistana, March 1, 1970, p. 3. JPRS,
50382; TOUTAS, 90.

41. Düsseldorf, Handelsblatt, April 22, 1970, p. 5. JPRS, 50664; Translation U.S.S.R. Resources, 100.

42. V. Shashin, Pravda, December 25, 1970, p. 2. CDSP, 22 (January 26, 1971), 25.

43. "Editorial: Larger Diameter Pipelines Planned," Stroitelstvo Truboprovodov, April 1970, pp. 1-4. JPRS, 50664; TOUR, 100.

44. See B. Ibrayev, "Siberia to Help the South," Pravda, April 27, 1972, p. 6. CDSP, 24 (May 24, 1972), 25; and "Irtysh-Aral Sea Canal," Pravda, December 11, 1972, p. 1. CDSP, 24 (January 10, 1973), 17.

45. "The Volga's Northern Spring," Izvestia, June 2, 1972, p. 1. CDSP, 24 (June 28, 1972), 33.

46. Robert N. Taaffe, "Volga River Transportation: Problems and Prospects," in Richard S. Thoman and Donald J. Patton, eds., Focus on Geographic Activity: A Collection of Original Studies (New York: McGraw-Hill, 1964), pp. 191-92.

47. A. Vasilyev, "Across Seas and Rivers," Pravda, June 9, 1972, p. 5. CDSP, 24 (July 5, 1972), 22.

48. A. Belodvortsev, "From River to Sea," Pravda, June 22, 1972, p. 2. CDSP, 24 (July 17, 1972), 32.

49. Helpful background on the evolution of the Soviet merchant fleet can be found in The Soviet Drive for Maritime Power, Committee on Commerce, U.S. Senate, 90th Congress, 1st Session (Washington, D.C., 1967). For the official reaction of a sector of the labor movement, see Andrew Pettis, "Ships Bringing Russian Revolution to Doorstep," Maritime, 5 (April-June 1971), 40-44.

50. M. Bruskin and P. Pustovoit, "High Goals of the Merchant Marine," Vodny Transport, November 30, 1971, p. 2. CDSP, 24 (February 2, 1972), 1-4.

51. S. Mikhailov, "The Development of the U.S.S.R.'s Maritime Economy," Voprosy Ekonomiki, July 1972, pp. 101-08. CDSP, 24 (November 1, 1972), 1-6, at 4.

52. Synthesized from extensive data in A Statistical Analysis of the World's Merchant Fleets, U.S. Department of Commerce, Maritime Administration (Washington, D.C., 1971); and Merchant Fleets of the World, U.S. Department of Commerce, Maritime Administration (Washington, D.C., 1969).

53. V. Novikov, "Soviet and Foreign Shipowners Pacts Discussed," Morscoy Flot, March 1970, pp. 60-62. JPRS, 50636; TOUTAS, 127.

54. N. Plyavin, "Merchant Fleet Awaits Good Fuel," Izvestia, June 29, 1972, p. 4. CDSP, 24 (July 26, 1972), 29.

55. B. Cherepanov, in Vodny Transport, July 8, 1971, p. 2. JPRS, 53679.

56. See D. G. Sokolov, N. N. Rodionov, and Y. G. Frid, "Design of First Soviet 150,000-Ton Tanker Explained," Sudostroyeniye, April

1970, pp. 14-17. JPRS, 50745; TOUTAS, 132; and V. Shmyganovsky, "Plans and Achievements: The Ocean Is its Element," Izvestia, December 4, 1969, p. 6. CDSP, 21 (January 6, 1970), 31.

57. See T. B. Guzhenko, "Following the Traditions of Maritime Friendship," Izvestia, September 24, 1972, p. 2. CDSP, 24 (October 18, 1972), 26-27; A. Knop and S. Bejger, "Maritime Cooperation Is Strengthening," Izvestia, October 23, 1971, p. 4, CDSP, 23 (November 23, 1971), 20; and Novikov, "Soviet and Foreign Shipowners Pacts Discussed."

58. Helpful background can be found in R. Badowski et al., Report from the Arctic (Moscow: Novosti Press Agency, 1964). This is a short book of 10 readings by Eastern and Western journalists on the Northern Sea Route.

59. See V. Zakharko, "Through the Ice," Izvestia, January 26, 1973, pp. 1, 3; and "The Ice Is Behind," Izvestia, January 28, 1973, p. 1. CDSP, 25 (February 21, 1973), 24.

60. Lavrishchev, Economic Geography of the U.S.S.R., p. 372.

61. G. Borisenko, "Where Should Fruit Be Marketed?," Pravda, July 21, 1965, p. 2. CDSP, 17 (August 11, 1965), 14.

62. I. Melnikov, "Back Country," Izvestia, January 15, 1972, pp. 1-2. CDSP, 24 (February 9, 1972), 27-28.

63. "Dirigibles for Siberia," Gudok, February 28, 1970, p. 4. JPRS, 50216; TOUTAS, 102.

64. Kosygin, Directives of the Five-Year Economic Development Plan, p. 45.

65. K. Respevin, "Clear Skies, IL-76," Pravda, May 19, 1971, p. 6. CDSP, 23 (June 15, 1971), 44-45.

66. Documents of the 24th Congress of the Communist Party, p. 167.

67. A. Segedinov, "Underground Urban Development," Stroitel'stvo i Arkhitektura Moskvy, no. 5 (1971), 13-15. JPRS, 53584; TOUTAS, 256.

68. D. Palterovich, "The Structure of Equipment," Pravda, December 6, 1971, p. 2. CDSP, 23 (January 4, 1972), 42-43.

69. G. Arakelyan, "Urgent Matter: The Demand Is There, but the Machines Are not," Pravda, November 11, 1969, p. 2. CDSP, 21 (December 3, 1969), 27-28.

70. Lavrishchev, Economic Geography of the U.S.S.R., p. 327.

71. Editor's note to P. Novokshonov, "Automation Comes to the Warehouse," Izvestia, November 28, 1972, p. 2. CDSP, 24 (December 27, 1972), 15-16.

72. Ibid.

73. For example, see Y. Kazmin, "Once Again on Containers," Pravda, April 29, 1970, p. 2. CDSP, 22 (May 26, 1970), 21-22.

74. Alexei Kosygin, "On the State Five-Year Plan for the Development of the U.S.S.R. National Economy in 1972," Pravda, November 25, 1971, pp. 1-4. CDSP, 23 (December 21, 1971), 12-24, at 16.

75. "Containers for Freight Shipping," Izvestia, January 15, 1972, p. 2. CDSP, 24 (February 9, 1972), 26.

The comprehensively planned Soviet economy traditionally isolated itself from changeable world market prices, fluctuating physical
volume of goods traded, and shifting comparative advantage. Planners, desiring to control outcomes carefully, tended to restrict their
plans to areas over which the state possessed political and economic
authority and tried to avoid embroilment with unpredictable foreign
trading partners.[1] However, it will be remembered that during the
1930s the U.S.S.R. participated as a seller in world markets for agricultural products, despite severe shortages and even rationing at
home, so that the imports needed for industrialization could be obtained. The Soviet Union has traditionally suspected the intentions
of non-Communist countries in international commerce, perceiving
trade overtures as covert designs for interfering with or weakening
the Soviet system. The modest foreign trade that occurred took place
through a ponderous bureaucracy headed by the Soviet Ministry of
Foreign Trade. No Soviet business enterprise was permitted to import and export except through this intermediary.

Entry of the U.S.S.R. into foreign trade presents some com-
putational problems. Comparative advantage is frequently impossible
to calculate because Soviet domestic prices do not reflect relative
scarcities and bear no relationship to world market prices or to
domestic prices in other centrally planned economies. A further
impediment to meaningful calculations is the artificial and unrealistic
exchange rate of the Russian ruble. For such reasons Soviet foreign
trade is often carried out as barter.

The Soviet fear and skepticism about foreign trade began to
crumble following World War II, when trade ties and economic commitments to the Comecon nations were an essential counter to the
Marshall Plan. The U.S.S.R. also began to see trade as an opportunity
to expand its sphere of influence among developing economies and to

spread its belief systems. The merchant fleet, which is a normal concomitant of foreign commerce, was perceived to have some military and propaganda value. Other factors have also influenced the drift toward more involvement in world trade. In the recent past there has been growing government acceptance of the goal of a higher standard of living, to which imports can contribute. Professionals are becoming more important, and many tend to be more interested in their specialties than in politics. Patterns of values are becoming more instrumental and less ideological.

Soviet planners are coming to believe more and more that imports and exports and international services can be sufficiently coordinated with national economic plans that they may be advantageous. International trade is even perceived to some extent as a potential remedy for defects in the master plan which appear as the plan is carried out. Nevertheless, the official Soviet stance toward international marketing continues to be characterized chiefly by caution.

SIZE OF TRADE AND COMPOSITION
BY PRODUCT TYPE

Soviet foreign commerce amounted to 25.8 billion rubles in 1972, more than eight times the 2.9 billion rubles of 1950 and 2.5 times the 10.1 billion of 1960. Already the world's sixth largest, this commerce is scheduled to grow by 33 to 35 percent during the 1971-75 Five-Year Plan. This goal appears reasonably attainable in light of a 6 percent gain in 1971 and about 9 percent in 1972.

Since the First Five-Year Plan the top category of products in Soviet imports has been machinery, equipment, and transport goods, except in the 1946-50 period of recovery, when foodstuffs took first place. Manufactured consumer goods as a percentage of imports have risen rapidly since the 1956-60 period. Fuels and electric power as a percent of imports have fallen drastically through the years. The category of chemicals, fertilizers, and rubber has remained fairly stable as a percentage since the 1930s.[2]

Machinery, equipment, and transport goods took first place in Soviet exports in the 1966-70 period. This category ranked second in the three previous planning periods. Ores, concentrates, and metal articles were second in the 1966-70 period and first in the two previous periods. Exports of fuel and power declined as a percentage for several early periods but turned up in the 1951-55 period and probably will rise again in 1971-75. The share commanded by timber and pulp has shown gains for three periods, while furs and skins and consumer goods have declined.[3]

ORGANIZATION STRUCTURE AND NEGOTIATIONS

The beginning point for foreign trade is the usually secret provisions on such intended sales and purchases in Gosplan's five-year plan. Outsiders typically know only the aggregates and a few rather gross categories. An operating enterprise may prepare a request for a foreign purchase and route it to the appropriate internal ministry for review and inclusion in requested budgets. Gosplan may approve, disapprove, or modify. If the purchase is authorized by Gosplan, the Ministry of Foreign Trade takes over. It normally tries to find enough exports to offset the cost of the imports. The initial request normally occurs months or even years before authorization. On the other hand, Gosplan may occasionally take the initiative to instruct the Foreign Trade Ministry to buy in some bottlenecked category.

The Foreign Trade Ministry is almost a monopoly. International marketing operations are performed by about 50 foreign trade organizations, sometimes termed combines, each of which specializes in a group of (usually) related product types. As Soviet foreign commerce has grown, there has been an increase in the number of foreign trade organizations. Their number approximately doubled between 1960 and the early 1970s. Examples are Traktoroexport, which deals in tractors and road-building equipment, and Exportles, which deals in timber, pulp, plywood, and paper products. Almost all of these organizations are subsidiaries of the Foreign Trade Ministry; but some, such as the organizations for tourism, cinema, maritime chartering, and insurance, are outside the Ministry's jursidiction. The Foreign Trade Ministry itself is divided on the bases of product type and geography. Financial activities are handled by Vneshtorgbank, the Bank for Foreign Trade. In addition, there is the State Committee for Foreign Economic Relations, which encourages economic contacts with other nations, supervises the sizable program of aid and technical assistance, and administers some scientific collaboration. Moreover, there are two noteworthy agencies of Gosplan. The Committee on Science and Technology gathers and evaluates intelligence from everywhere, while the All-Union Chamber of Commerce collects commercial information abroad, arranges trade exhibitions in the U.S.S.R., and assists in resolving trade disputes between foreigners and Soviet entities.

Another institution is the foreign trade delegation. Normally it is a team of experts from one or more industrial ministries, the Ministry of Foreign Trade, and perhaps engineers and accountants from the requesting enterprise and planners from Gosplan. The delegation makes preliminary arrangements for imports or barter deals but leaves the specifics to the central planners and suppliers. Sometimes the preliminary arrangements do not come to fruition.

The trade delegations sometimes coordinate their visits with cultural events or trade fairs. They tend to benefit from a closer cooperation between Soviet diplomatic officers, consular officials, and local business executives in the host country than do American businessmen abroad. Some quasi-permanent trade missions, such as those in Brazil and Malaysia, disseminate newsletters, films, and thousands of specialized advertising brochures. In Hungary and Czechoslovakia there are Soviet advertising-catalog bureaus that stock 12,000 different technical brochures and catalogs.[4] Most delegations are ad hoc, but a few have lengthy lives. Amtorg is a permanent delegation in New York incorporated under the laws of that state. It represents all the Soviet foreign trade organizations. However, it appears that Amtorg is being bypassed more and more frequently, thus making its future uncertain.[5]

Soviet traders normally use prevailing world prices or long-term moving averages of such prices in negotiating a transaction. They appear to disregard short-run price fluctuations in specific markets, even if it is a major market center, such as London or New York. The calculated figures then tend to become administered prices and tend to have a life of several months, if not longer.[6] Ostlund and Halvorsen conclude that the Russians are preoccupied with price, and that perhaps the other party in the dyad should cater to that factor.[7] Farrer apparently disagrees, noting that some negotiators are guided by past prices under like circumstances and that most negotiators are quite interested in additional factors, including timing, appropriate quality, and "willingness to take back specified bundles of domestic compensatory products, services, currency, and transferable roubles."[8] However, some of these would appear to be integrally related to price, taken in the broad sense. Farrer reports that the foreign trade combines utilize both fixed-price and cost-plus-fixed-fee contracts. Payment may be by cash or barter or a combination. American firms, generally not accustomed to barter, may need the services of European switch-dealers.[9]

If there are disagreements later between buyer and seller, Soviet-based arbitration is usually available and, according to both S. B. King-Smith and H. J. Berman, is normally competent and equitable.[10] However, the fine detail in Soviet contracts reduces ambiguity and thus the number of disputes. If there are conflicts, compromise rather than arbitration is typically used.[11]

The largest companies, especially the multinational, may attempt to reach the appropriate Soviet officials in other ways rather than waiting to be discovered through normal market investigation. The company may send a delegation to Moscow, an effort unlikely to succeed if for no other reason than bureaucratic delay. Another approach is to use an intermediary specializing in Soviet trade, of which

there are few so far.[12] The Western company may use its West
European subsidiaries and affiliates as representatives, especially
if they are in nations already active in Soviet commerce.[13] It may
enter into a subcontract with a firm holding a prime contract for a
major project or complete plant. Still another approach is to try to
open a small permanent office in Moscow. However, permission is
exceedingly difficult to get and only a few West Europeans have accomplished this feat. Chase Manhattan Bank received permission in
1973 for a branch in the Soviet capital, the first American bank to do
so in over half a century. Even if a Western organization receives
the authorization, facilities and services constitute a severe problem.

It is now standard practice for Soviet foreign trade organizations
to participate in trade shows, exhibitions, and fairs and to conduct
business there. These can be usefully divided into four common
types, each exemplified by some 1972 promotions. First, there are
exhibitions abroad composed entirely of Soviet goods, such as those
in Lagos and Beirut. Second, there are international exhibitions
abroad, such as the Paris Motor Show, Seattle Unimart-72, and the
International Fair of Algiers. Third, there are international expo-
sitions in the U.S.S.R. with exhibits from many nations, such as
Electro-72 in Moscow for electrical equipment and Container-72 in
Leningrad. Fourth, there are foreign shows in the U.S.S.R. devoted
to one nation or one industry of that nation, such as Hungary's Medim-
pex medical products show and the Polish Chamber of Foreign Trade's
exhibition of apparel and housewares. Most shows in the last category
are held by Comecon nations.

TRADE WITH OTHER COMMUNIST ECONOMIES

Comecon

The Comecon (Council for Mutual Economic Assistance) nations
are the principal trading partners of the U.S.S.R. What brought about
Comecon? First, it is conceivable that it is a logical culmination of
a century and a half of the Pan-Slavism movement.[14] Second, the
vastly superior military strength and larger economy of the Soviet
Union had a great deal to do with the founding and maintenance of
this organization. Third, the unfolding of the Marshall Plan in Western Europe was a major factor in organized politico-economic reaction by the Russians. It is now logical to surmise that Pan-Slavism
was only a philosophical palliative to the East European Six (and
culturally inapplicable in some cases) and a useful thought tool to the
involved theorists, and that the other two explanations are predominant.

171

Nations belonging to Comecon have been accounting for over 55 percent of the Soviet Union's foreign trade in recent years. Unlike the pattern prevailing before World War II, all six European nations in this group now purchase large shares of their imports from the Soviet Union, in most years 30 to 60 percent, and they sell similar shares of their exports to that country. Bulgaria is the most locked in, Romania the least. In most years the U.S.S.R. has a favorable aggregate balance of trade with its East European partners. The 1971-75 Five-Year Plan aims for Soviet-Comecon trade to grow somewhat faster than Soviet foreign trade in total.

Some Long-Run Developments in Comecon

The conjectured goal of the Russians to use the Comecon apparatus to divide and coordinate production capabilities and foreign sales among the member countries exactly as it might see fit has not materialized, and probably will not in the years ahead. Without question Comecon can point to major accomplishments, such as long-term agreements to trade certain products, pools of railroad rolling stock, electric power grid interconnections, international oil and gas pipelines, and Intervidenie (the multinational television network). Of course the fuel and power interconnections tend to create a dependence on the U.S.S.R. at a rather basic level. Another accomplishment is product standardization, which is the work of the Comecon Standing Commission for Standardization. Its most significant effects have been in metallurgy, industrial machinery and equipment, and the chemical industry. The U.S.S.R. is finding it necessary to revise nearly half of its state standards in light of Comecon agreements.[15] Nevertheless, there are problems, such as the pricing mechanisms of Comecon, alleged price discrimination by some members against other bloc members, and the mild competition between the Russians and East Europeans for markets in the developing countries.[16] More important, it is well known that the bloc countries have tended to seek a measure of independence in making their economic plans[17] and have labeled more matters internal and domestic than the Russians wished. W. Arthur Lewis put it concisely and provocatively: "Independence, interdependence, and dependence are found as much in the socialist as in the non-socialist world."[18] Czechoslovakia and East Germany, both with a higher living standard than the Soviet Union and both with a sophisticated industrial sector partially inherited from the years before World War II, have been fairly cooperative with the U.S.S.R. in recent years in moving in the general direction of a broad division of production, i. e., in Russian parlance "the international socialist division of labor." Of course, they have not been perfectly pliable. Some members hope to industrialize further

172

and faster by following a less integrated path. Romania, the most outspoken of the nations, has flaunted defiance of Soviet international marketing policy several times.

The trust or commission is the organization by which many Comecon decisions, such as product-line composition, channels, and plant location, are partially worked out. Comecon encourages industrial, commercial, scientific, and technical cooperation among member nations but leaves many specific ongoing activities to be carried out by as many of the members as care to participate in a specific trust or commission. One example is Intermetall, which Romania chose not to join. It arranges for exchange of metal products, such as hardware and pipe, and encourages and plans the construction of plants that are specifically designed for supplying several member countries rather than just one. For example, it has approved and is designing a rolled steel plant that will be built in the Soviet Union. It is planning a transformer metal-plate plant in Poland, for which the U.S.S.R. has agreed to provide the already mastered technology, and a sheet steel plant in East Germany. Other specialty steel plants are tentatively planned for other countries. At least six pipe plants, each specializing in particular bent shapes, are also tentatively planned. Agromesh, another commission, is on a smaller scale of operations and includes only the U.S.S.R., Hungary, and Bulgaria. Dealing in agricultural machinery, this arm of Comecon has assigned 13 kinds of farm equipment to particular nations to produce and market. For example, trenching plows are assigned to the Soviet Union and rotary plows to Bulgaria. Nineteen other kinds of farm equipment are being analyzed.[19]

There has been small but significant Soviet aid to the East European nations, even some to Albania (prior to the early 1960s) and Yugoslavia, which are not members of Comecon. This aid has on occasion taken the form of reductions and cancellations of reparations payments, debt reductions and cancellations, commodities, finished goods, and (very rarely) gold and convertible foreign exchange; but the dominant form has been credits with which to buy Russian goods. No accounting of the extent and exact composition of this aid has ever been released. Much of the public relations value for the Russians has never been tapped.

The aid extended from 1946 through the end of 1948, the trying initial recovery years, was extremely crucial in first linking the Eastern economies to the Soviet Union. One of the cornerstones of Soviet foreign policy in that era was to minimize American aid to Eastern Europe. After it was assured that there would be no significant American assistance, and after the establishment of the basic framework of the infant Comecon in 1949, Soviet aid virtually stopped. There was a brief resumption for the benefit of East Germany and

Romania immediately after Stalin's death and the famous East Berlin riots of 1953. Then there was a lapse until the Poznan uprising and Hungarian revolution in 1956, after which there was a large outpouring of Soviet aid in late 1956 and 1957.[20] Since that time there have been helpful but unspectacular amounts of assistance.

The 1971-75 Five-Year Plan of the U.S.S.R. includes export of 400 turnkey jobs to the Comecon countries. These complete plants will be in the following industries: electronics, chemicals, petroleum refining, power-engineering, building materials, and ferrous and non-ferrous metallurgy.[21] Moreover, there will be massive increases of Soviet exports to Comecon nations in several categories of goods. During the 1966-70 Five-Year Plan the U.S.S.R. sold 138 million tons of petroleum to Comecon, but the 1971-75 figure is 243 million tons. Similarly, natural gas deliveries will rise from only 8 billion cubic meters to 33 billion, electric power from 14 billion kwh to 42 billion, and iron ore (in terms of the resulting metal) from 72 million tons to 94 million. The largest category that the U.S.S.R. will import from the other members is 9.4 billion rubles' worth of manufactured consumer goods.[22] The previous plan called for 6.3 billion rubles.[23]

M. Lesechko, Vice-Chairman of the U.S.S.R. Council of Ministers and permanent representative to Comecon, recently noted two major problems in his country's relations with other members. One was that specialized ministries and economic associations of the concerned nations must play a much larger and more direct part. This was an unmistakable bow to the technocrats' importance and expertise. The other problem was that five years is not long enough for meaningful planning when one is dealing with several nations and their markets simultaneously. He concluded that "a more extended period" is an "urgent need."[24]

Promotion in Comecon

There is a problem in Comecon with promotional information and images. G. P. Lauter correctly notes that "serious attempts have been undertaken to develop an advertising industry."[25] Nevertheless, most firms and brands are not well known outside their home countries at this point. Even today engineers, architects, production managers, and industrial buyers generally know relatively little about specific enterprises in Comecon countries, their scientific-technological capability, and their product mix. During the 1950s they had so little information that astute West German traders occasionally acted as merchant middlemen between Comecon enterprises.[26] Many Western companies and brands are more familiar than Eastern, and on the whole they enjoy a favorable reputation in the Eastern economies. There has been considerable discussion of the need for more

174

advertising, exhibits, salesmen, and other promotional endeavors. Writing in a prominent Soviet journal, East German economist F. Tamme stated that "a definite information vacuum has formed in the international socialist economy. . . . And capitalist advertising can penetrate this vacuum."[27]

Other Communist Nations

Despite some deep-seated differences of ideology and occasional verbal clashes, there is a flourishing trade between Yugoslavia and the U.S.S.R., and some technical assistance as well. In the early 1970s trade ran just over half a billion rubles a year, versus only 97 million rubles in 1960.[28] The Soviet Union tends to export considerably more to Yugoslavia than it imports.

The hostile relations between the U.S.S.R. and China are well known. The U.S.S.R. supplied about half of China's imports at one time but now an extremely small fraction. Soviet-Chinese commerce grew throughout the 1950s and reached 1.85 billion rubles in 1959, accounting in that year for almost one-fifth of Soviet foreign trade. In that year 63 percent of Soviet exports to China were machinery and equipment.[29] After 1959, commerical relations between the two dropped off drastically. Soviet sales to China were only 22.4 million rubles in 1970 but more than tripled to 70.1 million in 1971. Even so, this represented only 0.50 percent of Soviet exports. Soviet imports from China rose from 19.5 million rubles in 1970 to 68.6 million in 1971, but the latter figure represented only about 0.60 percent of Soviet imports. Soviet trade with North Korea, in which the Russians have a favorable trade balance, is several times as large as its trade with China. The same is true of North Vietnam,[30] although in the case of that country the state of war has cast grave doubt on the data.

Soviet-Cuban commerce is clearly vital to the Castro regime and accounts for over 50 percent of Cuba's foreign trade. Much of Cuba's buying from the U.S.S.R. is on 10- to 13-year credits at 2 percent interest per year. Soviet exports to the island nation exceed imports by a large amount every year. Since Cuba reoriented its trade toward the U.S.S.R. in 1960-61, it has sold a substantial fraction of its sugar crop to the latter country. Both the absolute amount of sugar the Russians have bought and the percentage of the crop have fluctuated widely from year to year,[31] but not enough to endanger the Cuban economy. There is also seasonality. The Soviet Union requires that sugar deliveries be clustered in the first half of the year to take advantage of the off-season in Soviet sugar refineries. Soviet technical aid has been of modest importance.

Relations between the Soviet Union and the developed nations of the West, including Japan, account for about one-fourth of Soviet foreign commerce. The Russians tend to buy more from the West than they sell. Clearly desirous of expanding these activities, they are nevertheless cautious. Western Europe has received the bulk of Soviet attention aimed toward the West. The Soviet Minister of Foreign Trade, N. Patolichev, has stressed Soviet-West European cooperation in science and technology as a counter to the United States; exchange of patents and licenses; some production specialization; the need for joint transport, fuel, and electric power development; and the potential for reducing tensions in Europe.[32]

The level of commerce and channels of distribution are particularly well developed in Soviet relations with Finland, Belgium, France, and Italy, and significant progress is being made with Britain, West Germany, Austria, and Japan. Soviet raw materials and fuels are intriguing to the resource-poor Japanese. Chairman Brezhnev made a reasonably successful visit to France in 1971. The Russians are proud of their technical cooperation with the French on such matters as the Serpukhov elementary-particle accelerator, the Secam color television system, water desalinization, and transport of high-voltage electric power. In addition, the Russians have licensed a French company to manufacture a new type of steel electrode first developed in the U.S.S.R.[33] They have also bought computer equipment from the French-American company Bull-General Electric several times.[34] Italy's Olivetti Company is a major technical adviser in the Soviet attempt to raise the level of its computer technology, as is Italy's Montedison in the chemical industry. One of the largest single transactions in trade history was between these two nations when the U.S.S.R. sold Italy's E.N.I. 100 billion cubic meters of natural gas. Signed in late 1969, the contract calls for the Italians to deliver steel pipe, compressor and measuring devices, cables, road machinery, and other equipment.[35]

Soviet relations with Belgium and West Germany are interesting. Russian foreign marketing owes a considerable amount to Belgium with regard to transportation of its goods. Transworld Marine Agency Company, founded in Antwerp in 1969 with mixed Belgian and Soviet capital, services Soviet ships on the vital West European routes.[36] Russian and Belgian capital had already cooperated in buying a large tract in Antwerp for storing oil products and in operating a Brussels department store.[37] For several years there has also been a mixed Belgian-Soviet company, Scaldia-Volga, assembling automobiles in Brussels and selling them in Belgium, Holland, and Luxembourg. Brussels is perhaps the closest thing to a coordinating center for

Soviet business activity in Western Europe that one can find. The icy relations of West Germany and the U.S.S.R. have thawed, and more progress should come through Chancellor Brandt's Ost-Politik. Imitating earlier trucking agreements with France and Switzerland, the Soviet foreign trade enterprise Sovtransavto recently signed an agreement with Muth, a Hamburg shipping agency, for trucks of the two corporations to serve a regular route between that city and Moscow, a two-and-a-half-day trip.[38] However, importation of industrial technology is probably the overriding interest of the Russians in dealing with the West Germans. The Soviet government operates banks in Frankfurt, Zurich, Paris, and London.

The U.S.S.R. has found it expedient to buy a good many complete industrial plants from the West. The best-known transaction was the arrangement with Fiat of Italy in which the Italians granted a long-term credit of U.S. $360 million and built a large automobile factory in Togliatti.[39] Renault of France is a participant in building the Kama River truck plant. Pirelli of Italy has installed several tire plants in the U.S.S.R. Serete of France has built three plants that make perfumes and cosmetics and is being paid back over eight and a half years at 5.95 percent per year interest.[40] The French are also constructing a natural gas refinery. Belgian organizations have built several plants that manufacture glass containers and mini-plants that turn out pharmaceutical ampuls.[41] Zuckermann of Austria is now erecting two factories with a combined cost of U.S. $73 million to make flooring, windows, and doors.[42] Simon-Carves of Britain is building a polyester film plant and is also participating in the U.S. $96 million Polyspinners complex. BASF Company of West Germany has built a nylon plant, while two other West German companies, Mannesmann and Thyssen, have agreed to establish jointly a steel pipe factory near Moscow. Such projects as these are usually done on credits of 6 to 15 years' duration. Aggregate credits extended by Western manufacturing concerns for new plants in the Soviet Union appear to have averaged about U.S. $175 million per year during the period 1964 through 1970. In contracts for industrial installation imports, the typical Soviet practice is to buy spare parts for a short time and after that to buy only jigs and tools for new models. Sometimes there are industrial royalty payments as well. A desire for international respectability will encourage such payments. In 1973 the Soviet Union announced that it would begin adhering to the Universal Copyright Convention.

Commercial relations between the United States and the Soviet Union are essentially undeveloped. Until quite recently even a very small transaction was regarded as a novelty. The probability is high that in the absence of politics and ideological factors, there would be a substantial flow of commerce between these two economies directly and a substantial amount through third-party nations and world markets. However, to be realistic one must grant that international trade is always intermingled with geopolitics and ideology.

The volume and composition of commerce with the U.S.S.R. have been affected by a critical climate of opinion and by restrictions on American exports and associated credits to that country.[43] One reason that extremely few Soviet goods enter the United States is the high tariffs charged on them. The Soviet Union does not have "most favored nation" treatment. A proposal by Secretary of State William P. Rogers and Secretary of Commerce Maurice Stans in 1971 might have altered this legal situation, but it was rejected by President Nixon. However, prospects for a reversal have improved. Soviet emigration policies and past Soviet war debts have been stumbling blocks.

Several benchmark events in the recent progress of Soviet-American commerce must be identified. A distinct warming of relations occurred in mid-1971, when the United States approved export licenses for approximately $85 million worth of vehicle-making equipment to the U.S.S.R. That country and some of the American sellers had been waiting for nearly two years for licenses because the products had been considered strategic in nature. It is noteworthy that this change followed a relaxation of stringent restrictions on commerce between the United States and China. It is noteworthy too that the change benefited the depressed machine-tool industry of the United States and came at a time when there was great concern for the American balance of payments. This financial concern could well continue to lubricate the wheels of international commerce.

Another breakthrough came only a few days later, when the United States approved the U.S. $24 million sale of sophisticated computers by Britain's International Computers Ltd. to the Soviet Union. American approval was needed because a transaction involving delivery of such advanced technology in a strategic industry had to be reviewed by NATO and because the equipment included some American-made or -licensed components. Two more important events occurred in late 1971. Secretary of Commerce Stans made an 11-day trip to the U.S.S.R. to promote increased American-Soviet business. In addition, American companies made large sales of grain to the Soviet Union exceeding the normal yearly totals for all types of goods. President Nixon and the maritime labor unions reached workable agreements on implementing the President's removal of the old requirement that 50 percent of U.S. exports go in American ships. Perhaps the most important events were Secretary of Agriculture Earl Butz's visit to the U.S.S.R. in April 1972, President Nixon's visit in May 1972, and Secretary of Commerce Peter G. Peterson's visit in July 1972. In that month a sale of about U.S. $750 million worth of grain was made to the Soviet Union for delivery over several years. A joint commercial commission was set up to coordinate and improve business relationships between the two nations.

The large sales of grain in 1971 and 1972 aroused conjecture about future commodity sales and a continuing outlet for high agricultural production. It is not at all clear that the grain transactions are indicative of a long-term intention to purchase foodstuffs, even on an intermittent basis. Soviet economic history shows an effort to stay self-sufficient in food and a tendency to do without something if circumstances warrant. Prospects for machinery, equipment, complete plants, and technological expertise are much brighter. In fact, in early 1973 the Soviet Union and Occidental Petroleum Corporation of California signed an agreement in principle tentatively valued at about U.S. $8 billion. Although much further negotiation was necessary, the agreement involved creation of a chemical fertilizer complex near Kuibyshev and the trading of machinery and chemicals for chemical fertilizers over a 20-year period.

TRADE WITH LESS DEVELOPED COUNTRIES

In recent years the Soviet Union has conducted about one-seventh of its international trade with the non-Communist LDC's, but the proportion is slowly growing. It grew fairly rapidly during the 1960s. This commerce exhibits a large amount of concentration in two ways. First is regionality, a factor important for logistical reasons. Sales to the LDC's are highly concentrated in an arc extending from Morocco to Bangladesh, including North Africa, the Middle East, and the Indian subcontinent. Purchases from the LDC's are also concentrated regionally, but less so than sales. Second, Soviet commerce with the LDC's is concentrated with a small number of partners. India, Egypt, and Malaysia furnish slightly over half of Soviet imports from the LDC's in an average year, while India, Egypt, and Iran take over a third of Soviet exports to LDC's.[44]

There are some problems. Most of this commerce is conducted on a bilateral basis, which causes some bothersome rigidities for the LDC's. In addition, Soviet purchases of basic commodities have not exhibited the stability that the LDC's sought.[45] Moreover, the Soviet Union exports several basic commodities, such as iron ore, chrome ore, and gas, in competition with many of the developing economies. On the other hand, there is considerable Soviet aid to these nations, usually in the form of credits with which to buy Soviet products. These countries have been perplexed with the problem of what organizational form to use in their Soviet relations. Important because of the glaringly unequal bargaining situation between a small private company and the Soviet government, this problem also occurs in developed economies. Another aspect to the dilemma is the inter-mingling of Soviet political goals with international trade. Therefore some LDC's have centered the work in state agencies or in private syndicates. Bachmann argues that a policy under which private firms in an LDC cannot deal directly with Communist nations leads to better terms and stability and discourages political activity.[46]

NOTES

1. Thomas V. Greer, "Soviet International Marketing: Rationale and Practice," in Fred C. Allvine, ed., 1971 Combined Proceedings, American Marketing Association (Chicago: American Marketing Association, 1972), pp. 267-70.

2. Foreign Trade, no. 12 (1972), 52-54. This is a monthly magazine of the Soviet Ministry of Foreign Trade.

3. Ibid.

4. B. Karpov, "Advertising-Catalogue Bureaux at U.S.S.R. Trade Missions Abroad," Foreign Trade, no. 3 (1973), 52-53.

5. Lyman Ostlund and Kyell Halvorsen, "The Russian Decision Process Governing Trade," Journal of Marketing, 36 (April 1972), 3-11.

6. Thomas V. Greer, "Soviet International Marketing: Fear, Constraint, and Growth," Business Studies, 10 (Fall 1971), 19-23 (North Texas State University). For earlier years see F. D. Holzman, "Ruble Exchange Rate and Soviet Foreign Trade Pricing Policies, 1929-1961," American Economic Review, 58 (September 1968), 803-25.

7. Ostlund and Halvorsen, "The Russian Decision Process Governing Trade."

8. D. G. Farrer, "Soviet Foreign Trade Monopolization Practices: A Problem of Economic Growth and Development," Marquette Business Review, 14 (Winter 1970), 203-16.

9. See Marshall I. Goldman, "The East Reaches for Markets," Foreign Affairs, 47 (July 1969), 721-34.

10. Sandford B. King-Smith, "Communist Foreign-Trade Arbitration," Harvard International Law Journal, 10 (Winter 1969), 34-100; and Harold J. Berman, "The Legal Framework of Trade Between Planned and Market Economies: The Soviet-American Example," Law and Contemporary Problems, 24 (Summer 1959), 482-528. Also see Berman, "Unification of Contract Clauses in Trade Between Member-Countries of the Council for Mutual Economic Aid," International and Comparative Law Quarterly, 7 (October 1958), 659-90.

11. Ostlund and Halvorsen, "The Russian Decision Process Governing Trade."

12. Ibid.

13. William A. Dymsza, "East-West Trade: Types of Business Arrangements," M.S.U. Business Topics, 19 (Winter 1971), 22-28. Also see Dymsza and Alfred Daiboch, "Export Marketing in Eastern Europe," American Review of East-West Trade, August 1968, pp. 8-15.

14. For background on Pan-Slavism, Slavophilia, and Slavophobia, see Hans Kohn, Pan-Slavism: Its History and Ideology (South Bend, Ind.: Notre Dame University Press, 1953); Michael Boro Petrovich, The Emergence of Russian Panslavism, 1856-1870 (New York: Columbia University Press, 1956); and Merle Kling, The Soviet Theory of Internationalism (St. Louis: Washington University Press, 1952).

15. See V. Kartsev and V. Kotov, "Standardization—An Important Aspect of Economic Cooperation Between the CMEA Countries," Foreign Trade, no. 1 (1973), 10-13.

16. For example, on pricing mechanisms see Pavil Bozyk, "Domestic and Foreign Trade Prices in the Process of Integration in Comecon Countries," Soviet and East European Foreign Trade, (Summer 1970), 125-40; "Changes in Domestic and Foreign-Trade Pricing," Economic Bulletin for Europe, 20 November 1968), 47; and Frederic L. Pryor, The Communist Foreign Trade System (Cambridge, Mass.: M.I.T. Press, 1963), pp. 131-62. For background on price discrimination see Nicolas Spulber, The Soviet Economy: Structure, Principles, Problems (New York: Norton, 1962), pp. 245-56. On competition in developing countries, see Arnost Tauber, "Mutual Cooperation Between Socialist States and Developing Countries," International Development Review, 13, no. 2 (1971/72), 12-15, at 14, 15.

17. For example, see O. Bogomolov, "Problems in Production Specialization Among CMEA Countries," Soviet and Eastern European Foreign Trade, 4 (Spring 1968), 68-90; and N. Bautina, "International Socialist Production Relations," Soviet and Eastern European Foreign Trade, 4 (Fall 1968), 87-104.

18. W. Arthur Lewis, "Economic Development and World Trade," in E. A. G. Robinson, ed., Problems in Economic Development (New York: St. Martin's Press, 1965), pp. 485-86.

19. M. Odinets, "Promising Results," Pravda, March 2, 1971, p. 4. CDSP, 23 (March 30, 1971), 17.

20. See Marshall I. Goldman, Soviet Foreign Aid (New York: Praeger Publishers, 1967), pp. 23-59.

21. M. Lesechko, "The Main Direction," Pravda, March 27, 1971, p. 4. CDSP, 23 (April 27, 1971), 32-33.

22. Alexei Kosygin, "The 24th Congress of the Communist Party of the Soviet Union: The Directives of the 24th C.P.S.U. Congress for the Five-Year Plan for the Development of the U.S.S.R.

National Economy in 1971-1975," Pravda, April 7, 1971, pp. 2-7. CDSP, 23 (May 18, 1971), 1-11, at 10.

23. M. Loshakov, "Economic Cooperation Between the Socialist Countries," Foreign Trade, no. 12 (1972), 12-20, at 19.

24. Lesechko, "The Main Direction."

25. G. Peter Lauter, "The Changing Role of Marketing in the Eastern European Socialist Economies," Journal of Marketing, 35 (October 1971), 16-20, at 19.

26. Pryor, The Communist Foreign Trade System, pp. 69-70.

27. F. Tamme, "The Socialist Nations and Advertising," Nauka i Tehknika, no. 10 (1969), 8-10. JPRS, 50229; TOUTAS, 103.

28. Foreign Trade, no. 6 (1972), 57. no. 12 (1972), 58.

29. V. I. Zolotarev, "Main Stages of Development of U.S.S.R. Foreign Trade, 1917-1967," Voprosy Istorii, no. 8 (1967). Reprinted in Soviet and Eastern European Foreign Trade, 4 (Summer 1968), 3-34, at 19-20.

30. Foreign Trade, no. 6 (1972), 56-58.

31. See V. Vladimirsky, "Soviet-Cuban Trade and Economic Relations," Foreign Trade, no. 10 (1972), 14-18.

32. N. Patolichev, "The Present Day and Problems of European Security: May Economic Ties Grow Stronger," Izvestia, December 11, 1969, pp. 2-3. CDSP, 21 (January 13, 1970), 5, 7.

33. "French Firm Licensed to Produce Soviet Electrodes," Neümunster Informationen Ueber den West-Ost Handel, April 1969, p. 45. JPRS, 48336; TOUTAS, 29.

34. For example, see "French Computer Equipment for U.S.S.R.," Neümunster Informationen Ueber den West-Ost Handel, May 1969, p. 25. JPRS, 48336; TOUTAS, 29.

35. L. Zamoisky, "Record Contract," Izvestia, December 12, 1969, p. 2. CDSP, 21 (January 13, 1970), 5.

36. "New Soviet-Belgian Shipping Agency Formed," Morskoy Flot, November 1969, p. 21. JPRS, 50010; TOUTAS, 92.

37. Goldman, "The East Reaches for Markets."

38. "Automotive Transport Agreements," Neümunster Informationen Ueber den West-Ost Handel, May 1969, p. 25. JRPS, 48336; TOUTAS 29.

39. For example, see "Giant on the Volga Goes into Operation," Izvestia, March 28, 1971, p. 1. CDSP, 23 (April 27, 1971), 36.

40. "French Cosmetics Plants for Soviets," Düsseldorf Handelsblatt, June 4, 1969, p. 5. JPRS, 48336; TOUTAS, 29.

41. Ibid.

42. Düsseldorf Handelsblatt, June 13/14, 1969, p. 8. JPRS, 48336; TOUTAS, 29.

43. See Marshall I. Goldman and Alice Conner, "Businessmen Appraise East-West Trade," Harvard Business Review, 44 (January-

February 1966), pp. 6-16, 21-28, 168-172; and Sumer Aggarwal and C. M. Korth, "Pitfalls and Prospects of U.S. Trade with Communist Countries," California Management Review, 15 (Winter 1972), 5-16.

44. Calculated from data appearing annually in June or July issues of Statistical Office of the United Nations, Monthly Bulletin of Statistics.

45. Egon Neuberger, "Is the U.S.S.R. Superior to the West as a Market for Primary Products?," Review of Economics and Statistics, 46 (February 1964), 287-93.

46. Hans Bachmann, The External Relations of Less-Developed Countries (New York: Praeger Publishers, 1968), p. 311.

8

SOME CONCLUDING
REMARKS

Many aspects of Soviet marketing have been examined in the preceding chapters. More emphasis has been given the technical process of marketing, but the social process has not been neglected. One wishes that some aspects, such as marketing research and consumer behavior, could be tied down more concretely and even measured. To be able to say, for example, that marketing research is relatively small, underdeveloped in techniques and personnel, diffused, and constrained by political and ideological factors is certainly not enough to satisfy either the scholar or the practitioner in the West. It is to be hoped that academicians will be able to conduct further research on such subjects.

Some readers may have wished for a more concise rendering of the book's material. However, the subject is complex. The U.S.S.R. is developing a more sophisticated marketing process within ideological constraints quite foreign to those of nations now advanced in marketing. Placing this development in its proper sociological and ideological context has been a major objective of this book. New phenomena such as "market socialism" can be well understood only by appropriate consideration of the culture and philosophy of their architects, time-consuming though this approach may be. If the Soviet marketing process is not set in its Soviet context, the examination of the process is apt to be rather artificial and unrewarding.

The author does not find the current hypotheses of convergence between the Soviet Union and the United States particularly convincing from the point of view of the business disciplines. They seem simplistic and tenuously reasoned. If the West is moving to the left and the Soviet Union and its bloc to the right, it may mean an increasing ability to understand each other and communicate better and more fully. It may mean accommodation. But it does not necessarily mean convergence to a common model. A more likely outcome is an uneven, irregular interface, where the two are far apart on some things and not so far apart on others. If pluralism continues to grow in the U.S.S.R. the Westerner may find that he is much closer to some identifiable groups in that country than he is to others. As a matter of conjecture, perhaps the Muscovite or Leningrader will be more like the New Yorker or Londoner than he is like the goatherd in the Uzbeki hills or the Siberian lumberjack. There may be a culture of large cities, as there is of a nation. Despite present or future similarities of culture and environment within the two nations, the comprehensive trade policy of each nation at a given time will act as a set of constraints on market participants.

Hypotheses of convergence also seem to make an implicit assumption that two entities considerably different from one another will necessarily move toward each other. It does not strike the author as inevitable. Marketing has to be performed in any economy and becomes progressively more important as affluence rises, but the specific ways in which it is carried out can vary greatly. Lenin himself admonished his followers not to be afraid to borrow from the West; but the extent to which they will be willing to borrow the technologies of marketing, as contrasted with technologies like automotive engineering, is still an unknown. Adoption of the Western social process of marketing is a still more sensitive question. The Soviets are hostile to any implication that they are compromising their ideology in the interests of progress, as the following tirade from the pages of Pravda will illustrate:

> Westerners are clutching convulsively at a new weapon:
> hope for an "evolution" of the Soviet system in the
> direction of capitalism.
> However, the liars who compose these stupidities
> evidently are aware of the absurdity of such fabrications.[1]

In all the discussion about convergence one must not lose sight of the parallelism, and yet competition, between the Communist Party and the Soviet state. The Party has been rather ideological in the past, the state somewhat instrumental but not unideological. The two could move toward each other in philosophy, or away from each other. Multinational convergence requires first a sizable degree of convergence within the Soviet Union between these two hierarchical entities, and a convergence toward instrumentality rather than ideology. As recently as Khrushchev, the power structure was loaded on the side of the Party; and he made some relatively unsuccessful efforts to strengthen its hand further. The present leadership is made up mainly of technicians. Although grounded in orthodox theory, they are pragmatists. Many men and many cultures in history have practiced faiths selectively. They did not demand perfect intellectual consistency of themselves. Marxism is a faith that can be practiced with deletions, altered emphases, and new interpretations. If it is so practiced in the future, a closer resemblance between the U.S.S.R. and the United States in marketing practices is certainly possible.

In addition, one must realize that just as behavior can change, so perceptions of unchanged behavior can change. Sometimes behavior of a group or nation does not actually change much; and yet we become satisfied with it, or at least learn to tolerate it, to live with it, and to work within its constraints.

Churchill said that Russia was "a mystery wrapped in an enigma." Phrases such as this have helped deter some from thinking, and perhaps furnished succor to those who did not really desire to understand but could not afford to say so. Leopold Labedz has noted that there is a "special resistance to learning"[2] in Soviet affairs. One encounters "all sorts of pseudocertainties, ranging from mild misconceptions to wilful ignorance."[3] Frederic Fleron has emphasized that a decided policy orientation is typically found in scholarly Western studies of Communist states, and has reminded scholars of the fundamental need for the fact-value distinction.[4] It is difficult to separate oneself from one's culture and one's politico-economic values in studying that which is different, foreign, or even hostile. However, the study of another society, even when one cannot completely free his mind of impeding thoughts, helps one to understand one's own society better. One cannot help but emerge a bit more sensitive, perceptive, and inquisitive.

NOTES

1. Vitaly Korionov, "Barking from the Gateway," Pravda, September 11, 1967, p. 4. CDSP, 19 (October 4, 1967), 17. See also Jeremy R. Azrael, Managerial Power and Soviet Politics, Russian Research Center Studies, vol. 52 (Cambridge: Harvard University Press, 1966).

2. Leopold Labedz, in Walter Z. Laqueur and Leopold Labedz, eds., The State of Soviet Studies (Cambridge, Mass.: MIT Press, 1965), p. 163.

3. Ibid.

4. Frederic J. Fleron, Jr., in Frederic J. Fleron, Jr., ed., Communist Studies and the Social Sciences (Chicago: Rand McNally, 1969), pp. 28-29.

THOMAS V. GREER is professor and chairman of the Department of Marketing in the College of Business and Management at the University of Maryland. Formerly he taught at the University of Texas and Louisiana State University. He received his Ph. D. in business administration from the University of Texas, where he was a Ford Foundation Fellow. In 1966-67 he was a Fulbright Professor in Mexico. Earlier he spent four years in industry. He has taught in the management development programs of several American and Latin American companies.

Dr. Greer has conducted research in the Soviet Union, Western Europe, and Latin America, and has written extensively on international topics. He has published more than 40 articles in academic and professional journals and was the editor of the combined annual proceedings of the American Marketing Association in 1973.

THE POLITICS OF EAST-WEST TRADE WITH
THE SOVIET BLOC STATES
Robert W. Dean

THE POLITICS OF ECONOMIC REFORM IN
THE SOVIET UNION
Abraham Katz

SIBERIA AND THE PACIFIC: A Study of Economic Development and Trade Prospects
Paul Dibb

SOVIET FOREIGN TRADE: Organization, Operations, and Policy, 1918-1971
Glen Alden Smith

THE SOVIET QUEST FOR ECONOMIC EFFI-
CIENCY: Issues, Controversies, and Reforms
(expanded and updated edition)
George R. Feiwel